MARRIAGE IN BLACK AND WHITE

Marriage
IN
Black
AND
White

JOSEPH R. WASHINGTON, JR.

BEACON PRESS *BOSTON*

Library of Congress catalog card number: 77-121828
International Standard Book Number: 0-8070-4172-6 (*hardcover*)
International Standard Book Number: 0-8070-4173-4 (*paperback*)
Beacon Press books are published under the auspices
of the Unitarian Universalist Association

Published simultaneously in Canada by Saunders of Toronto, Ltd.

Printed in the United States of America
First published as a Beacon Paperback in 1972.
The author gratefully acknowledges the following permissions to reprint
copyright material:

   Horace Mann Bond, the *American Journal of Sociology* and its publisher,
the University of Chicago Press, for material from "Two Racial Islands
in Alabama."

   Milton L. Barron, the *American Journal of Sociology* and its publisher,
The University of Chicago Press, for material from "Research on
Intermarriage."

   John H. Burma, the *American Journal of Sociology* and its publisher,
the University of Chicago Press, for material from "The Measurement
of Negro 'Passing.' "

   The *American Journal of Sociology* and its publisher, the University of
Chicago Press, for material from "The Legal Status of Negro-White
Amalgamation in the United States" by Ulysses G. Weatherby, and from
"The Negro-White Intermarried in Philadelphia" by Joseph Golden.

   Kingsley Davis and the American Anthropological Association for
material from "Intermarriage in Cast Societies." Reproduced by permission
of the American Anthropological Association from *American Anthropologist*,
Vol. 43, No. 2, Yr. 1941.

   "Cross" by Langston Hughes, copyright 1926 by Alfred A. Knopf, Inc.,
and renewed 1954 by Langston Hughes. Reprinted from *Selected Poems
of Langston Hughes* by permission of the publisher.

   Commonweal for brief quotations from Allen C. Brownfield's
"Intermarriage and the Court."

   Social Forces and its publisher, the University of North Carolina Press,
for material from "Social Control of Negro-White Intermarriage" by
Joseph Golden and "Interethnic Marriage in Los Angeles" by
John H. Burma.

   Harper and Row, Publishers, Inc., for material from *An American
Dilemma* by Gunnar Myrdal; *Characteristics of the American Negro* by
Otto Klineberg; *If You Marry Outside Your Faith* by James A. Pike.

   McGraw-Hill Book Company for quotations from *Race Mixture* by
Edward B. Reuter and from *Negroes in American Society*
by Maurice Davie.

   Syracuse University Press for material from *People Who Intermarry:
Intermarriage in a New England Industrial Community* by
Milton L. Barron.

   Abingdon Press for material from *Segregation and the Bible*
by Everett Tilson.

FOR SOPHIA

CONTENTS

ACKNOWLEDGMENTS

It gives me special pleasure to acknowledge the contribution of my secretary, Mrs. Susan Dowding, who not only typed the first and second drafts of this manuscript, but who, as well, encouraged me with earnest enthusiasm and critical appreciation. Miss Roberta Fitzsimmons has contributed immeasurably to the clarity of my thought.

Chapter One

CLEANSING THE AMERICAN PSYCHE

We suffer most in our society because of our obstinate hypocrisy, the result of our pervasive fear of unmitigated honesty. We are bold to claim leadership of the free world through espousing the American Creed of freedom, justice, and equality—as if we practiced what we preach. Far from freedom from fear, we are bound by the fear of freedom in thought, word, and deed.

The touchstone of America is egalitarianism, which means a truly open society. This rational Creed is stymied by the irrational heart of America expressed in our adamant refusal of black-white social equality. So bound are we to "no social equality" that the key to our fundamental fear, marriage in black and white, is not openly discussed for fear we will truly educate and therefore liberate. If we could begin to be honest in this area, the other problems between blacks and whites would rapidly fall into their proper perspective and pale into insignificance. Instead, we compound our fears by refusing to face *the* fear. Until we begin to liberate ourselves from this keystone fear of black-white marriages, the nitty gritty of white racism and therefore of the American dilemma, we shall continue to chase the shadow of our conflict as if it were the substance. It is not too much to hold that the fear of candidly facing black-white marriages is our only problem. To the degree we come clean on marriage in black and white, everything else can be worked out, and to the degree we are dishonest about

I

marriage in black and white, nothing else will work. Put another way, our problems will increase until we create in ourselves clean hearts and a right spirit vis-à-vis black-white marriages. Gunnar Myrdal came to this conclusion more than a quarter of a century ago in *An American Dilemma:*

> Our practical conclusion is that it would have cleansing effects on race relations in America, and particularly in the South, to have an open and sober discussion in rational terms of this ever present popular theory of "intermarriage" and "social equality," giving matters their factual ground, true proportions and logical relations. Because it is, to a great extent, an opportunistic rationalization, and because it refers directly and indirectly to the most touchy spots in American life and American morals, tremendous inhibitions have been built up against a detached and critical discussion of this theory.[1]

Part of the reason the liberal establishment which gives intellectual leadership to America has become so ineffectual is due to its tenacious ignoring of the importance of marriages in black and white. Liberals will not shake loose from the notion that the black-white conflict is a class problem as opposed to a group or caste problem. It is frequently assumed that if blacks are given legal, public, and economic opportunity, combined with educational advantage, they will enter the American mainstream. The liberal bias is that the black masses, like all disadvantaged groups, are naturally unprepared to handle fundamental problems in society and if they were it would do neither them nor the society at large any good. Liberals have put all their eggs in the basket of providing blacks with security. To hold that the black-white crisis is a class problem is to have faith that it will fade away when blacks are given an economic stake. Were this the case, there would be no point in candidly discussing black-white marriages. It is a dream to hold that we can go around the problem forever by pushing education, jobs, legal relief in the expectation that the rise of blacks in the economic sphere will eliminate the sharp conflict implicit in black-white marriages. The practical and pragmatic aspects of the problem were never in doubt; the engineering of equal opportunity is a matter of committing resources to know-how, but that is not the problem. The issue is the full acceptance of blacks and their exercise of freedom of choice which would allow whites to be free. The problem is nothing less than one of social exclusion.

To presuppose there will be no social exclusion with economic opportunity is to assume blacks do not want freedom of choice, which is manhood, or it is to assume that this push for unrestricted opportunity is a problem for the future generations, when it is hoped it will be no problem. The ideological preoccupation with class instead of caste is not explanation enough for the liberal failure to deal with the heart of the matter. Of course liberals are sincere in their adherence to the practical, but they are sincerely wrong. It would be one thing if society were slowly moving toward economic opportunity without rupture. The truth is, society is badly ruptured and the prospects are that the rupture will get worse. This would appear to be reason enough to open the society fully up once and for all, instead of doing it on the installment plan. One suspects that the liberal failure to break through with leadership on the social level is due to the concern to protect the order of things as they are. Liberals, in the spirit of Edmund Burke, oppose tampering with society to any serious extent. Thus, the black concern for a radical reordering of society is as opposed by liberals as are demands for educational change, and for the same reason.

Irrespective of the liberals' cautious ideas and cost accounting idealism, we can no longer afford to allow this traditional source of leadership to impede full discussion of marriage in black and white. We shall be a stronger America when we come to grips with this issue as we do with all other issues, in open and free discussion at every level of our society. For the only thing to fear in black-white marriages is the fear of black-white marriages— nameless, unreasoning, unwarranted fear. It is imperative, as well, that we do not pooh-pooh the value of this discussion as a truly cleansing power because we can name some prominent persons who have married across color lines, or because liberals pretend this is no problem since it occurs outside their family, or because it comes about largely among marginal people. Marriage in black and white is not an issue for intellectuals to enjoy or dismiss as irrelevant. It is an American problem to be worked out by all; indeed, it is *the* American problem for the vast number of Americans who pay for the tune to which we all dance.

The issue of black-white marriages will be advanced if in the beginning a distinction is made between marriage in black and white and the much more malignant concepts with which it is often associated—amalgamation, miscegenation, assimilation, intermixture—concepts which ignore fidelity in marriage. These latter concepts vary in their import, but they all concern themselves with solving the crisis of black and white through interbreeding or breeding out black people with "all deliberate speed."

Marriage in black and white is not a devious biological escape from *the* American problem. It is a public and visible symbol of the private and invisible American spirit of egalitarianism. It is not American to require marriage, but the opportunity for marriage in black and white must be open to all without fear of recrimination. Marriage in black and white is the will to the unity of the spirit as well as the flesh, the unity of the soul of America as much as the body. In a word, marriage in black and white is a call to honesty in the present as the precondition for an open society. Marriage in black and white as a free choice available to all does not require that it be the individual choice of each person; the possibility of the former should not deter us from the impossibility of the latter. Erich Fromm, speaking of the *Revolution of Hope,* put it this way: "It is not up to us to complete this task, but we have no right to abstain from it." [2]

The inclination of the old line liberal spirit toward assimilation as the solution to the black-white issue in America failed us with respect to marriage in black and white because it sent us down the wrong track of escapism rather than that of resolution. This approach to the issue was best exemplified by Franz Boas, Professor of Anthropology at Columbia University, in 1921:

> It is claimed by many that the negro problem is economic rather than racial, that the fear of negro competition causes racial opposition. Obviously, this explanation also would not

hold good if the tendency did not exist to treat the negro as a class, not as an individual. . . . It would, however, be an error to seek in these sources the fundamental cause for antagonism; for the economic conflict, as well as the other conflicts, presuppose the racial recognition of the classes. . . .

If my view is correct, it is clear that the only fundamental remedy for the situation is the recognition that the negroes have the right to be treated as individuals, not as members of a class. . . .

But the greatest hope for the immediate future lies in a lessening of the contrast between negroes and whites which will bring about a lessening of class consciousness. . . . Intermixture will decrease the contrast between the extreme racial forms, and in the course of time, this will lead to a lessening of the consciousness of race distinction. If conditions were ever such that it could be doubtful whether a person were of negro descent or not, the consciousness of race would necessarily be much weakened. In a race of octroons, living among whites, the color question would probably disappear. . . .

It would seem, therefore, to be in the interest of society to permit rather than to restrain marriages between white men and negro women. It would be futile to expect that our people would tolerate intermarriages in the opposite direction, although no scientific reason can be given that would prove them to be detrimental to the individual.[3]

Assimilation, as Professor Boas perceived it, was in the best interest of the white community, a continuation of interbreeding from slavery as a one-way process. Clearly, this solution could not be acceptable to blacks, for whom equality with reciprocity is necessary. Moreover, his pitch to whites was a futile attempt to meet head on the fundamental hypocrisy. The American Creed of equality for all has meant an "Americanizing" of all groups through assimilation, except for blacks, and this conflict in American values is resolved by the general proposition that even blacks can and will be assimilated in the very distant future. Boas was bold to remind his fellow old-line liberals what they preferred to forget:

> Intermixture between white males and negro females has been common ever since negroes were brought to our continent, and the efficacy of the modern attempts to repress this intermingling is open to grave doubts.[4]

But he was not helpful in setting forth an ideal without any concern for manhood of the black male, or, for that matter, any strategy for accomplishment. Whether he advocated the wrong thing for the right reason or the right thing for the wrong reason, he was right in what he affirmed and wrong in what he denied:

> Thus it would seem that man being what he is, the negro problem will not disappear in America until the negro blood has been so diluted that it will no longer be recognized, just as anti-Semitism will not disappear until the last vestige of the Jew as a Jew has disappeared.[5]

Assimilation—amalgamation, interbreeding, intermixture, miscegenation—in the long run has some support among Americans, but not in the short run. Every generation of Americans sets forth as its dominant and guiding light what amounts to a doctrine or interposition in the form of antiassimilation. Blacks are unassimilable in the sense that they are undesirable:

> Considerable efforts are directed toward "Americanizing" all groups of alien origin. But in regard to the colored peoples, the American policy is the reverse. They are excluded from assimilation. Even by their best friends in the dominant white group and by promoters of racial peace and good-will, they are usually advised to keep to themselves and develop a race pride.[6]

So uniform is this antiassimilation doctrine in the American way of life that there is not one shred of difference between whites on this score in any region of America. To support this doctrine a white folklore has developed based on the biological inferiority of the black stock to the white stock, a doctrine which asserts that blacks like to be separated and unequal and that whites would not stand for social equality. A bumper sticker I saw recently provides a good illustration of how this folklore is expressed: "This is white man's country; what kind of man are you?"

The intensity with which whites cling to assimilation of all segments of the society, except the colored and especially blacks, is irrefutable:

> Except for a handful of rational intellectual liberals—who also, in many cases, add to their acceptance in principle of amalgamation an admission that they personally feel an irrational emotional inhibition against it—it is a rare case to meet a white American who will confess that, if it were not for public opinion and social sanctions not removable by private choice, he would have no strong objection to intermarriage.[7]

There are those like Gunnar Myrdal who claim that the walls are tumbling down on this score, but if wishes were horses, beggars would ride:

> But even a liberal-minded Northerner of cosmopolitan culture and with a minimum of conventional blinds will, in nine cases out of ten, express a definite feeling against amalgamation. He will not be willing usually to hinder intermarriage by law. Individual liberty is to him a higher principle and, what is more important, he actually invokes it. But he will regret the exceptional cases that occur. He may sometimes hold a philosophical view that in centuries to come amalgamation is bound to happen and might become the solution. But he will be inclined to look on it as an inevitable deterioration.[8]

In the light of antagonisms to marriage in black and white, it is difficult to see how one and the same man can hold as Myrdal does that "the Negro's friend—or the one who is least unfriendly —is still rather the upper class of white people, the people with economic and social security" [9] while proclaiming this unexceptional dictum:

> *This attitude of refusing to consider amalgamation—felt and expressed in the entire country—constitutes the center in the complex of attitudes which can be described as the "common denominator" in the problem.* It defines the Negro group in contradistinction to all the non-colored minority groups in America and all other lower class groups. The boundary between Negro and white is not simply a class line which can be successfully crossed by education, integration into the national culture, and individual economic advancement. The boundary is fixed. It is not a temporary expediency during an apprenticeship in the national culture. It is a bar erected with the intention of permanency. It is directed against the whole group.[10]

The white upper class is no true friend to blacks any more than are the liberal intellectuals, both of whom have put a good distance between their day-to-day lives at home and the black community. On the issues that count, liberal or upper class whites are alike, with few exceptions. In order that we do not fool on this count, it is important to have Myrdal tell it as he, an outsider, perceives it:

> The response is likely to be anything but pleasant if one jestingly argues that possibly a small fraction of Negro blood in the American people, if it were blended well with all the other good stock brought over to the new continent, might create a race of unsurpassed excellence: a people with just a little sunburn without extra trouble and even through the winter; with some curl in the hair without the cost of a permanent wave; with, perhaps, a little more emotional warmth in their souls; and a little more religion, music, laughter, and carefreeness in their lives. Amalgamation is, to the ordinary American, not a proper subject for jokes at all,

unless it can be pulled down to the level of dirty stories, where, however, it enjoys a favored place. Referred to society as a whole and viewed as a principle, the anti-amalgamation maxim is held holy; it is a consecrated taboo. The maxim might, indeed, be a remnant of something really in the "mores." It is kept unproblematic, which is certainly not the case with all the rest of etiquette and segregation and discrimination patterns, for which this quality is sometimes erroneously claimed.[11]

The white man's folklore of caste is set forth in the basic concern for "race purity," to prevent amalgamation or assimilation and "social equality" or black-white marriages. This folklore is a rationalization, and yet potent as a caste line between blacks and whites. The whole basis of antimiscegenation or antiassimilation is to prevent marriage in black and white. The emotional opposition to black-white marriages is paradoxical in that while a great concern is exercised over legal marriage between whites and blacks, illicit relations involving the white male and black woman are met with almost sheer indifference. In fact pre-marital, post-marital, or extramarital relations with a black woman constitute less of a breach of morality in the eyes of whites than illicit relations with a white woman. However, the tirade of antiassimilation operates effectively and ubiquitously when a black man and white woman are involved. In effect, intercourse between black men and white women causes the antiassimilation fever to rise to a fervor of high passion, whether this intimacy be in the form of marriage or less formal relations. Antiassimilation does not rise with respect to white men and black women in any relation outside of marriage.

Opposition to assimilation and its primary object of preventing marriage in black and white is chiefly the protection of white women from illicit or legal arrangements with blacks. The white male is exempted because it is assumed he would not give up his status to marry a black woman, especially since illicit intercourse is not a taboo. With respect to intercourse in black and white it is basic to the white folklore that there be no white maternity though there may be white paternity, the black woman may be raided but the white woman (and therefore white race) remains pure under this arrangement—all children of black-white unions being considered black—and no white woman is expected to engage in this fusion. To further protect the white woman, there is not only the antiassimilation doctrine with its legacy of the once widespread state laws, there are social sanctions as well. The double standard holds that a white woman must be degraded by marriage with a black. The exclusion of blacks from the mainstream of society or caste by color is built around marriage in black and white. Of course all these defenses of white womanhood are expressions of the fear that white women would not only be open but would respond positively to black men were they not protected from themselves. In the end, the whole antiassimilation doctrine in defense of "no social equality" with its prohibition of marriage in black and white revolves around sexual taboos summarized by Thomas Bailey: "For, say what we will, may not all the equalities be ultimately based on potential social equality, and that in turn on intermarriage? Here we reach the real *crux* of the question." [12] It all comes down to that conversation stopper: "Would you want your daughter to marry a Negro?" In effect, there is not the inherent repulsion between blacks and whites that so many love to proclaim, for if there were, the restrictions placed on marriage in black and white would not be necessary.

White people wish to keep blacks in their place, in a status which will not tempt white women to act as if black men were their social equals. This anti-intermarriage end of the antiassimilation doctrine is an indirect way of stating that blacks are not and should not be equal to whites in all things social or essential. It may be that the puritan ethos of America with its officially antisexual thrust supports this hypocrisy and at the same time salves the consciences of white males. What is certain is that blacks have to this day carried the burden of the white man's sins and virtues, the personification of the doctrine of double damnation.

In the face of antiassimilation doctrines, a defense of marriage in black and white has placed black people in a most precarious position. Up to this point in history, the attitudes and behavioral patterns of whites have been so dominant that blacks have been unable to carve out their own free response. The overwhelm-

ing majority of blacks has been against assimilation and by implication against marriage in black and white. Given the white edict,
blacks could hardly take any other position. Furthermore, on the
question of marriage in black and white, whites stress the value of
there being two races, both of which in this context are held to be
good, and go on to encourage in blacks race pride, which in fact
means keeping blacks black and untainted with whites. Blacks
have at times reacted in the "pure blood" spirit of whites. Yet, this
has always seemed phony since whites have been able to violate
the "pure blood" theory by having white and black women. Further, there has been a wholesale exchange of blood between
blacks, Indians, and whites which is most difficult to ignore.

We suggested earlier that the old-line liberals were less than
helpful in their advocacy of assimilation in that it has led to a misunderstanding of the meaning of marriage in black and white.
The obsession with assimilation as the cure-all of the black-white
problem is so strong that it is believed that blacks must be in
favor of assimilation. No less a liberal than Myrdal holds this
view, believing as he does that blacks have no principle or experience persuasive enough to make antiassimilation more than just a
perfunctory gesture of conciliation:

> Race pride, with this particular connotation of the
> undesirability of miscegenation, has been growing in the
> Negro group. This is, however, probably to be interpreted as
> a defense reaction, a derived *secondary* attitude, as are so
> many other attitudes of the Negro people. After weighing all
> available evidence carefully, it seems frankly incredible that
> the Negro people in America should feel inclined to develop
> any particular race pride at all or have any dislike for
> amalgamation, were it not for the common white opinion of
> the racial inferiority of the Negro people and the whites'
> intense dislike for miscegenation. The fact that a large
> amount of exploitative sexual intercourse between white men
> and Negro women has always been, and still is, part of
> interracial relations, coupled with the further fact that the
> Negroes sense the disgrace of their women who are not
> accepted into matrimony, and the inferior status of their

mixed offspring, is a strong practical reason for the Negro's preaching "race pride" in his own group. But it is almost certainly not based on any fundamental feeling condemning miscegenation on racial or biological grounds.[13]

In truth, the rapid rise of race pride in this century that culminated in the civil rights movement has meant that blacks believed the American Creed will overcome. Therefore, no black leader has found it expedient to support miscegenation. This was obviously a political necessity to gain the cooperation of whites, the crux of civil rights and so blacks had no alternative but to condone antiassimilation. While blacks have never worked out a theory based on "pure blood" or other biological grounds to oppose miscegenation, it does not follow that they were not as adamant in opposition to it on other grounds. To hold that the only reason blacks have not advocated marriage in black and white is the fact that whites in the majority dislike the idea, "independent of the Negroes' wishes," is to mistake practicality for causation.

It should first be understood that blacks opposed assimilation or miscegenation because it supported the condition of slavery rather than freedom. That is, assimilation has historically meant the absorption of blacks into whites since its underlying assumption was that white men and black women would cohabit but not black men and white women. Such a prescription for the black-white issue is tantamount to saying that blacks have no past or present value, that they are but tools for the cultivation of white culture. Beyond this, the liberal white call to assimilation furthered the exploitation of the black woman. Moreover, as W. E. B. Du Bois stated, "it is quite conceivable that the advance of the American Negro might mean not more but less intermingling of blood." [14] This determination to counter the white doctrine of "no social equality" by appealing to the American Creed in black solidarity was not a confession that blacks deemed themselves inferior to whites; rather, it was a step toward honest relations.

The touchstone of black honesty in race relations, its wholesale opposition to miscegenation as a denial of black manhood and the exploitation of black womanhood, was set forth by Robert R. Moton: "Theoretically Negroes would all subscribe to the right of freedom of choice in marriage even between the two races." [15] This position of blacks is in keeping with the American Creed and transcends thereby both the purer white doctrine of antiassimilation and the expression of assimilation made by liberal whites. Moton was stating the situation as it existed, not begging the question, when he wrote, "As for amalgamation, very few expect it; still fewer want it; no one advocates it; and only a constantly diminishing minority practise it, and that surreptitiously." [16] In the Twenties and Thirties, blacks who were counterparts to the old-line liberals saw through the unreality of supporting assimilation which they distinguished from marriage in black and white. Du Bois wrote to the point:

> A woman may say, I do not want to marry this black man, or this red man, or this white man. . . . But the impudent and vicious demand that all colored folk shall write themselves down as brutes by a general assertion of their unfitness to marry other decent folk is a nightmare. [17]

Moton, a member of the Talented Tenth, held that the black man,

> even in the matter of the mingling of racial strains, however undesirable it might seem to be from a social point of view, he would never admit that his blood carries any taint of physiological, mental, or spiritual inferiority. [18]

Thus, throughout the period of rising race pride, blacks opposed shortcut assimilation proposed by the old-line liberals and concluded marriage in black and white to be a matter of freedom of choice. In the long run, blacks have not held assimilation to be unnatural or immoral. The point of blacks was summarized by Kelly Miller:

> The amalgamation of the races is an ultimate possibility, though not an immediate probability. But what have you and I to do with ultimate questions, anyway? [19]

In the perspective of blacks, assimilation was not a means of manipulating people and problems. The emphasis was upon respecting the manhood of blacks and whites. If assimilation was necessarily an issue to be discussed vis-à-vis its advocacy by white liberals of the past, it was viewed as an evolutionary process that would in time become natural, rather than a revolutionary solution of moment:

> It must be taken for granted in the final outcome of things
> that the color line will be wholly obliterated. While blood
> may be thicker than water, it does not possess the spissitude
> or inherency of everlasting principle. The brotherhood of
> man is more fundamental than the fellowship of race. A
> physical and spiritual identity of all people occupying
> common territory is a logical necessity of thought. The clear
> seeing mind refuses to yield or give its assent to any other
> ultimate conclusion. This consummation, however, is far too
> removed from the sphere of present probability to have
> decisive influence upon practical procedure.[20]

What needs clearly to be seen is that assimilation has been on the far periphery of the black vision and even then it has been deemed a consummation rather than an operating principle. Where blacks have given ground on the question, it has been in the form of mutual respect centered in marriage in black and white.

It has been sixty-five years since Kelly Miller penned his assumption, "in the final outcome of things . . . the color line will be wholly obliterated." But we now know that even in the twenty generations ahead this obliteration shall not come about, for, as Edwin R. Embree has remarked: "Improved standing and self-respect of the Negro is the only thing that is likely to retard interbreeding of the white and colored groups." [21] Our present is a time of dynamic pluralism rather than one of ultimate assimilation or amalgamation or miscegenation. What is new in this pluralism is the emergence of black consciousness as a fourth dimension added to the old triumvirate of Protestant, Catholic, Jew.

In his classic *Protestant, Catholic, Jew,* written a decade ago,

Will Herberg successfully demonstrated America to be a trans-muting pot in which immigrants from diverse cultures and heri-tages found it imperative to shed their culture, including language and nationality, in order to participate fully in the American mainstream. To be an American mainliner means that one can identify with one's past, and thereby find one's identity, only as a Protestant, Catholic, Jew, or Eastern Orthodox, and then only to the extent the religious heritage is transmuted into the "American way of life."

As far as blacks in America are concerned, Herberg made it clear that they are excluded from the mainstream. The black man is not accepted as a Protestant, Catholic, Jew, or an Eastern Or-thodox, as is a white man, and he cannot find his identity therein as do other Americans. Blacks are like other Americans in that it has been unacceptable for them to identify with their past culture, but they are unlike other Americans in that the loss of a past cul-tural identity was neither voluntarily given up nor were they pro-vided a substitute way of becoming mainliners.

This double jeopardy coupled with a vision of some distant amalgamation and civil rights advancement had been largely ac-cepted as inevitable by black and white old-line liberals until the recent emergence of militant blacks who not only dare to defy the American way of life by nurturing the African past as a fourth or fifth addition to old-line pluralism, but who also claim that they do not wish to become mainliners—injecting into their veins the deadly poison of white America. Old-line liberals and the new lib-eral establishment have not differed from the common American in reacting as if they had been deeply wronged and wounded when the people they ruled out of bounds draws upon a resource which purports to leave them out. For the most part, however, white liberals of all stripes react in disbelief. The old-line liberals believe that the black-white issue will not be resolved until blacks are bred out. They therefore hold that blacks not only have no past heritage and no present culture but that they have no basis but defensive reaction to oppose assimilation, which, after all, old line liberals have held up as the process in direct confrontation to popular will. The present liberal establishment simply holds there is no black culture. There are a few who now say it is acceptable for the old pluralism of Protestant, Catholic, and Jew to give way to a new pluralism of black, Protestant, Catholic, and Jew. This verbal concession is made on the grounds that blacks cannot pull it off, and if they can pull it off the new pluralism is preferable to a radical disruption of society and its structures.

Liberals have held onto their vision of gradualism through eventual assimilation and the resolving of the conflict through elimination of what they hold to be a class problem, because the only "status" blacks have had in America was in slavery. It is against the American faith for blacks to gain status in America apart from the shackles of slavery. It is against the grain of the American way of life for blacks to realize their identity and accept it and transform it into assets, for it is viewed, if at all, as a liability. Negative responses to black rhetoric about black reality and black experience and black perspectives and black power are only symptomatic. The real source of white reaction to black pride and black consciousness is the myth that refuses to be demythologized. More than a quarter of a century ago, Melville J. Herskovits, writing in *The Myth of the Negro Past,* exploded the great American myth that "the Negro is a man without a past." Old myths do not die, they simply become dysfunctional or meaningless if they are not demythologized in the new reality structured by different values, norms, attitudes, experiences, and actions.

The combination of the old-line liberals' belief in the efficacy of assimilation, or the wiping out of black culture and blood, and the new liberal establishment's affirmation of a class struggle lead us away from the true potency of black-white marriages, thus preventing it from becoming a dynamic part of the American way of life. Whatever their differences in strategy, all liberals have a common faith. It was expressed some years ago by two scholars who have subsequently gained national recognition, Nathan Glazer and Daniel Moynihan, in their book entitled *Beyond the Melting Pot* where they asserted that "the Negro is only an American and nothing else. He has no values and culture to guard and protect." [22] Abram Kardiner and Lionel Ovesey developed the same viewpoint in *The Mark of Oppression*:

He [Negro] had no culture, and he was quite green in his semi-acculturated state in the new one. He did not know his way about and had no intrapsyche defenses—no pride, no group solidarity, no tradition. This was enough to cause panic. The marks of his previous status were still upon him—socially, psychologically and emotionally. And from these he has never since freed himself.[23]

Arnold Toynbee gives this liberal position vis-à-vis blacks historical support:

His [Negro] primitive social heritage was of so frail a texture that, save for a few shreds, it was scattered to the winds on the impact of our Western Civilization. Thus he came to America spiritually as well as physically naked; and he has met the emergency by covering his nakedness with his enslaver's cast-off clothes.[24]

In *Crisis in Black and White,* Charles Silberman continued the revisionism:

In contrast to European immigrants, who brought rich cultures and long histories with them, the Negro has been completely stripped of his past and severed from any culture save that of the United States.[25]

In the face of this white perspective, the rising black consciousness holds that the black man has a cultural past and cultural present with which he needs to identify. Briefly, it is recalled that the captive Africans were ripped from African culture and that the strangeness of this culture was excuse enough for Northern white Europeans, unlike slave traders and masters of South America, to promote and perpetuate the myth that this strange culture was no culture. It is true, Africans became acculturated faster here than in the other Americas. This was largely due to the fact that small farmers owned the vast majority of slaves which allowed them to have more total control over their slaves than was possible in other slave countries where the slaves were not so parceled out on small farms.

In Bahia, as well as Haiti, Guiana, and Cuba, the African attitudes, customs, politics, social and economic systems, technology of iron working, wood carving, weaving, and, of course, religion are readily discernible today. The rapid acculturation of Africans in the United States resulted from their ancient belief that the more powerful gods of other tribes were to be respected. These two factors, combined with white America's insistence that everything African was inferior primitivism and that its elimination would speed acceptance, advanced the general capitulation of Africans here to the dominant white mode and model.

The emergence of black consciousness as refutation of the liberal denial of a black culture from the past or in the present is illuminated best for our purposes in religion. Africans in general, and those from West Africa where the majority of the captives brought to America were found in particular, were rooted in a society highly determined by intense religion at all levels. This affirmation of the supernatural in every nook and climb of the culture was one of the heritages which Africans found congenial in the new culture. In Bahia, blacks were massed together under the impact of Roman Catholicism, a highly ritualistic religion which allowed them to continue their rites by adaptation. Stark Protestantism in America, however, forced the Africans to drastically change their rituals and patterns of worship. Thus the reason syncretism (which did occur in Bahia) or African worship did not become the form or response or new religion in America was the fact that the white masters early perceived the worship of African gods through African rituals to be a major deviation from Puritanism, in which rituals played little or no part. Not only this, but the African rituals were viewed as primitive and as effective instruments of escape, rebellion, and insurrection. Unlike Brazil where assimilation became a way of life, antiassimilation in the United States became a way of life. There was no respect for the African as a mate or as a man of culture to be cherished. The process of total intimacy and assimilation in Bahia, for example, made escape of limited interest. In the United States any reference to African gods or customs of worship was immediately squashed on pain of brutal beatings or death. Clearly, in the United States, the African's native drum was not allowed the slave because it was as readily adaptable for a call to escape or insurrection as a call to dance. The slaves, who were so overpowered by total suppression here, chose uncertain life over certain death more often than not, but this is not perceived in the black consciousness as a lack of courage or a lack of culture.

When we look just to religion we can see what black consciousness means in its claim that not every strand of the African culture was eliminated from the black man. African culture did not distinguish between music, dance, song, rhythm, and worship of the gods. Through the medium of music, dance, song, on the beat of rhythm, religion survived the slave repression experience. Of course blacks here had a much more difficult time holding onto their past than did their brothers in South America, but they came from the same stock, and it is sheer propaganda to broadcast that there is no black culture. Here the language and concepts were changed, but the rhythmic beat of religious music and the total outpouring through dance and song survived and can be found to this day in the praise houses of black folk. There is in black religion an aliveness, an intensity of joy and ecstasy which is infectious because it is uninhibited. In addition to the rhythmic beat, the religious service continues to be driven by antiphonal singing, as in African music, where the leader sings a lead line and is answered by a congregation in chorus. Another important survival in the worship of black folk is the African dependence upon improvisation. Even today, then, if one searches hard enough, in isolated areas of the rural South and some urban communities, the mixture of spirit-power and other African animistic beliefs with Christianity can be found—especially where Roman Catholicism is dominant, as in New Orleans or Detroit.

There is an old African dictum that "the spirit will not descend without a song." In African religious rituals emotional frenzies were a dynamic and integral part. The ritual dances and songs and emotional frenzies of the African religious "total letting go" are among the lasting contributions to the religion of black folk in America. Black folk religion is highly charged with emotion to this day. "Spirit possession" of the African religions has become the "getting happy" or "getting religion" so indispensable to Southern rural and nonmiddle-class urban folk religion. Dancing, though frowned upon by the Puritan white culture in worship, has persisted in ingenious ways among the "sanctified" black religious folk. It is true that music or drama or dance or poetry are now, to a very large extent, black forces independent of black folk religion. It is also true that black folk religion is still dependent upon these forces for its life, power, and uniqueness.

Black folk religion created music of pure African heritage that was changed in response to the American restrictions. Nowhere is the African melody clearer than in the spirituals whose words were changed to fit the English language, the American experience, and biblical teachings. The development of black folk religion in America cannot be understood apart from the singular role African music plays in it, a fact that was true of African religion as well. Without elaborating upon this theme, it is well to point out that the importance of music in the religion of blacks as inherited from Africa is further evidenced in the singular role of the black preacher.

The black preacher made superb use of African folk tales, parables, riddles, and proverbs, which were increasingly left behind for biblical stories and the American slave experience, for the chief method of educating the young in African culture consisted of passing the wisdom of the elders on to them through these tales, parables, etc. Not only was the black preacher a superb artist in telling a story, but his dramatic presentations were more often than not accented by his musical leadership in the most emotional parts of the sermon or story. Sermons were rhythmical, sometimes sung in parts to gain added feeling and emphasis. The power of this verbal-rhythmic combination was a continuation in a new mode of the ancient African tradition of call-and-response or participation by the gathered, which the music of Africa demands. The chants, the hollers, the shouts in rhythmic syncopation and shifted accents with full vibrato all were African in form, if not in content. The key to the black preacher was his ability to so dramatize the sermon that the people were pulled into a direct response. His slow beginning, stuttering, stammering at key points for dramatic effect so that the people would feel forced to say it for him, the repetition, all are demonstrated in black folk services.

If we were to focus on the wider aspects we could see how the blues and jazz and dance were initially formulated in the black church and rooted in Africa. Here it is enough to point out how black folk religion is rooted in Africa and how Africa is rooted in black religion. In the beginning was the black church, and the black church was with the black community, and the black church was the black community. The black church was in the beginning with the black people; all things were made through the black church, and without the black church was not anything made that was made. In the black church was life, and the life was the light of the black people. The black church still shines in the darkness, and the darkness has not overcome it.

The root of black folk religion in African rhythm, music, dance, and participating sermons has flowered among blacks as frenzied dancing, tambourine playing, speaking in tongues, screaming sermons, instrumental groups, hand clapping, and total congregation participation in worship. Black folk religion today is to be found among the masses as has always been the case. The flowering of black religion from its root in Africa is important because therein is the locus or special domain of black culture. This religion of ritual and drama and "dialectical catharsis" is best perceived, today, as a real blend of the sacred and the secular, not limited to the churches or the sacred. Those who possess this ritual power are black preachers, musicians, comedians, singers, and disc jockeys, with an occasional athlete now and then. These ritualists are in the long line of black ritualists, they have soul power because they have tapped the soul tradition at its African roots.

The flowering of black folk religion may be perceived in black music, composed of the blues and jazz, spirituals, jubilees, and gospels. The fusion today of the blues, jazz, and gospel music into what is known as soul music is a special instance of the integration of the church and secular dimensions of black folk religion and culture. Soul music is a music of the soul of the masses, the black folk, the black culture. Black culture has come forth from the black experience in America, the black reality. This black reality or expression or experience is unmistakable among the black folk in their dance, religion, music, and drama which have penetrated the white culture.

It is not by accident that our brief exploration into the

flowering of black religion, an example of black culture, takes the form of discussing soul. Soul is a dynamic part of black consciousness, and black consciousness is a challenge to the liberal desire to determine what is best for blacks. Soul, the communication of the black experience which forges the black reality, took root in the earliest religious experiences of black folk. The black church served the black folk as the matrix of their life in the past. Today soul music is the life and the black church continues as the matrix. The center of black folk which gave shape to the black experience and structured the black reality, the black church, is no longer the dominant, all-embracing center of the black culture. Yet the black culture cannot be grasped—or better still, you cannot be grasped by the black culture—apart from coming to grips with the black church.

It is obvious that many blues and soul singers began their careers in gospel choirs. Some become, in time, preachers or gospel singers or both. The battle of gospel choirs is not different in style and tone from that of soul groups, a fact that leads one to suggest the radical possibilities of black music, especially soul music, as a subversive force in the unity of black masses vis-à-vis white America. Black music is subversive: it has power of revolutionary dimensions, as well as a means of conversion. The gospel music, blues and jazz, are so intertwined that few blues singers, or "soul singers," today have not made their way to the top via a church choir. The words of the Supremes or Aretha Franklin may differ from those of the gospel singers in the churches, but the beat and the rhythm and message are of the same African root, for the medium is the message and the message of soul is the medium.

In response to the American demand that whites engage in assimilation or pluralism and the demand that blacks bow to the antiassimilation doctrine, and, at the same time, miraculously and inconspicuously blend into America without developing a viable pluralism—the rise of black consciousness has tapped these roots of black culture and taken the initiative in determining the destiny of blacks. Black consciousness says that America cannot continue with business as usual. It says that America cannot hold out the carrot of the American Creed to tempt blacks and then withhold it from them. Black consciousness says there cannot be assimilation for whites and antiassimilation for blacks; there cannot be pluralism for whites and antipluralism for blacks; there cannot be penetration of black women without penetration of white women. Black consciousness opposes assimilation now and in the future because it means in the American experience the elimination of black culture and black identity rather than, as in the Bahia experience, the full acceptance of black culture and black integrity. But, black consciousness is not opposed to marriage in black and white because it can be an affirmation and extension of blackness—it is saying "Yes" rather than "No" to blackness. Assimilation and marriage in black and white are not the same, either in their immediate intentions or ultimate results.

In the American experience, to be against (racist), or for (old liberal), or indifferent to (establishment liberal) assimilation is to be against black manhood and womanhood and equality. Marriage in black and white, as distinct from assimilation-amalgamation-intermixture-interbreeding-crossbreeding-miscegenation and its artificial manipulation of black people by white people, is not the white man's approach. Assimilation, as envisioned by American whites, is synonymous with underhandedness, surreptitiousness, inequality, inauthenticity. Assimilation is the white man's pattern because he is unable to receive, he can only give. Marriage in black and white is the black man's pattern and initiative because he has the grace, the courtesy, the sense of appreciation, and the joy to receive as well as to give. Herein lies the superiority of the black man, his superior strength over the white man. This superiority is humility—not that humility which takes the form of ingratiating knee-bending, but the humility which holds that one may be wrong and in the face of that truth one will change. The superior quality of blacks, their humility, means they do not have to force themselves upon whites to prove their value, as whites must do. Here lies the essential meaning and difference vis-à-vis assimilation and marriage in black and white.

Given the unhealthiness of the dominant American psyche, its psychasthenia with regard to blacks, racism, and sex, there is only one resolution: marriage in black and white.

Marriage in black and white is not a unique or unilateral or independent factor in the resolution of the black-white conflict.

There are multiple factors the strength of which will be increased to the extent their essentials are interwoven in the warp and woof of marriage in black and white. Marriage in black and white is a substantial imperative, the ultimate criterion of an open society. Marriage in black and white is the resolvent not in the sense that it will singularly bring the black-white conflict to a conclusion, but, in the sense that the conflict will not be concluded without it. Marriage in black and white is not an end to be consummated by some mysterious or magical happening in the far distant future but demands participation at various levels by the whole community in the present, for, like all things, that which will be already is. Marriage in black and white is the end of the beginning and the beginning of the end. It is the eye of the needle which the camel must thread. It is not a euphemism for miscegenation nor a clandestine call to eugenics. Marriage in black and white is in no manner extremism, nor is it despairing pessimism or undisciplined optimism. It is the precept by which we find our wholeness in the union of the saving remnant, the efficacy of which is directly dependent upon the full measure of our enthusiastic and open support whereby we give our blessing and receive one in return.

Marriage in black and white is not inevitable, but it is an indispensable ingredient in the solution of our American dilemma. Clearly, America may not be interested in a solution of the conflict and may, like Rhodesia under Ian Smith, seek only those measures which are necessary to keep the pot from boiling over. If the hypocrisy of a double standard with respect to the American Creed is invincible in the foreseeable future, one would have to be extraordinarily sanguine to presuppose that the presently escalating tension can be permanently controlled and prevented from erupting into a race war of such magnitude that the Civil War and race riots would pale into insignificance in comparison. This impossible possibility—war between blacks and whites—would only be a desperate effort to turn this society inside out and upside down, in the hope of turning it right side up and right side out. It would be a very anguishing beginning on the way to living out the National Creed of freedom and justice and equality without respect to color or creed or race; it would not be the solution. However, there is no solution either if the holocaust is escaped through political and economic enfranchisement with "all deliberate speed" in separate but equal housing and education. The National Creed may be battered and crushed down, but it is so much the truth of America that it will rise to its natural hegemony. Whether out of conflict or out of cooperation, out of war or out of peace, out of fear or out of hope, we must finally come to the resolution of marriage in black and white, and, if we do not, we will know that the American experiment is the impossible dream.

There is no way to marriage in black and white, it has been sighed, but, it must be exclaimed, marriage in black and white is the way. We have repressed for too long this ultimate, though not singular, resolution. Whatever justification existed in the past is no longer relevant. We have come to the crossroads of late. We have finally, recently, committed America to the necessary supporting penultimates, equality of opportunity in every sphere except intimacy; and although these penultimates have only begun to take effect, their emergence makes the ultimate resolution possible, meaningful, and realizable.

The rise to the surface of black consciousness would seem to be the most powerful refutation of marriage in black and white as the resolution. Black consciousness, given the American experience, is absolutely inevitable, indispensable, and necessary for the freedom of blacks and whites. It is not, however, sufficient. Black consciousness is the process whereby American blacks become indelibly impressed with the fact that they are descendants of slaves and continue to be captives without freedom and justice and equality. This historical perspective and present awareness both provide the urgency for a truly integrated society in which blacks and whites who so choose may live together in ebullient equality and, at the same time, demand the resources and freedom to develop a separate black community as a live option for blacks who wish it. It is the minor price we have to pay, and therefore ought to be willing to pay, for slavery. Black consciousness—beauty, pride, politics, religion, economics, education, history, community—is a two-edged sword and it sharply cuts both ways. In the short run, the demand for a separate but equal stake in the society cannot be denied because it is a passionate concern to provide blacks with initiative thrusts in atonement for the past and as hope for the future. Black consciousness seeks to have the whole history of the black man accepted by the black man and, subsequently, by the white man for the purpose of equality. Essentially, this history is one of disinheritance, and the cancer to be eradicated is the dithyrambic and diabolical effects of slavery. At its best, black consciousness, now the initiating force forging real community, works against separation. True, the slave, the disinherited, must be singularly concerned at this point with wrenching freedom from his captor. Once he has gained freedom, however, he then is in a position to determine how the freedom he has won by his own action is to be used with respect to the previous captor. So, while it is natural and right that black consciousness focus on self-awareness, self-realization, self-actualization, nevertheless, black consciousness would be meaningless if it did not desire the enrichment of all through the enrichment of self. The love and respect of self, like charity, begins at home and then spreads abroad. That is, black consciousness is not only a call to the authentication of the disinherited, although it must first and foremost be this; it is as well a call to all to join in the enrichment and cleansing of the American psyche through identification with the disinherited at all levels. This is obvious when it comes to politics, employment, education, and housing. It is less obvious when it comes to immediate family and social intimacy. Black consciousness is neither informed by nor is the extension of masochism or sadism. The suffering of the disinherited has as its purpose the creation of a new society of true community, not the continuation of suffering alone for either black folk or white folk. It is an infectious call for the inherited to join in the suffering, to become those who suffer most, and therefore to participate as initiators in the creation of the new community. Here is the contagious but fiercely "mind blowing" power of black consciousness. In the decades immediately ahead of us, identification with the suffering disinherited, the high road of black consciousness, without vicarious participation by the majority and full participation by the minority in marriage in black and white, is no less a contradiction than marriage for the purpose of celibacy.

Put another way, black consciousness outdoes itself by being extremely attractive. The very fact of the black demand for full recognition and the nurture of the black past in the present as the necessary requirement for achieving radical change and a new future brings the black man and black woman to a new stage of appreciation by white women and white men. The contagion of the black movement is self-evident in its impact upon the larger society, which has taken its methods and put them to use in education, politics, and the peace movement. However, these issues we will have with us always if men continue to be men—they are not in fundamental clash with the American Creed. Blacks bring to the American experiment a cause which neither poor nor affluent whites can duplicate with all of their despair or frustration. The cause of blacks is not manufactured, it is not a new thrill; it is real blood and guts supported by moral rightness. To see an intrepid people rise with intestinal fortitude to meet the intractable is irresistible.

Black culture and black commonality have created an extraordinarily electric force whose time has come just when white culture and society are the least challenging and pioneering and valuable to white youth. It is not the object of black consciousness at this time to win white converts, but the undeniable worth and value of this movement increases daily the numbers of those quality white youth who seek to belong. Despite the extremity of the insistence of black consciousness, black power, and even black nationalism or separation by some black advocates, notably the Black Panthers, white men and white women have never sought union with black with such verve. By any measure, it is the best of white youth who find true life a venture in black. Those who have paid their dues are, for the most part, not rejected.

In the absence of black consciousness in all of its ramifications there would be no value in viewing seriously the ultimate resolution to the black-white embroilment. Above all else, men and women give their lives to those who show promise of giving purpose and meaning to their lives beyond providing for the basic needs. This is the true and universally significant adventure in black, the opportunity to identify with men and women who really know what they intend that is so dynamically contagious in black consciousness. It is this very ingredient which has so long been missing in our society, and has made previous concern with marriage in black and white a misplaced emphasis. It is too early for marriage in black and white to be of potent significance for more than the few. Black consciousness will need to do more of its work in attaining real freedom for blacks at every level for there to be participation in marriage in black and white by more than the avant-garde. But we can begin now to see the ultimate resolution emerging and the importance of bringing into being the solution, as opposed to letting the future do it.

To be consciously black is to be a hero and to be heroic for whites as well as blacks. Freedom, power, and equality are not granted blacks in the American experiment—they must be taken by means of self-esteem and assertiveness with solidarity. The old working assumption that blacks would gain in the mainstream to the extent their blood was mixed with whites, or that mixed blood is the singular solution, has now come to be seen as a rank red herring. Black consciousness, whether as an aggressive demand for integration, for separation, or both, advances blacks on their own militant initiative with a power envied by whites without a cause.

Instead of blacks begging to be let in, whites are begging to join the black movement. The very fact of black consciousness, popularly perceived by whites as antiwhite, has moved blacks to the near brink of unity in spirit, if not in deed, by disavowing intimacy with whites. Nothing has shattered the white ego more than apparent rejection. It is generally known how humans react when they are told not to eat of the forbidden fruit. This important independence of blacks and advance on their own has made them all the more attractive to white youth in search of an ideal to preach by practice. Historically, whites intermingled with blacks when blacks possessed what whites could not attain elsewhere, and then on white terms. Blacks are marching from pride to pride and as they advance from civil rights to local control and black power, there is a manhood expressed which is repulsive to the average adult middle class white and therefore exceedingly exciting for the perceptive white child.

There is no doubt about the fact that a profound wind of change is blowing through America. As blacks continue to open up the society to radical change, they find themselves inextricably involved with whites who seek them out at any cost.

The paradox of black assertiveness, which but a few years ago was the thing to avoid, is that the simultaneous push toward integration, separation, and black solidarity increasingly becomes sought after by whites who are permitted to participate to the extent they think and act black, under the hegemony of blacks— even to the point of intimacy. This intimacy has barely begun, but its minimal beginning is a sign that blacks are for humanity in their black consciousness and that whites can only find their humanity through unquestioning identification with the disinherited on the way to their inheritance—a new humanity. What is clear in all of this is that the advance of blacks in the society is only one thing, their acceptance is another. Not many years ago it appeared that some blacks denied their blackness wherever possible in order to identify with whites through *passing* for whites. The black consciousness movement has made it abundantly clear that there is no escape for any black as long as some blacks are denied their humanity. At the same time, it has given all blacks a new sense of their real worth and of possibility for changing the society.

Further, black consciousness has unleashed the reality that while the advance of some blacks is one thing, the final resolution of the black-white dilemma is quite another. There can be an advance of blacks through black consciousness in separation, but such an advance will not be the end to the American dilemma. The new thing in our time is the acceptance of black by blacks which ends escapism through "passing" by blacks or "interbreeding" as exploitation by whites. It barely opens the wholly new ground rule of equality through marriage in black and white, if at all. In this new era blacks are the determiners. Once upon a time it was held that "the bed of the Negro woman has been a leveling ground of democracy, a doctrine upon which all could agree." Here in one sentence is the old humanity—antiassimilation and antiblackness. The crisis of our time is acute. We are in dire need of a new humanity, a true community, and, there is awareness that this real meeting can only come through a new family of blacks and whites together in America. It is not helpful to hold that the marriage bed of the white woman will be the leveling ground of democracy, a doctrine upon which all can agree. There are some whites who set forth this response when their fellow whites ask what they can do. This is a hard answer, but one only whites can make to fellow whites, though it may be no more difficult than ending the night of wrong. This is not the pathway to the new humanity, it is too dogmatic. The new humanity will not be born of a large number of black-white marriages. Where once we thought interbreeding or intermingling, the invasion of blacks by whites, would solve the conflict through creating a society mustard yellow in color, we now know that the solution lies in a society where blacks are accepted and acceptable at every level, including marriage. How many engage in black-white marriages is not what counts. It's how the many count the black-white marriages which are engaged in! For there to be a new humanity we will need a new spirit. There is only one way to this new spirit, and that is the way of reconciliation. The price of reconciliation in the American experience is a very high one for whites. They will literally have to change their lives, die in their old selves and be reborn. Marriage in black and white is the imperative resolution because it demands reconciliation, the suffering of whites through what has heretofore been unsufferable.

By the power of black consciousness we can now see the advance of blacks toward separate but equal opportunity in the areas of politics, economics, housing, and education. This is known as pluralism. As we advance toward this first stage of freedom, some blacks will be satisfied to contribute to and live out of this pluralistic condition. But there will be blacks who will find no conflict between black consciousness and full humanity. They will be the man! They will demand equal but no separate opportunity in every sphere of life, including the social. What blacks really want is what true humanity demands—freedom of choice.

There is an unconscious sense of this black demand among whites. Some are willing to pay the price, but not enough. We know that the faith of Thomas Jefferson and Abraham Lincoln is still dominant, but no longer sufficient—that blacks and whites cannot live together in real equality. The old humanity, the American way of life, will not change because change is right. It will change only as the real world changes, as the new community, and the new humanity and the new family of blacks and whites create a new society.

Such a radical change will not be easy. Whether it comes by escalating fury or shared sensibility there is no alternative to real union in body and soul—for black consciousness will allow the society to rest on no other basis. The hope is in the present isolated, but illuminating, unity of a few blacks and whites in conscious black commonality. The fear is in the present suppressive, repressive, and oppressive responses to black-white unions which seek to stamp out our hope in the name of tradition. Those who will to crush our hope are not evil men. They are good men doing what they believe is necessary to hold on to what has been good for them. It is these good men who do the most evil in the name of good. They are all the more dangerous because they are good, sincere, well meaning. It is only as we face with candor our black-white intimate relations of the past that we will be able to decrease fear with increased hope.

Our real concern is the final resolution of black-white crisis in America, not marriages in black and white. But we cannot come to the final resolution, let alone solution, without marriages in black and white. Marriage in black and white is the key to resolving the black-white conflict because by destroying the taboo against marriage of blacks and whites in all of its expressions in contemporary America, white America would be affirming in the most total and meaningful way available to her that she accepts the personhood of blacks, and until she accepts the personhood of blacks there will be no end to the conflict. Thus it is imperative to focus on marriage in black and white. Those who stand opposed, oppose the ultimate resolution. Facts cannot be argued with; they can only be accepted or rejected. Since those who oppose the final resolution oppose marriage in black and white and those who oppose marriage in black and white on principle oppose the final solution, we have reason enough to face our history in order to accept it and thereby prepare ourselves and our children to be men and women of the future.

For the first time in our history, marriage in black and white can be faced as other than whites stooping down to pull up blacks or exploit them for the sake of making easier the bed whites have made so hard. That is, it is no longer a matter of turning black people white. The day which whites have dreaded is near at hand. The rise of black consciousness, though it be by way of separation, is too powerful a demand to be so limited. It is a call for fundamental change, for a right to be ready. It is not a call to marriage of blacks and whites but in its call to the right an image has been created that cannot be misperceived. It is a call to solve the problem of blacks and whites and therefore an unknowing commitment to marriage in black and white.

In the demand of black consciousness for the right, it must accept all those who seek to do the right. To the extent the black man stands up and fights for the right, to that extent he gains strength through freedom of choice and the choice of free men. The sexual attraction of white for black and black for white has been with us all along. It has been denied expression by keeping the black man and woman chained to slavery and its resulting image of inferiority. Freedom is gained to the degree that slavery is faced and accepted, and with this acceptance arises the demand for a new orientation. Freedom cannot now be put back. The free black man seeks to be himself and finds himself sought after as the only hero left for an affluent people in need of life.

We have stated the problem of cleansing the American psyche. We now engage in that process through turning to the truth and consequences of our sexual past.

Chapter Two

IMPROVIDENT AMBIGUITY AND IMPUDENCE
IN OUR SEXUAL PAST

Geeorge E. Simpson and J. Milton Yinger, two distinguished social scientists, conclude their study of black-white intermarriage with this statement:

> Intermarriage on a large scale would produce a relatively
> homogeneous population, physically and culturally. The
> elimination of intergroup conflicts based on race and culture
> would have societal advantages, although some would
> lament the passing of cultural pluralism.[1]

When asked by a newspaper reporter if marriage in black and
white would increase in the United States, former President Harry
S Truman replied:

> "I hope not; I don't believe in it." Then Mr. Truman asked
> the reporter that hackneyed question often spouted at
> anyone advocating racial integration, "Would you want your
> daughter to marry a Negro?" The reporter responded that he
> wanted his daughter to marry the man she loved whoever he
> might be. "Well, she won't love someone who isn't her
> color," the former President continued, and, as if he had not
> said enough, added that racial intermarriage ran counter to
> the teachings of the Bible.[2]

These two statements, by prominent white leaders in the 1960's, reflect the polarization on the issue of marriage in black and white in the United States and express in a nutshell the intellectual elite and the dominant popular view of our fundamental ambiguity. It is important for us at this juncture to understand how this American ambiguity came to be. To understand the history of our sexual past is not to change it, but in order to change the direction of our history an understanding of our sexual ambiguity is basic.

CROSSINGS OF PRIMARY STOCK

We do not know how many slaves were imported to the United States prior to 1808, when Federal law prohibited the slave trade. A figure between 333,000 and 400,000 is generally agreed to be reasonable. Slaves were smuggled in between 1808 and 1860 in numbers approximating those prior to 1808. It is probably accurate enough to assume the maximum total slave importation to have been under 1,000,000. We know even less precisely where all the slaves in the United States were located. Undoubtedly, the majority came by way of the "middle passage" from West Africa. However, a significant proportion were imported from the Mediterranean area and others were imported from Guinea and the West Indies. What we do know is that the imported slaves to America between 1620 and 1820 were not all "pure African." A number of our slaves were a cross between Portuguese and African or Spanish and African, for extensive miscegenation had taken place in Spain, Portugal, and in Africa, a pattern which was developed later among these colonists in the New World. The optimum figure for those slaves with some trace of white genes prior to their landing in the United States is fifty per cent.

Intercourse with pure Africans was not the sole prerogative of Mediterranean people, although the Spanish and Portuguese were more persistent:

> Alexandre Dumas was the son of a Haitian planter and a
> Negro woman. Alexander Pushkin, founder of modern
> Russian literature, was the offspring, on his mother's side, of
> a full-blooded Negro. Alessandro de' Medici, first hereditary

Duke of Florence, was the illegitimate son of Giulio, who later became Pope Clement VII, and a mulatto servant girl; he married Margaret, the illegitimate daughter of Charles V. John VI, King of Portugal, was a dark mulatto; his son, Pedro I, became the first emperor of Brazil. The Empress Josephine is alleged to have been a near white. Rogers claims that Robert Browning, Beethoven, and Haydn, among others, had Negro ancestry and calls attention to the fact that thousands of Guinea Negroes were imported into Europe in the early centuries of the African slave trade (1440 to 1773) and that today not one of these pure blacks remains. The absorption was probably greatest in Portugal and Spain. Among notable Americans, the story persists that Alexander Hamilton, who was born in the Island of Nevis, British West Indies, was of Negro descent. Complete proof or disproof of this allegation is difficult, since he was born out of wedlock. If Hamilton was not Negro, he certainly brought two Negro sons into the world. One married a very light-colored wife; the other married into a white family and lived as white.[3]

That the first children of African and European descent were born off the coast of Africa and on the Mediterranean shores cannot be attributed to the lack of desire on the part of Englishmen. It just so happened that the Spanish and Portuguese were the first to explore the coast of Africa and discovered as early as 1440 the value of Africans in European ports. By 1540 they were importing 10,000 slaves annually into the West Indies. The Dutch entered the slave trade in 1621, but lost their hegemony to the English through a series of naval wars. Though the English sea captain James Hawkins broke the Portuguese monopoly on the slave trade in 1562, it was not until 1631 that Charles I of England granted English traders exclusive rights to trade in Guinea, Benin, and Angola for 31 years. With the later defeat of the French on the high seas and the development of a large navy, the English dominated slave trading in the New World as well as in Europe. Though they were late in starting, the English were not slow about intimacies with Africans. For example, England completely absorbed the substantial African slave population in her midst in the seventeenth and eighteenth centuries. English slave traders and their crew not only penetrated the African people on African shores, but during the "middle passage" as well:

> Indeed, in those early days many a negress was landed upon our shores by her captors already pregnant by one of the demonic crew that made up the company of the slave ship that brought her over.[4]

Our purposes do not include an exploration here into the psychological ramifications of these somewhat exotic human intercourses or into the theory of the attraction of opposites. Whatever the psychological dynamics, or sociological ones for that matter, it is sufficient here to be reminded of the fact that from the beginning of contact between Africans and Europeans, the latter had no hesitancy regarding intimacy with the former. The historical record has implications for the present. As the social scientist Maurice Davie points out:

> There is nothing unusual about such intermixture. Wherever and whenever races have come together, they have intermingled. This fact, incidentally, is the best possible indication of the absence of any innate aversion of races to one another. What is uncommon in the American situation is the intensity with which the Negro element is disparaged.[5]

The popular mind contends that such intermixing is unusual, and in the unwitting writings of a scholar like Edward Byron Reuter, the contention of the popular mind finds a measure of fortification:

> The Negroes have never shown any marked aversion to crossing with other races. Their women at all times and places have entertained the men of all races and people with whom they have been in contact.[6]

Davie and Reuter may both be wrong; they cannot both be right. Reuter makes some allowances which appear to put him in line with Davie:

While all the advanced races have, under certain conditions, mixed with the women of the lower races they have not done so with anything like equal readiness. Of the white races, the Spanish and the Portuguese have mixed most easily and in the largest numbers. They have mixed, moreover, with almost equal readiness with the Malay, the American Indian, and the African Negress; and with less repugnance than any other people with whom these lower races have come in contact. "They have never acquired, or had lost as the result of experience, any aversion to race mixture." The French mixed readily with the American Indians but in contact with the Negroes in Haiti they mixed relatively little. The English have crossed with all the lower races, but much more slowly than have the Latin peoples. Moreover, the English mix less readily with the Negroes than the Indians, and more slowly with these than with certain of the brown races.[7]

Nevertheless, in all of this, Reuter's biases are obvious, and they are numerous. Reuter was a representative of a school of social scientists which was not consciously antiblack but nonetheless supported the idea of "superior" and "lower" races:

The simple fact of the case seems to be that the women of the lower races everywhere seek sex relations with the men of the superior race or caste. Ratzel comments upon "the ease with which Malay women form transitory alliances with foreigners," and adds that "nearly all the so-called Chinese women in Banca are half-breeds from Malayan mothers." Keller says of the Eskimo women that "illicit relations with white men are rather a glory than a disgrace." Of the Indian women, Lee says "she is the seducer and it is the proudest moment of her life when she has allied herself with a man of a superior race," while Crooke points out the fact that a failure on the part of girls of certain castes to attract the attention and have sex relations with men of a higher class ruins their chances to secure husbands in their own group, and that for a girl to claim such an honor falsely is legal grounds for divorce on the part of the outraged husband.[8]

Surely there are visions of grandeur in this view that the "lower race" female is the aggressor while the "superior race" white male is passive. Reuter was so caught up in an elitist position that it was impossible for him to accept another cultural perspective as of value. When the black princes of Africa permitted their black women to entertain the first white men, they did so as an expression of hospitality. African culture, among other nonwestern cultures, has not held to the monogamous or even marital code of the West. From the perspective of African culture, this sharing of one's women was not considered illicit as it is in our western sense. Such positions as Reuter's led Frantz Fanon to comment:

> When the question arises of understanding why the European, the foreigner, was called *Vazaha,* which means *honorable stranger;* when it is a matter of understanding why shipwrecked Europeans were welcomed with open arms; why the European, the foreigner, was never thought of as an enemy, instead of explaining these things in terms of humanity, of good will, of courtesy, basic characteristics of what Cesaire calls "the old courtly civilizations," scholars tell us that it happened quite simply because, inscribed in "fateful hieroglyphics"—specifically, the unconscious—there exists something that makes the white man the awaited master.[9]

As distinguished from racial superiority (a biological statement), Reuter holds to a cultural superiority of whites. In order to defend this cultural superiority, he does not deny that the "superior" whites mix with the "lower" blacks, browns, and beiges. Instead, he takes the position that the "superior" white culture is so irresistible that the contact between the "lower" and "superior" cultures turns the normally passive female of the "lower" culture into the aggressor and causes the normally aggressive male of the "superior" culture to become passive. Reuter and company could not hold that in the initial contact between the two different civilizations or cultures, black or brown or beige people were simply gracious. Furthermore, the readiness of the whites to mix with all manner of nonwhites did not appear to be in keeping with their "superior" status. Thus, it was necessary for him to underscore the white bias that these involvements were illicit, on the "outskirts of civilization." That is, the protection and maintenance of the "superior" culture led Reuter to make the case that the superior aspects of the "superior" culture were not involved in the initial, illicit intercourse, just the inferior aspects of the "superior" culture:

> In most of the early contacts of the white race with the darker races, the white race has been represented by its adventurer and outcast classes. In Central and South America, the adventurers and the clergy were reinforced by convicts sentenced to death or mutilation who had their sentences commuted on condition that they emigrate to the colonies. Greenland was practically a Danish penal colony with a forced immigration of orphan boys to recruit the teaching force and the inferior clergy. South Africa was made the dumping ground for Asiatic convicts. Portugal unloaded on her Brazilian colony not only her convicts but her prostitutes as well. Aside from the criminal and the vicious, however, the military and the adventurer classes are hardly more typical of the moral sense of a community, but they usually have been the first representatives of the superior race with whom the native peoples have come in contact.[10]

This attempt to maintain the moral as well as cultural superiority of white values (and to be fair, Reuter does not hold to white superiority) is rather strained. Even the suggestion that black people received only the dregs of the white society, while the whites gained the best of black culture is spurious:

> The mixed-blood group was of course in its origin the product of extramatrimonial association between the white men and the Negro women. From the Caucasian side the mulattoes' ancestry has not as a rule been of a particularly high order. The great mass of the mulattoes must trace their ancestry back to the association of their women with the lower classes of the whites. Certainly some mulattoes of

today can trace their ancestry back to men of great ability and prominence. But on the whole the Caucasian side of the mulattoes' ancestry has been, if not an inferior one, at least not above the average.

But from the Negro side the mulattoes are descended from the best of the race. In this respect America is but a single case of what appears to have been the general rule: the choicer females of a subject race have always been selected as the concubines and auxiliary wives of the master race. It is sometimes asserted that only the vicious members of the backward race entered into such relations, but this is not in accord with the facts.[11]

Reuter failed to consider seriously Edward Wilmot Blyden's suggestion that

the black man who was weak enough to be caught and shipped away as a slave was naturally inferior in mind and body to the black man who possessed ingenuity enough to escape from the toils of slavery and remain at home as a slave hunter.[12]

Of course the claim that inferior whites and the best of blacks intermingled gives the edge to whites and supports the contention that their "superior" culture will out. It takes no special genius to figure out that the initial contacts with the African culture would have been made by those members of western civilization who for various reasons were the most mobile. To count them as inferior therefore is suspect. Moreover, to make blacks the dumping ground where they give their best to the worst is highly questionable. We know that Alexander Pushkin's maternal great grandfather, named Hannibal, was the black of Peter the Great; that Benjamin Franklin was supposed to relate intimately with a number of black women, which he never affirmed or denied (his response being, "What is sauce for the goose is sauce for the gander"—"An humble attempt at scurrility"); that Thomas Jefferson had at least five black children; that Patrick Henry's black son was named Melancthon.* These exceptions only give rise to the suspicion that either there must have been many more involvements between "superior" whites and blacks which were not considered abnormal in periods past, or that prominent persons who engaged in black-white intercourse were not under attack from political enemies and were able to keep their private lives separate from the public. What is important is that blacks and whites engaged in sexual intercourse from the time of the initial contact between the two races and in America white-black intimacies were practical at all levels of the society because members of both races had the desire as well as the opportunity for it.

We shall see how it was that whites in our society maintained the figment of "superior" culture out of which the figment of white superiority grew—not through natural evidence but through the making of the rules which determined that blacks could become white but that whites could not become black:

> The actual amount of Negro blood introduced into the white
> race through the incorporation and marriage of mulattoes
> able to pass as white is of course very small. It requires eight
> or sixteen or more such crossings to introduce Negro blood
> equivalent to that of one full-blooded Negro. But each such
> case is a loss to the mulatto group and slows up by so much
> the process of amalgamation.[13]

However blacks are manipulated so that whites come out on top, the truth is, with respect to America, that in the beginning was the black people, and the black people were with white people, and black people were united with white people. Black people were in the beginning with white people; all things were made through black people, and without black people was not anything made that was made. In black people was life, the life was the light of

---

* No hyperbole is intended when we call George Washington "the Father of our country." Arnold Toynbee reminds us that "the planters had illegitimate children by Negroes. George Washington caught a cold while visiting Negro quarters on his estate for this purpose. It is never put into the official biographies, but this was the cause of his death. After all, it was a normal thing for a gentleman to do." (Arnold Toynbee talks on "Peace Power Race in America," with J. Robert Moskin, *Look,* March 18, 1969, p. 26.)

America. The light still shines in the darkness, and the darkness has not overcome it.

It is important now to see the variety of ways in which intercourse developed between blacks and whites on these shores.

EARLY FRUCTIFICATION IN THE COLONIES

The first permanent black settlers were the twenty let ashore at Jamestown in 1619 by Dutch slave traders. These blacks were not slaves, but indentured servants, reinforcements for white indentured servants in Virginia who supplied the primary labor needed for clearing the forests and enlarging the tobacco crops. The social condition of black and white servants was identical, and they were "bound together by a fellowship of toil." The white servants consisted of a group of poor people who signed off for a period of servile labor as payment for their passage to America. Others were kidnaped, among them children, on the streets of Europe and sold into servitude. There were prisoners of war, political prisoners, and criminals. Some of the white servants consisted of once successful persons fallen on hard times. Others were simply the poverty stricken of Europe. Criminals, prostitutes, convicts, and generally disadvantaged whites made up a sizable servile class in Virginia and Maryland.

Little time passed before servant blacks and whites engaged in intercourse. The earliest record available of a case against the cohabitation of black-white servants was the case of Hugh Davis, a white servant in Virginia who was sentenced to a public beating on September 17, 1630, "before an assembly of negroes and others" for "defiling himself with a negro." "It was required that he confess as much the following Sabbath." [14] The intimate relations between these servant groups were so natural and so widespread that the first slavery law was worked out to determine the status of children born to black and white servants; this took place in Virginia in 1662. The first law regarding slavery in Maryland was proposed in 1663; its aim was to prevent English women from marrying with slaves and to determine the status of slaves who had intermarried or would seek to do so in the future.

It is clearly evident that intermingling commenced early in the colonies and proceeded at a rapid rate. One historian wrote that "during the first half to three-quarters of a century there was an indiscriminate mingling and marrying" in the colonies. The records make clear that affection, sympathy, and intimate association between black and white servants continued even after blacks sunk from servitude to slavery. Indeed, black-white intercourse and children born of these relations had become fairly common before a variety of laws were enacted in a desperate, if successful, attempt to curb their situation. The Virginia Act of 1691, for example, was enacted

> for the prevention of that abominable and spurious mixture which hereafter may increase in this dominion as well by Negroes intermarrying with English or other white women as by their unlawful intercourse with one another.[15]

Nevertheless, during the period of servitude for blacks and whites a number of black-white marriages, as opposed to mere sexual intercourse, took place and the male partner was often black. There is some real evidence that at first marriage between the black male servant and the white female servant was encouraged by white masters who expected to gain more servants from the children of these unions.

In the bond of servitude, whites and blacks did not develop antagonisms or hate based on competition. Poor whites often shielded fugitive slaves. In all of this a great body of mulattoes were produced, children of white servant women by slave, servile, and free black men as well as children by black women cohabiting with white servants. The commonality and compatibility of black servants and slaves with white servants apparently developed into a very high degree of mutual acceptance. It was from without, not within, that the conflict between lower class blacks and whites developed:

> The miscegenation of these servile elements early came to be a matter of concern throughout the colonies. Thoughtful men saw the dangers of this in a frontier society and denounced such unions, but the miscegenation was already advanced before the whites realized the need of efforts to control it and maintain racial integrity. Numerous laws were designed to

stop racial fusion and to determine the status of mixed-blood offspring. Other laws were designed to restrain white women from marrying or cohabiting with Negroes and to fix the status of the children of such unions as had already been formed.[16]

It is not altogether clear why "the decent" elements of the society determined that black and white cohabitation and intermarriage, which had begun so well and naturally in the early years of the colonies, should be halted or why they felt the need to preserve "racial integrity" so strongly. It can be speculated that the increased number of black slaves and the less efficient performance of white indentured servants made the need for the latter less important, and therefore there was less need for children born of black and white unions. It can also be speculated that the children born of these unions were too often expected to be free, especially where the mother was white, and so the reaction was against the loss in capital investment. It may be that the blacks born of these unions grew to think of themselves as free to a degree that challenged too radically their purpose of being as the dominant white society had defined it. Looking back on the situation, one writer described the dominant white perspective this way:

> The contact of these two elements of slaves and convicts was neither prudent nor healthy. The halfbreed population increased and so did the free negroes. The negroes suffered from the touch of moral contagion of this effete matter driven out of European society.[17]

Another writer viewed the matter in this light:

> The women grew unchaste, the men dishonest, until in many minds the term "free negro" became a synonym of all that was worthless and despicable.[18]

Whatever the basis of the dominant white view, popular opinion became translated into law. It is not possible to determine the frequency of black-white marriages in those early years, but the fact that numerous laws were passed to prevent black-white marriages is an indication that the number was significant. The

1681 Maryland law developed around "Irish Nell," a servant to the Lord Proprietor, who had married a slave and the issue was the status of her children. Moreover, the first slavery act in Maryland, in 1663, outlawed what was apparently common:

> And be it further enacted, that all issues of English, or other free born women, that have already married negroes, shall serve the master. . . .[19]

In 1677 in Pennsylvania a white servant was indicted for intercourse with a black woman and in 1698 Chester County Court forbade race mixture:

> Again in 1722, a woman was punished for "abetting a clandestine marriage between a white woman and a Negro." The same year the Assembly received a petition praying for relief from the "wicked and scandalous practice of Negroes cohabiting with white people." A general law of 1725–26 forbade the mixture of races.[20]

There were legislative enactments regarding mulattoes in Connecticut in 1690, in New York in 1706, in Delaware in 1721, in New Hampshire in 1714, in New Jersey in 1704, and

> North Carolina in 1715 passed an act carrying a heavy penalty on any white man or woman who should marry a Negro, mulatto, or Indian and also provided a heavy penalty on any minister who should officiate at such a marriage.
>
> In North Carolina in 1727 "a white woman was indicted in the General Court because she had left her husband and was cohabiting with a Negro slave." [21]

In substance, then, whether within the conventional bounds of marriage or without, whites with the power to put their opinions into law found *honorable* cohabitation between blacks and whites undesirable. The marriages were contrary to public sentiment before they were contrary to public law. In defense of white culture, it was believed that intermingling took place only among blacks and "the meanest classes of whites," or, put more strongly:

> Among the servants imported into the colony, there were often women of a very low type, who during their term of servitude intermarried with negro slaves.[22]

What is important in all of this is that whether in the South or in the North the attitudes toward black-white marriages among dominant whites did not vary one iota. The attitudes in both the slave and nonslave-holding states could be described as they were in Pennsylvania:

> After a while a strong feeling was aroused, so that in 1821 a petition was sent to the Legislature, asking that mixed marriages be declared void, and that it be made a penal act for a negro to marry a white man's daughter. In 1834 such a marriage provoked a riot at Columbia; while in 1838 the subject caused a vehement outburst in the Constitutional Convention then assembled. Three years later a bill to prevent intermarriage passed in the House, but lost in the Senate. From time to time thereafter petitions were sent to the Legislature, but no action was taken; the obnoxious marriages continuing to be reported, and even being encouraged by some extreme advocates of race equality. Nevertheless what the law left undone was largely accomplished by public sentiment and private action. As time went on marriages of white people with negroes came to be considered increasingly odious, and so became far less frequent. When a case occurred, it was usually followed by swift action and dire vengeance. The fact that a white man was living with a negro wife was one of the causes of the terrible riot in Philadelphia 1849.[23]

The fact that the nonslave-holding states did not enact laws against marriage in black and white was undoubtedly due to the limited number of blacks in these states where, as in Massachusetts, there was "no problem":

> For a period of 138 years Massachusetts prohibited intermarriage between whites and Negroes or mulattoes. The statute of Queen Anne of 1705 may be said originally to have been tinctured by the religious objection to a union between

Christians and pagans. But it was several times reenacted long after such influences had ceased to exist. It was finally repealed in 1843. By such action Massachusetts did not by any means intend to declare in favor of racial intermarriage. The real significance of the repeal was that, whether consciously or unconsciously, the numerical insignificance of the Negro population had finally brought possibly a majority of the whites to a point from which they were able to view with entire indifference any possible consequences of a formal reversal of the ancient policy of the state.[24]

The thoughtful, decent, respectable, good white folk increased the public intolerance of intercourse and marriage in black and white during the first seventy-five years of the colonies' existence and deemed it necessary to put this public sentiment in the laws. Undoubtedly advocates of popular opinion were sincere in their efforts to stamp out black-white marriages, but their fanaticism proved to be neither good will nor will to the good. Instead of encouraging and teaching blacks and whites to continue in the civil, legal, and honest interrelationships, the white community promoted infidelity, promiscuity, and sexual irresponsibility, to say nothing of nurturing the seed bed of family disorganization among blacks. Public sentiment and public laws stamped out public marriages and served only to appease the sensitive eyes of whites who found it so unbearable that whites would be so attracted by blacks. It was as if the natural sexual attraction that had advanced to a remarkable degree could suddenly be eradicated by fiat or without permanent damage to whites and blacks. So, in the name of white folklore, open intercourse between blacks and whites withered, and clandestine intercourse flowered. The amount of black and white intercourse did not decrease, just the amount of marriage. Illegitimate children of white servants and black slaves increased. Indiscriminate sexual relations became the rule with few exceptions, with the price of social ostracism and legal punishment being paid most often by the children and only infrequently by their biological parents.

With the increase in laws and in the number of black slaves, and the definition of blacks as enslaved for life while whites were

bound only for a term of years, the natural affection and enthusiastic courting between whites and blacks ended with the same
certainty as marriage in black and white. There can be no doubt
that blacks were sought after by whites as the most agreeable of
companions until the laws against sexual intimacy emphasized racial and social differences, and thus increased race pride among
the "poor whites" which gradually developed into a bitter hatred
that still characterizes relationships between poor whites and
blacks. It is understandable that the healthy intercourse between
blacks and whites which had led to marriage when forced to the
level of clandestine relations would end up in hatred, especially
when the white woman guilty of bearing a black child gained five
years of punishment and "there were not a few cases of such offspring." Exacting penalties were meted out to slaves and free
blacks, and the children born of free blacks and whites were often
bound out for thirty years by church wardens. Add to these penalties the fact that the heaviest work load shifted from whites to
blacks, with black women working in the fields with men while
white servant women were placed in domestic service, and it is
understandable that white servants began to see themselves as a
class and exaggerated the difference between themselves and the
blacks: "Yet, in spite of the strong social antipathies, there were
some illicit relations between shameless white persons and Negroes." [25]

In time, this attitude that whites intimate with blacks were
"shameless" made its impact with vengeance. Where once blacks,
servants or slaves, were actively courted by poor whites, poor
whites came to treat blacks worse than did the slave traders, slave
overseers, and slave masters. It should be clear by now that the
hatred of blacks by poor whites was most unnatural, that it resulted from manipulation by those who governed the "superior
culture." And it may be added with some objectivity that in the
past, perhaps in the present as well, the true enemy of the black
man was the intellectual and opulent classes, not the least of
whom were the founding fathers, whom we know to be the foundling fathers as well. The great documents of America were written
by a class of men, who, in not a few cases, engaged their slaves in
"the pursuit of happiness" with pleasure, as well as labor. We

have long since come to terms with the ambiguity of the founding fathers; we have yet to grapple with their impudence as foundling fathers.

The intimacy between white indentured servants and black servants and slaves from 1620 was paralleled by intercourse with blacks by influential and affluential, intellectual and middle class whites. But unlike the poor whites, only the white male was involved, and of course marriage was a sometime thing. The name of their game was "I've got mine—you try and get yours." There would be no equality between black men and white men, no reciprocity. This is what is meant by "the mental superiority of the white race." There was no question of opportunity for the white male. There was even less question of his desire to bed and not to wed with black women. When the sympathy between servant whites and blacks had tailed off into social caste and rigid racial prejudice and jealousies, the white middle and upper class male stepped up the fructification. It is not to be wondered that the colonial period was a time of rapid intermixing and reproduction, for the white slave-holding class had unrestricted access to black women who were largely grouped in isolated rural farms or plantations. In this segregated arrangement, with the freedom between poor whites and blacks sharply curtailed, the only restriction on reproduction was the stamina of the relatively few white males. The effective barriers erected to limit relationships between black men and white women and relationships between poor white men and black women gave opportunity for the white overseers and slave masters to fulfill their desires:

> There were no formidable barriers to intercourse between
> slaves and the upper-class whites. The opportunities for
> association were practically unlimited. There was no attitude
> of racial jealousy to interfere, and the caste distinction was so
> clear that the relations of the sexes raised no question of
> social equality.[26]

The uninhibited sexual relations between native African women and members of the "superior culture" was explainable— what can you expect from adventurers and military men "on the outskirts of civilization"? As for the poor whites of the "superior culture," they were obviously inferior and "hardly more typical of the moral sense" of the superior race. But how does one explain the free but repugnant association of the intellectual and upper and slave-owning class with their female slaves? First, it is argued that these whites of "superior culture" did not have any natural attraction to black women and sought them only because of the absence of their own women: "The paucity of white women was an important factor in overcoming any racial repugnance and in stimulating the sexual use of Negro women." [27] It is difficult to determine how this fact makes the superior class of the "superior culture" superior to the inferior class "on the outskirts of civilization," especially when it is known that the slave holders and overseers were always and everywhere without their wives and the cultural elevation of white womanhood to the pedestal of near untouchability no doubt increased the desire for playmates.

Second, the superiority of the white male in the upper classes and his association with his black female slaves are defended on the grounds that he was not so much the seeker as the sought, not so much the seducer as the one seduced. Somehow the white man is the awaited master:

> It must be remembered that a sex relation between a slave woman and a white man was in no sense forced: it was in general a relation to which the Negro girl aspired and one which she courted.[28]

When the defense of the white male of good breeding revolves around the position that "the women of the lower races everywhere seek sex relations with the men of the superior race or caste," the conclusion follows that the starch has been taken out and these men are but poor victims whose only defense is benevolence:

> It seems to be the usual situation everywhere that the women of the lower races or the lower castes desire, seek, feel honored by the attention of the higher class men, and are enormously proud of their light-skinned half-caste children.[29]

This is sheer demonic rationalization, even when tempered:

The association of the slave-holding class and the slave
women is not properly to be considered as a forced
relationship. There were no doubt cases of the involuntary
use of the female slaves. But it was more usual for the
relationship to be courted by the slave women and girls as a
mark of distinction and this was especially true as social
distinctions arose between the house servants and other
occupational groups of the slave population.[30]

When the defense of a class takes such malevolently extreme
forms, blacks must thereby become rank fools:

The Negroes recognized the superiority of their masters and
attributed that superiority, as did the white man himself, to
the fact of his race and color. They accepted their inferior
status as a consequence of their inferiority. No Negro
questioned the superior ability of the white, and probably
there is no Negro today who does not subconsciously believe
the white man superior. Certainly the assumption is less
questioned among them than among whites.[31]

The simple truth is that the restraining of relationships between
poor whites and black slaves simply increased the indiscriminate
sexual relations of white men preying on black women with reck-
less abandon. In the colonial period, from the earliest days, males
in the higher classes "had given a share to the paternity of the
growing Negro population of America," [32] and, if the black
women could propose the white men could dispose: "From the
beginning the much larger portion of the intermixture occurred
between white men and Negro women and most of it was extramarital." [33]

THE PECULIAR INSTITUTION: 1776–1865
In the South throughout the early slavery years there was a considerable excess of black and white males and a scarcity of black
and white women, which meant that sexual desire tended to find
satisfaction without respect to race. However, the theory that
states that the pure African woman was repugnant to the upper

class white male holds very little water. Perhaps it was the case that white males preferred mulatto to pure African women, but we shall never know this was in fact the case because as white men engaged the pure African, they naturally increased the number of mulattoes. Some scholars claimed, and Gunnar Myrdal accepts the claim, that

> when a mulatto generation came into existence, it served as a new stimulus to relations between the Negro and white groups, as mulatto women were preferred to pure-blooded Negroes as sexual objects.[34]

This is a specious argument, however, born of white males "playing God" and creating black children in their own image:

> The choicest females of the black group became the mothers of a race of half-breeds. The female offspring of these mixed unions became chosen in turn to serve the pleasure of the superior group. By this process of repeated selection of the choicer girls of the black and mulatto groups to become the mothers of a new generation of mixed-blood individuals there has been a constant force making for the production of a choicer and choicer type of female.[35]

Furthermore, if one holds that the pure African was a less attractive object for sex than the mulatto, one also must hold that this very selection was a process engineered from the top down and not from the bottom up as some social scientists have suggested.

There is something unsettling in the argument that the paucity of white women led the white male to seek the black woman for sexual satisfaction and that since the black woman was the aggressor in these relations it is improper to label them as forced intercourse. What is missing in this justification of the upper class white male is the fact that he had no difficulty in converting his slave property into whatever kind of an object he desired, even a sexual object. To argue that the black slave woman had some choice in the matter neglects the fact that the hard laws preventing black-white marriages did not provide legal protection for the black woman to reject the advances of her white master or of his friends and workers. It is doubtful that fornication—voluntary sexual intercourse on the part of an unmarried person—was so much the initiation of the black woman as it was the privy of the white male. We are fully aware of the situation that blacks were not able to be witnesses against whites and that legal obstacles which might have prevented the seduction of black women were nonexistent. In fact, the North Carolina Supreme Court held in the nineteenth century that no white man could be convicted for fornication with a black slave woman. In the North Carolina Constitutional Convention of 1835 one man declared:

> A white man may go to the house of a free black, maltreat and abuse him, and commit any outrage upon his family, for all of which the law cannot reach, unless some white person saw the act.[36]

Only massive guilt would cause the fabrication of the notion that in a world where there were limited women and where black men were prevented from access to white women, black men would be indifferent or resigned to this raiding of their province by white males. Only a tremendous reservoir of guilt could break forth with the implication that the black female was the aggressor and the black male without rage especially in a world where a father heard the screams of his daughter being taken behind the barn or a son heard his mother yelling, waylaid in the next room by a white male.

On the plantations and the farms of the slave-holding Southern states, the white male was checked neither by legal redress for the black people nor by social responsibility. In fact, the sex mores tended to aid and abet misuse of black women. There certainly was no Puritan ethic at work among Southern "gentlemen" that might have acted as a humane control or tripper of the conscience. Fair game was underlying consensus, not fair play. In such a condition, where the seduction of black women by any means possible was not offensive, it is no wonder that some children thereby produced—and they were numerous—failed to be raised in the knowledge and admonition of family virtues or develop for themselves a solid family tradition.

There were many contemporary observers and reports lamenting the excessive numbers of bachelors in the South and the high rate of mulatto children. In such a situation, not all of the black-white unions were coerced, although far more of them were than is usually conceded. It is extremely evident that here, in these black-white unions, the white man created and perpetuated the idea that mixed-blood blacks or mulattoes were superior to pure Africans. This idea was followed by special treatment of mixed-bloods, perhaps because it was believed that the inferiority of blacks was lessened to the degree their genes were dominated by white ones. This exceptional treatment of mulattoes at first took many forms, as the white man saw in these mixed-bloods his own image:

> Some of the mulattoes were the children of white mothers and Negro fathers. When the question of the legal status of the Negroes came to be defined in law a distinction was made on the basis of parentage. It became a rule at law that the status of children should follow that of the mother, with the result that some percentage of the mulatto children were free persons. This group perhaps did not include a very considerable proportion of the total mulatto population but it contributed to the increase of the group of free Negroes and the percentage of mulattoes in the group.[37]

Obviously, if whites were going to treat blacks unequally, especially their children, this was a very potent power for corruption. The stakes were high and rewards often considerable and some black women were led to engage in uncoerced sexual relations with white men. Given considerable inducements, we can understand how some black women without the opportunity for merit advancement (and the male without any authority or power for achievement or justice) could, in the absence of personal freedom, be overwhelmed by the temptations of white men. It is in this context that the following statement of an observer is to be understood:

> Among the slaves, a woman apart from mere natural bashfulness, has no inducement to be chaste; she has many

inducements the other way. Her person is her only means of purchasing favors, indulgences, presents. To be the favorite of the master or one of his sons, of the overseer, or even of a driver, is an object of desire, and a situation of dignity. It is as much esteemed among the slaves as an advantageous marriage would be among the free.[38]

This is a very sad if revealing commentary upon the inhumaneness and inhumanity of slavery. What is important is that we see clearly that this prostitution was not that of free persons choosing this way, but a condition placed upon slaves by the will of whites who used naked and subtle power to create obedience to their will. Force is force, however, whether it be by coercion or seduction, when power is absolute.

Given the pressure chamber in which the black woman operated (and recognizing how the black male was largely out of it), the advantages of unions with white men, when not coerced but seduced, are plain. One, mulattoes were considered by whites to have "greater native ability," and because they were so considered were better treated and became those who were trained for skilled and semi-skilled tasks—the example par excellence of the self-fulfilling prophecy or vicious circle:

> The house servants throughout the slave period were a selected class. Appearance was one element entering into their choice for the occupation; natural intelligence another. The females of this class represented both physically and mentally the best of the race [in the sense that the female offspring of these mixed unions became chosen in turn to serve the pleasure of the superior group, to become the mothers of a new generation of mixed-blood individuals being a constant force making for the production of a choicer and choicer type female].[39]

Two, at first those sons and daughters of white men or women in union with blacks resulted in there being, often,

> a sentimental factor operating to favor the child. The relations between the parents of the mixed-blood children, at

least in some cases, were based on mutual affection. White men were sometimes inordinately fond of their colored babies. This matter of relationship and personal affection was a thing of first-rate importance in those cases where the mulattoes were children of the slave owner or some member of his family. Being the owner as well as the father or uncle of the mulatto child, he was in a position to give it special consideration. The cases where the masters were the slave owners of their own relatives and favored them above other slaves are numerous. Such children were often freed, sometimes they were educated, and generally they were directed into the more stimulating and less deadening sorts of occupations.[40]

Three, a class of mulattoes was created that looked up to whites and down on blacks because of cultural advantages sealed in blood distinctions:

Such families were, therefore, of more or less successful men and selected Negro girls. The children of such unions had on the whole a better ancestry and were more advantageously situated socially than were the children resulting from casual contacts or even the offspring of mixed marriages of a more conventional sort.[41]

Four, this special relation with the important man was also the only way the black woman had of not being molested by every Tom, Dick, and Harry.

In addition to the coerced and sentimental relations, white men sought intercourse with black women for purposes other than sexual desire and affectionate expression. Slave women were the legal property of the owner, and, whatever the going rate on the auction block, it was in every case cheaper to breed than to buy slaves. Nevertheless, sexual intercourse for the purpose of optimum propagation was motivated less by the low cost of breeding as opposed to buying, than by the real incentive of the higher value of mulatto slave women especially, although the mulatto male was desirable as well. Given the fact that slaves were first and foremost capital and personal relations quite secondary, to the point of being exceptions on the periphery, the high value placed on mulatto slaves became a matter of economics in which increased wealth was gained only through black-white unions. In the slave period this generally required the white male to be in wholesale copulation with the black woman. The percentage of mulatto women who gained personal advantage from sexual unions with white males was minute compared with the economic rewards reaped by the slave owners and in particular those who engaged in large scale breeding. To make the kind of profit breeders were after, the process had to be wholesale because of the unproductiveness of the early period of childhood. The high death rate in early childhood reinforced the encouragement of high fertility and thus the promptings that slave women "bear a long succession of children." A sufficient number of white males engaged in studding to influence generations to play because it paid, rather than to pay to play, and the repercussions of this attitude remain the root of our sociological, psychological, economic, and judicial problems:

> Great solicitude is often manifested that the breeding
> wenches, as they call them, should be the mothers of mulatto
> children, as the nearer the young slaves approach to white
> the higher will their price be, especially if they are female.
> Some affirm that rewards are sometimes given to white males
> who will consent to be the fathers of mulattoes.[42]

The sexual relations between white males and black women were consummated largely for personal profit and desire, as we have seen, but there were also some fairly stable, if socially unrecognized, relations. A form of polygamy was very common in which the white man maintained a white and one or more black households. This form of sexual engagement was exclusively that of the white male and the black woman. Over all, the relations were not indiscriminate sexual relations or promiscuous ones so much as the master cohabiting with his "favorite slave girl," and his son following suit. In the antebellum beginnings, children of these polygamous relationships were frequently given freedom (and occasionally the mothers as well) and sent away. Since the restriction placed on black slaves in the South generally applied to the free blacks, the master would often send his natural children as well as other faithful slaves he wished to spare the general fate, north to freedom. Booker T. Washington spoke of this arrangement succinctly in quoting a free black who was speaking of the period around 1850:

> At this time says Mr. Brown: "Cincinnati was full of women, without husbands, and their children. These were sent by planters of Louisiana, Mississippi, and some from Tennessee, who had got fortunes and had found that white women could live in those states, and in consequence, they had sent their slave wives and children to Cincinnati and set them free.[43]

Booker T. Washington underscored this development with relation to a settlement in Wilberforce, Ohio, named for the abolitionist:

> The thing that gives a peculiar and interesting character to many of these ante-bellum Negro settlements is that they were made by Southern slave-holders who desired to free their slaves and were not able to do so under the restrictions that were imposed upon emancipation in the Southern states. Many of the colored people in these settlements were the natural children of their master.[44]

Just prior to the Civil War, the polygamous relations which had developed on the plantations spread into a system of prolonged relations and mutual devotions which were carried on in the large cities. This system was referred to as concubinage, since it nearly approached the marriage condition. Concubinage, operating as "a substitute for marriage in institutionalizing and ritualizing interracial unions," expanded between the free mulatto women and the nonslave-holding men in the cities, far beyond the polygamous relations between the slave-holding men and their female slaves. At its height, the system flourished wherever there was a large number of black free women of mixed ancestry who had gained a degree of culture and sophistication. In Charleston, Mobile, and, especially New Orleans, concubinage was all but a socially sanctioned institution. Here light-colored black women or mulattoes tentatively emerged into a separate class popularly referred to as creoles. Frederick Law Olmstead described this system best in his *A Journey in the Seaboard Slave States,* set forth at length here because it is amply illustrative:

> I refer to a class composed of the illegitimate offspring of white men and colored women (mulattoes or quadroons), who, from habits of early life, the advantages of education, and the use of wealth, are too much superior to the negroes, in general, to associate with them, and are not allowed by law, or the popular prejudice, to marry white people. The girls are frequently sent to Paris to be educated, and are very accomplished. They are generally pretty, and often handsome. I have rarely, if ever, met more beautiful women, than one or two of them, that I saw by chance, in the streets. They are much better formed, and have a much more graceful and elegant carriage than Americans in general, while they seem to have commonly inherited or acquired much of the taste and skill, in the selection arrangement, and the way of wearing dresses and ornaments, that is the especial distinction of the women of Paris. Their beauty and attractiveness being their fortune, they cultivate and cherish with diligence every charm or accomplishment they are possessed of.
>
> Of course, men are attracted to them, associate with them, are captivated, and become attached to them, and not being able to marry them legally, and with the usual forms and securities for constancy, make such arrangements "as agreed upon." When a man makes a declaration of love to a girl of this class, she will admit or deny, as the case may be, her happiness in receiving it; but, supposing she is favorably disposed, she will usually refer the applicant to her mother. The mother inquires, like a Countess of Kew, into the circumstances of the suitor; ascertains whether he is able to

maintain a family, and, if satisfied with him, in these and other respects, requires from him security that he will support her daughter in a style suitable to the habits she has been bred to, and that, if he should ever leave her, he will give her a certain sum for her future support, and a certain additional sum for each of the children she shall then have.

The wealth, thus secured, will, of course, vary—as in society with higher assumptions of morality—with the value of the lady in the market; that is, with her attractiveness, and the number and value of other suitors she may have, or may reasonably expect. Of course, I do not mean that love has nothing at all to do with it; but love is sedulously restrained, and held firmly in hand, until the road of competency is seen to be clear, with less humbug than our English custom requires about it. Everything being satisfactorily arranged, a tenement in a certain quarter of the town is usually hired, and the couple move into it and go to housekeeping—living as if they were married. The woman is not, of course, to be wholly deprived of the society of others—her former acquaintances are continued, and she sustains her relations as daughter, sister, and friend. Of course, too, her husband (she calls him so—why shouldn't she?) will be likely to continue, also, more or less in, and form part of, this kind of society. There are parties and balls and all the movements and customs of other fashionable society, which they can enjoy in it, if they wish. The women of this sort are represented to be exceeding affectionate in disposition, and constant beyond reproach.

During all the time a man sustains this relation, he will commonly be moving, also, in reputable society on the other side of the town; not improbably, eventually he marries, and has a family establishment elsewhere. Before doing this, he may separate from his *placée* (so she is termed).

If so, he pays her according to agreement, and as much more, perhaps, as his affection for her, or his sense of the cruelty of the proceeding, may lead him to; and she has the world before her again, in the position of a widow. Many

men continue, for a long time, to support both estab-
lishments—particularly, if their legal marriage is one *de
convenance*. But many others form so strong attachments,
that the relation is never discontinued, but becomes, indeed,
that of marriage, except that it is not legalized or solemnized.
These men leave their estate at death, to their children, to
whom they may previously have given every advantage of
education they could command. What becomes of the boys,
I am not informed; the girls, sometimes, are removed to
other countries, where their color does not prevent their
living reputable lives; but, of course, many continue in the
same society and are fated to a life similar to that of their
mothers.[45]

Concubinage and other forms of illicit relations in which the
white male held sway were on the ascendancy throughout the antebellum period, in spite of the rigid laws and social sanctions
which existed to deter them. The simple truth that a natural
affinity between blacks and whites is thwarted and twisted into an
unnatural one cannot elude us. In all this we see that the deepest
dimension of man is not reason but passion, and it is passion
which conjures up in the reasoned rationalizations that turn
blacks into objects of prey at the same time it creates the false
myths that intercourse between blacks and whites is a violation of
the divine purpose manifested in color differences; that western
civilization will fall by the rise of barbaristic blacks, who would
contaminate the Nordic stock; that the nation will fall as a result
of its genius being diluted. In order to forestall any or all of these
evils, the nice, decent, God-fearing, good white folk bring to bear
external control and use the state to deny black-white marriages
the protection of civil society; they force the church to withhold
its sanction and blessing; they ostracize those who dare to ignore
public sentiment, the law, and the church; and, in times past, the
best of white folk were enraptured on the sidelines as white mobs
were unleashed to regulate and discipline persons violating the
basic passions. In the name of white womanhood and social in-

tegrity, American whites did not prevent interracial intercourse—
they simply drove it into the dark recesses of clandestine, cheap,
and dishonest impudence, there to permit ambivalence, but never
resolution, of the ambiguity.

The effect of slavery was to increase the instability of blacks
with respect to pride in person and in family. The wanton use of
black women by white men, however refined, taught very well the
sex code expected of blacks. The children of white fathers and
black mothers were generally disowned by their fathers, despite
the exceptional patterns set by those living in the limited spheres
of polygamy and concubinage. The children were not only disowned by the father but despised by the society. After the first
generations of familial feelings toward their black children among
a small number of notable upper class or wealthy white men,
white people in general did not see in mulattoes their own image
to be revered. Instead of developing the mulattoes as a separate
group, as an advance between blacks and whites, white American
society placed all blacks among the outcast. All blacks are held in
contempt; no blacks are social equals. The pure African or black
is held in contempt because he is believed to be from an inferior
ancestry. The mulatto is held in contempt because his approximation of the white group is evidence of his irregular and illicit origin, and combined with the other known half of his origin, the
mulatto excites as much or more prejudice as his darker brother.

Yet, despite being "forbidden by the decent elements of the
white community," intermarriage, as well as various other forms
of sexual unions between blacks and whites took place, if infrequently, in the antebellum days. Perhaps they were only incendiary where whites were concerned, but they do indicate that black-
white intimate relations can be full and honest even in a dishonest, hostile society. Following the hardening of the laws in the
slave states, black-white marriages did not occur there except in
Louisiana among whites and creoles, and then rarely. Frederick
Law Olmstead quoted a resident of New Orleans:

> White men, sometimes, married a rich colored girl; but he
> never knew of a black man to marry a white girl. [Olmstead
> adds: "I subsequently hear of one such case."] [46]

In the light of what we have previously set forth in this chapter, the surprise is not that black-white marriages took place infrequently, but that they took place at all. In the antebellum North black men married white women with some frequency, but these marriages have usually been explained away by saying either that "these unions take place without the girl realizing that she is marrying a Negro," [47] and thus,

> cases where such facts are made the grounds for divorce proceedings [because the man is so light he is taken for white], appear from time to time in the daily press,[48]

or, "the women in most of the unions are recent immigrants and often, no doubt, contract the alliances without realizing the social consequences." [49] It was generally felt that no knowledgeable, decent, self-respecting white woman would engage in marriage to a black of course unless she was a "very low type." Even where such a distinguished American as the former slave Frederick Douglass, who married a white woman as his second wife, is concerned it is necessary to place such a relationship in an explanatory context:

> In the period just preceding the Civil War, the emotional tension in the North and the preaching of amalgamation of the races by Phillips [Wendell] and others brought about a few intermarriages.[50]

Every conceivable argument has been used to pooh-pooh intimate relations between blacks and whites by rationalizing the dishonest ones and downing those that are honest. If a white woman becomes intimate or even dares to marry a black man she is written off as decadent:

> The few white women who have given birth to mulattoes have always been regarded as monsters; and without exception, they have belonged to the most impoverished and degraded caste of whites, by whom they are scrupulously avoided as creatures who have sunk to the level of the beasts of the field.[51]

It soon becomes evident in the research on sexual unions between blacks and whites that we know very little about our historical past, and what we do know comes forth less as a description of reality than a projection of what writers believe reality should be.

The suspicion is justified when we recall that during the antebellum period upper class whites engaged in concubinage widely and with some regularity (to say nothing of black men engaged with white women in the North), and then read the following "observation":

> Comment on these cases is hardly necessary. They tend to prove that as a rule neither good white men nor good white women marry colored persons, and that good colored men and women do not marry white persons. The number of cases is so small, however, that a definite conclusion as to the character of persons intermarrying is hardly warranted. However, it would seem that if such marriages were a success, even to a limited extent, some evidence would be found in a collection of thirty-six cases. It is my own opinion, based on personal observation in the cities of the South, that the individuals of both races who intermarry or live in concubinage are vastly inferior to the average types of the white and colored races in the United States; also, that the class of white men who have intercourse with colored women are, as a rule, of an inferior type.[52]

As the antebellum days drew to a close the number of free blacks increased. A great many of these blacks were women, and, as we have seen, their freedom was, often enough, at the behest of their former master whom they had well pleased. These free black women were concentrated in the cities without legal husbands and had great mobility. The women were not only free but more often than not came to the cities bearing children who grew up free. There in the mobility and anonymity of the urban centers, with few free black males, black women engaged in sexual unions with white men whom they otherwise would have had no opportunity to meet. It is the case that with the precedent of polygamy and its resultant concubinage and with the freeing of the black woman for past favors in far greater numbers than the black male, a pattern of black-white unions had not only been set, but most alternatives effectively eliminated, except for spinsterhood or the lesbian life. Given this development, it is not surprising to learn that in the antebellum and postbellum eras the amount of black-white intercourse surpassed its beginnings on the plantations. Of course black-white unions increase wherever whites and blacks are together, and blacks are a small fraction of the number of whites. This was the case in the cities of the slave and postslavery periods and there the frequency of contacts multiplied over those on the plantations where the number of whites were small, though amazingly prolific.

POSTBELLUM AND RECONSTRUCTION
INTERRACIAL INTERCOURSE

In the era of slavery interracial unions between upper class whites and their favorite slave girls or women were very common. Upper class whites had the pick of the lot, and the more they bred, the lighter became their results and choices as well. This plantation custom spread to the cities as these women with children were released for various and sundry reasons. It has been traditionally assumed that the immediate postbellum and subsequent Reconstruction eras drastically reduced the number of the upper class whites with black mistresses. It is probably the case, however, that the decline was more apparent than real. As John Dollard wrote of the decline, "a rising social pressure has brought people to exaggerate the actual decline in these patterns since slavery days." [53] The freeing of the slaves increased their numbers in the cities and also the opportunity for interracial intercourse. In the period between Emancipation and Reconstruction, the selective processes of breeding and harboring favorite black women by white upper class men gave way to a more pervasive and less exclusive intermixture.

It is most difficult to determine the turning point when the more stable relations of upper class and middle class whites with black women gave way to the dominant pattern of promiscuous relations of lower class white men and black women. Emancipation increased interracial intercourse for the following reasons.

First, slavery was largely a rural institution where the great bulk of blacks was not in contact with great blocks of whites. It was a peculiar institution in the sense that black women were kept, and most blacks were kept from involvement with those not accepted by the masters. Second, slavery taught no code of ethics with respect to sex. Family life was not the exception to the rule among blacks, though unrestrictive intercourse between blacks and blacks and blacks and whites was the order of the day. Emancipation changed the institutionalized relations of the rural areas and set blacks free in the urban areas armed with social disorganization and personal demoralization that resulted in "a prolonged period of sex irregularity and racial intermixture." Third, the freedom of the blacks to move at will in urban centers increased their contact with whites of all stations and standards. Fourth, personal demoralization and social disorganization of family relations, the mobility and desertion of the husband who had a freedom of movement formerly enjoyed largely by women, provided the women with real susceptibility to unstable sex interests of the white male. Fifth, despite the freedom of blacks, the power of whites was still unchallengeable and the intimate associations were "pretty much at the will of the white man":

> Although the legal relations between the races had been drastically altered, the ascendant position of the whites still enabled them to utilize this for sexual purposes.[54]

Sixth, black women who had been used to the favors only white men could provide did not immediately give up concubinage and the rewards of the status they had achieved in their relationships with white men for what some believed to be the less prestigious relation of marriage to a black man.

The sufficient means of determining the relative amount of increase in interracial intercourse with Emancipation are no longer available. But the turning point from stable concubinage to free sexual exploitation, from the unique sexual relations of white upper class and middle class men with black women to a more universal promiscuity among all white male elements, resulted. The increase in the white male's interracial experience in intercourse was less productive of stable relations and children. There was little opportunity for formal prostitution; few prostitutes could make a living when black women were so vulnerable. Yet, the pattern of the white male and black female more and more took on the form of prostitution, and this casual relation did more than anything else to speed "race consciousness" among blacks and the demand for equal protection of their women. Reporting on one county in North Carolina, E. Franklin Frazier pointed up this need:

> Illicit unions between white men and mulatto women, which were responsible for the large mulatto class, continued on a large scale until the opening of the present century.[55]

The formal concubinage with responsibility where the white father expressed interest in his mulatto child as in the following ended with some abruptness:

> They care for their children, clothe and educate them, and may even live with them. In some cases the white fathers send their Negro children away to be educated and in a number of instances have provided for them in their wills.[56]

With the passing of the stable old days, fornication without responsibility was as common, as W. E. B. Du Bois states:

> In many an instance a prudent negro mother finds it wise to send her good-looking yellow daughter to some institution to save her from the temptation of association with the lowest grade of white boys in the neighborhood.[57]

It is of course not our concern here to deal with the black family since we are interested singularly in interracial intercourse, but the impression is not to be left that the majority or all of the black families were in disarray. E. Franklin Frazier reminds us that

> the disorders arising from the Civil War and Emancipation often provided a proof of the strength of marital and family

ties that had developed during slavery. Many mothers kept their children with them and cared for them at tremendous sacrifice.

The family life of the emancipated Negro was influenced to a large extent by his social development under slavery. Even during slavery some of the free men had engaged in semi-free economic activities in order to support their families. Among the better situated slaves, the family had acquired considerable stability and the transition to freedom did not result in disorganization.[58]

It is clear that in the colonial period laws were enacted against illicit intercourse and marriage between blacks and whites. It is also clear that laws were active against black-white marriages only, and that they were virtually dead letters when it came to the white male having his fun at the expense of the black female. Though the legal situation if anything increased cohabitation, laws were of paramount importance for the mode, model, and ambiguity of the twentieth century.

Chapter Three

PERIL AND PARADOXES IN
THE DOUBLE STANDARD

At the turn of the century, when Reconstruction was ended before it had a good beginning, the South had so fixed blacks "in their place" that to be mistaken for one required legal redress:

> In 1900, a Reverend Mr. Upton delivered a temperance address near New Orleans. The reporters, desiring to be complimentary, referred to him as a "cultured gentleman." In the transmission of the dispatch by wire to the New Orleans paper, the phrase was, by mistake, changed to "colored gentleman." The *Times-Democrat* of that city, unwilling to refer to a member of the Negro race as a "colored gentleman," changed it to "Negro," and that was the word finally printed in the report. As soon as he learned of the mistake, the editor of the paper duly retracted and apologized. But Mr. Upton, not appeased, brought a suit for libel and recovered fifty dollars damage.[1]

By 1900, the white man in the South had indisputable control and once again held the reins tight beyond challenge. Yet, the black people remained a disturbing presence. Perhaps the most troublesome nightmare was the persistence of reports concerning interracial equality in the North and the fear that the chickens might come home to roost. Southern whites knew that

> occasionally a white man goes completely native, living openly with a Negro woman in a Negro section of a town, associating only with Negroes, withdrawing himself from the world of whites.[2]

Such a development was too rare to be distressing, and posed no immediate threat to the established way of life:

> The usual version of the sexual inequality in Cottonville (pseudonym for a town in Mississippi) is that the white men and colored women "have the run of both races." [3]

If this situation were to be reversed by bold black bucks, however, a whole way of life would be ended. To preserve this dual way of life, Southern states made their existing miscegenation laws more exacting, as we shall see. For example, Virginia and Georgia went the route of requiring every citizen to register and state his "race."

In the North, black males were marrying white women in noticeable numbers. Such unions were generally rationalized by Northern moderates as a phenomenon of light-skinned black males and lower class European immigrant girls:

> In the majority of intermarriages the white women belong to the lower walks of life. They are German, Irish, or other foreign women, respectable but ignorant.[4]

It was widely held that the black man was a victim of untoward circumstances: "The desire of the Negro in this respect is, when he becomes wealthy, frequently taken advantage of by white adventuresses of questionable virtue." [5] The danger of this condescension lies in not giving the black man his due, for it was the case that Jack Johnson, former heavyweight champion of the world, was stripped by the white power structure and not by any of his white wives. Despite the mind sets with respect to certain personalities, a sufficient number of acceptable interracial unions occurred to promote the idea in some quarters that the final solution to the black-white antipathy would take the route of marriage between upper class black males and lower class white females. This was a prediction underscored by the nearly universal vision that interracial marriages took place between important black grooms and unpromising white brides:

> For this reason the idea, unpopular, to be sure, but still indicated by the facts, that the races in America are amalgamating is not unwelcome to many thinkers.
>
> That simply goes to show that we are now part way along in the process, which I do not hesitate to say will be accomplished in time. The black race is to be absorbed.
>
> In fact, things will not be so repellent in a few hundred years as it is now. As it is, those who say the relation between whites and blacks is a symptom of mental defect on the part of the whites fail entirely to consider that times without number the scions of our best Southern families have shown signs of such degeneracy.
>
> Is it not more reasonable to expect that as time goes on the more cultured blacks will more or less naturally intermingle with the least cultured whites in the South until eventually the whole process will have been complete and our race will have absorbed the other? Surely, there is every reason to believe that the condition will result.[6]

Given such demeaning aspirations to blacks, such incendiary suggestions for Southern whites, such illiberal ideas to Northern whites—it is easily understood why blacks opposed miscegenation, why Southern whites despised it and why Northern whites were unreceptive to it. In this context, Booker T. Washington's December 4, 1911, estimate of amalgamation is instructive:

> I have never looked upon amalgamation as offering a solution of the so-called race problem and I know very few negroes who favor it or even think of it, for that matter.
>
> What those whom I have heard discuss the matter do

object to are laws which enable the father to escape his responsibility, or prevent him from accepting and exercising it when he has children by colored women.

Those who are fighting race distinctions are doing so, I think you will find, not because they want amalgamation or because they want to intermingle socially with white people, but because they have been led to believe that where race distinctions exist they pave the way for discriminations which are needlessly humiliating and injurious to the weaker race.

Let me add that I do not wholly share this view myself. While there may be some serious disadvantage in racial distinctions, there are certainly real advantages to my race, at least.[7]

In all of this we can perceive why the real as well as potential sexual intercourse between blacks and whites immediately following the Civil War is highlighted in the legislation enacted against black-white marriages.

We pointed out in an earlier chapter that the greatest bulk of anti–black-white marriage legislation was packaged prior to Emancipation. The exception in the South was Louisiana which did not legislate against marriage in black and white until 1908. Only Western states enacted such laws after 1910: North and South Dakota, Wyoming, and Montana. However, due to the fears we have seen, many states both in the North and in the South amended their laws following 1910.

While all states opposed marriage in black and white and therefore miscegenation or amalgamation, no state (with the possible exception of Florida) enacted at any time a statute forbidding fornication or adultery between blacks and whites which it intended to be enforced. The undoubted assumption behind this loophole was the feeling that where black-white fornication or adultery would occur it would involve the white male and black female. The closest approximation to statutes forbidding illicit interracial intercourse were those which made cohabitation (the act or state of living together as though married) and concubinage (habitual cohabitation) illegal. The key to these statutes was the universal interpretation that *casual* or *promiscuous* relations between blacks and whites were not considered illegal nor were these laws intended to curb them, unless a white woman were involved, and when a white woman was involved, a statute of this sort was rarely tested in the courts for its constitutionality:

> *Louisiana:* "Concubinage between a person of the Caucasian or white race and a person of the colored or black race is hereby made a felony. . . . For the purpose of this act concubinage is hereby defined to be the unlawful cohabitation of persons of the Caucasian and of the colored races whether open or secret."

> *Nevada:* "If any white person shall live and cohabit with any black person, mulatto. . . . in a state of fornication . . ."

> *South Dakota:* "Illicit cohabitation of any persons belonging to the African . . . race, with any person of the opposite sex, belonging to the Caucasian or white race, is hereby prohibited."

> *Alabama:* "If any white person or any negro. . . . live in adultery or fornication with each other, each of them must, on conviction, be imprisoned. . . ."

Obviously, these laws were designed to prohibit black-white intercourse only so far as this act included an intention of future commitment. Furthermore, though Alabama was the only state which on the face of its legislation sought to cover every instance of black-white sexual intercourse, the statute as interpreted did not have this intention. It is to be noted as well that with the exception of Alabama these states passed their laws after 1908.

Among the states that prohibited black-white marriages in their constitutions are the following:

> *Alabama* (Sec. 102 of the amended 1901 Constitution): "The legislature shall never pass any law to authorize or legalize any marriage between any white person and a negro, or descendant of a negro."

> *Florida* (Constitution of 1892, Art. 16, sec. 24): "All marriages between a white person and a negro, or between a

white person and a person of negro descent to the fourth
generation, inclusive, are hereby forever prohibited."

South Carolina (Constitution of 1895, Art. 3, sec. 33): "The
marriage of a white person with a negro or mulatto, or person
who shall have one-eighth or more negro blood, shall be
unlawful and void."

Tennessee (Constitution of 1896, Art. 11, sec. 14): "The
intermarriage of white persons with negroes, mulattoes, or
persons of mixed blood, descended from a negro to the third
generation, inclusive, or their living together as man and wife
in this state is prohibited. The legislature shall enforce this
section by appropriate legislation."

During the nineteenth century thirty-eight states, including nearly
every former colony, passed legislation prohibiting black-white
marriages. A number of states repealed their laws years before the
Civil War, others in the period following the Civil War and the
freeing of the slaves (Pennsylvania—1780, Massachusetts—1843,
Rhode Island—1881, Maine—1883, Michigan—1883, New Mexico—1886, and Ohio—1887).

The nationwide concern about black-white marriages was
reflected in the rash of bills prohibiting black-white marriages
proposed to state legislatures in 1913. These bills were defeated
that year in Connecticut, Kansas, Illinois, Iowa, Michigan, Minnesota, New York, Ohio, Pennsylvania, Washington, and Wisconsin. In the South, however, the advance of interracial sexual
intercourse did not lead to the repeal of laws in the wake of
Emancipation and the freeing of the slaves, but often led to more
stringent laws.

Twenty-eight states had active anti–black-white marriage
statutes in 1913, Montana and Wyoming acting later. Excerpts
from these state statutes follow to illuminate two significant facts.
First, with the exception of California, these laws were embedded
only in criminal statutes and therefore were not within the jurisdiction of civil courts. Second, the variety and content of the
amount of blood it took to be criminally defined as a black person
discloses the extent to which whites insisted that blacks were ruled

out of bounds for social equality, marriage by religious or civil matrimony:

Alabama: "If any white person and any negro, or the descendant of any negro, to the third generation, inclusive, though one ancestor of each generation was a white person, intermarry, or live in adultery or fornication with each other, each of them must, on conviction, be imprisoned in the penitentiary for not less than two, nor more than seven years." [Criminal Code, 1896.]

Arizona: "All marriages of persons of Caucasian blood, or their descendants with Negroes, . . . and their descendants, shall be null and void." [Revised Statutes, 1901; *penalty:* fine of not more than $300, imprisonment of not more than six months.]

Arkansas: "All marriages of white persons with Negroes or Mulattoes re declared to be illegal and void." [Kerby's Statutes, 1904; *penalty:* imprisonment of one month to one year.]

California: "All marriages of white persons with negroes, . . . or mulattoes are illegal and void." [Kerr's Code, 1906; *no penalty*.]

Colorado: "All marriages between Negroes or Mulattoes, of either sex, and white persons are declared to be absolutely void." [Mill's Annotated Statutes, 1891; *penalty:* fine of no less than $50 and no more than $500, imprisonment of three months to two years.]

Delaware: "Marriage shall be unlawful between a white person and a negro or mulatto. If a marriage, prohibited by this section, be solemnized, it shall be void, and the parties thereto shall each be deemed guilty of a misdemeanor and shall be fined one hundred dollars and if any preacher shall knowingly and willfully procure or aid in the contracting or solemnizing such marriage, he shall be deemed equally guilty and shall be fined in like manner. Or if the parties to any marriage prohibited by this section, although the same may have been solemnized in another state, shall cohabit as husband and wife in this state, they shall each be deemed guilty of a misdemeanor, and upon conviction thereof shall be fined one hundred dollars." [Revised Code, 1893; *penalty:* no less than one hundred dollars, imprisonment of not more than thirty days.]

Florida: "It shall be unlawful for any white male person residing or being in this state to intermarry with any negro female person; and it shall be in like manner unlawful for any white female person residing or being in this state to intermarry with any negro male person; and every marriage formed or solemnized in contravention of this provision of this section shall be utterly null and void." [General Statutes, 1905; *penalty:* fine of not more than $1,000, imprisonment of not more than ten years.] "Every person who shall have one-eighth or more negro blood shall be deemed and held to be a colored person or negro."

Georgia: "The marriage relation between white persons and persons of African descent is forever prohibited, and such marriage shall be void." [II Code, 1895; *penalty:* fine of not more than $1,000, imprisonment of not more than six months.]

Idaho: "All marriages of white persons with negroes or mulattoes are illegal and void." [Revised Code, 1908; *penalty:* fine of not more than $500, imprisonment of not more than six months.]

Indiana: "No person having one-eighth part or more of negro blood shall be permitted to marry any white woman of this state, nor shall any white man be permitted to marry any negro woman or any woman having one-eighth part or more of negro blood, and every person who shall knowingly marry in violation of the provisions of this section shall, on conviction, be fined not less than one hundred dollars, nor more than ten years." [Burn's Annotated Statutes, 1908.]

Kentucky: "Marriage is prohibited and declared void between a white person and a negro or mulatto." [Carroll's Statutes; *penalty:* fine of not less than $500 and not more than $5,000.]

Louisiana: "Marriage between white persons and persons of color is prohibited [one-sixteenth], and the celebration of all such marriages is forbidden, and such celebration carries with it no effect and is null and void." [Civil Code, 1908; *penalty:* imprisonment of one month to one year.]

Maryland: "All marriages between a white person and a negro or between a white person and a person of negro descent, to the third generation, inclusive, are forever prohibited, and shall be void; and any person violating the provisions of this section shall be deemed guilty of an infamous crime, and punished by imprisonment in the penitentiary not less than eighteen months nor more than ten years." [General Laws, 1904.]

Mississippi: "The marriage of a white person and a negro or mulatto or person who shall have one-eighth or more of negro blood, . . . shall be unlawful, and such marriages shall be unlawful and void; and any party thereto, on conviction, shall be punished as for a marriage within the degrees prohibited by the last two sections; and any attempt to evade this and the two preceding sections by marrying out of this state and returning to it shall be within them." [Code, 1906; *penalty:* fine of $500, imprisonment of not more than ten years.]

Missouri: "All marriages between white persons and negroes, . . . are prohibited and declared absolutely void, and this prohibition shall apply to illegitimate as well as legitimate children and relatives. No person having one-eighth part or more of negro blood shall be permitted to marry any white person, nor shall any white person be permitted to marry any negro or person having one-eighth part or more of negro blood; and every person who shall knowingly marry in violation of the provisions of this section shall, upon conviction, be punished by imprisonment in the penitentiary for two years, or by fine of not less than one hundred dollars, or by imprisonment in the county jail not less than three months, or by both such fine and imprisonment; and the jury trying any such case may determine the proportion of negro blood in any party to such marriage from the appearance of such person." [Annotated Statutes, 1906.]

Nebraska: Void marriages: "First—When one party is a white person and the other is possessed of one-eighth or more negro . . . blood."[Laws, 1913; *penalty:* not more than $100 fine, imprisonment of not more than six months.]

Nevada: "If any white person shall live and cohabit with any black person, mulatto, . . . in a state of fornication, such person so offending shall, on conviction thereof, be fined in any sum not exceeding five hundred dollars, and not less than one hundred dollars, or be imprisoned in the county jail not less than six months or more than one year, or both." [Revised Laws, 1912.]

North Carolina: "All marriages between a white person and a negro, . . . or between a white person and a person of negro . . . descent to third generation, inclusive, shall be void." [Revised Code, 1905; *penalty:* imprisonment of four months to ten years.]

North Dakota: "It shall be unlawful for any white male person, residing or being in this State, to intermarry with any negro female person; and it shall be in like manner unlawful for any white female person, residing or being in this State, to intermarry with any negro male person, and every marriage hereafter formed and solemnized in contravention of the provisions of this section shall be utterly null and void and either or both of the contracting parties to such surreptitious marriage shall be punished by imprisonment in the State penitentiary for a term not exceeding ten years or by a fine exceeding two thousand dollars or by both fine and imprisonment." [Compiled Laws, 1913.]

Oklahoma: "The marriage of any person of African descent as defined by this constitution of this state, [wherever in this Constitution and laws of the State the word or words "colored" or "colored race," "negro" or "negro race" are used the same shall be construed to mean or apply to all persons of African descent. The term "white race" shall include all other persons.] to any person not of African descent, or the marriage of any person not of African descent to any person of African descent, shall be unlawful and is hereby prohibited within this state." [Revised Laws, 1910; *penalty:* fine of not more than $500, imprisonment of one to five years.]

Oregon: "What marriages are void: 3. When either of the parties is a white person and the other negro, . . . or one-fourth or more of negro . . . blood." [Bellinger and Cotton Code, 1902; *penalty:* imprisonment of three months to one year.]

South Carolina: "It shall be unlawful for any white man to intermarry with any woman . . . negro, . . . or any mulatto, . . . or for any white woman to intermarry with any person other than a white man, or for any mulatto, . . . negro, . . . to intermarry with a white woman; and any such marriage, or attempted marriage, shall be utterly null and void and of no effect." [Civil Code, 1902; *penalty:* fine of no less than $500, imprisonment of not less than one year.]

South Dakota: "The intermarriage or illicit cohabitation of any persons belonging to the African . . . race, with any person of the opposite sex, belonging to the Caucasian or white race, is hereby prohibited, and any person who shall hereafter enter into any such marriage, or who shall indulge in any such illicit cohabitation shall be deemed guilty of a felony and upon conviction thereof shall be punished by a fine of not exceeding one thousand dollars or by imprisonment in the State prison for a term not exceeding ten years or both such fine and imprisonment." [Compiled Laws, 1913]

Tennessee: "The intermarriage of white persons with negroes, mulattoes, or persons of mixed blood descended from a negro, to the third generation inclusive, or their living together as man and wife in this state, is hereby prohibited." [Code, 1896; *penalty:* imprisonment of one to five years.]

Texas: "If any white person and negro shall knowingly intermarry with each other within this state, or, having so intermarried, in or out of the state, shall continue to live together as man and wife within this state, they shall be punished by confinement in the penitentiary for a term not less than two or more than five years. The term 'negro,' . . . includes also a person of mixed blood descended from negro ancestry to the third generation inclusive, although one ancestor of each generation may have been a white person. All persons not included in the definition of 'negro' shall be deemed a white person within the meaning of this article." [Willson's Criminal Statutes, 1906; *penalty:* imprisonment of two to five years.]

Utah: "Marriage is prohibited and declared void: between a negro and a white person." [Revised Statutes, 1898; *penalty:* fine of no less than $300, imprisonment of not more than six months.]

Virginia: "What marriages are void: All marriages between a white person and a colored person, . . . shall be absolutely void, without any decree of divorce or other legal process." [Pollard's Code, 1904; *penalty:* imprisonment of two to five years.]

West Virginia: "Void marriages: 1. All marriages between a white person and a negro." [Code of 1906; *penalty:* fine of not more than $100, imprisonment not more than one year.] [8]

These laws owe their origin to the first definite legislation concerning black-white marriages passed in 1691 in Maryland; the penalties changed, but the intent remained fairly constant:

Forasmuch as divers free-born English women, forgetful of their free condition, and the disgrace of our nation, do intermarry with negro slaves, by which divers suits may arise, touching the issue of such women, and a great damage doth befall the master of such negroes, for preservation whereof for deterring such free-born women from such shameful matches, be it enacted: that whatsoever free-born woman shall intermarry with any slave, from and after the last day of the present assembly, shall serve the master of such slave during the life of her husband; and that all the issues of such free-born women, so married, shall be slaves . . . And be it further enacted: That all the issues of English, or other free-born women, that have already married negroes, shall serve the master of their parents, till they be thirty years of age and no longer.[9]

These massive laws served well to extend the quagmire of black-white relations. Their very numbers and variety, however, attest to the reality that the color line was being crossed and that public opposition was insubstantial against the floodtide. Extensive interracial intercourse took place after the Civil War between black and white lower class people. These relations were more exploitative in the South than in the North since in the South the black woman was defenseless because of the black man's powerlessness. In a word, the uninhibited black-white intercourse which had occurred in the early days of the colonies, before laws tampered with the natural relationships, was again possible, but only for the exploiting white male of all classes. Slavery had provided the upper and middle class white males of the South with exclusive rights to black women. As long as black women were their special province and special domain, upper class white males yielded to their natural inclinations. The freeing of the slaves created a more competitive and dynamic situation in which the former master was no longer in absolute control. Upper class whites retreated from black women and limited their conquests to occasional rather than frequent involvement.

That upper class Southern males pulled back from intimate association with black women (a relationship which upper class Northern whites tended not to enjoy because of their puritan upbringing and because of the sparse numbers of blacks in the

North) was due less to their repulsion of black women than to their loss of exclusive rights. Upper class white males always operated on the double standard; public laws and morality did not curb their sex appetite for black women prior to Emancipation, and it is doubtful that they suddenly gained religion. Whatever antiblack feelings the planters may have possessed, they were largely denied by their intimate association with black women.

Close association with black women, which during slavery days only upper class whites had had, with great numbers of blacks became a new way of life for lower class whites after the War. If close association between black slaves and white upper class males led to intimate sexual intercourse, the same development among blacks and whites of similar cultural, economic, and social advantages should not be treated as evidence of low morality or considered unnatural. It is the case that whites and blacks of similar stations in life tend through association to move to marriage, but they have neither the power nor the influence nor the wealth nor the prestige to publicly adhere to custom while privately responding to their natural inclinations. When all is said and done, after the paralysis of analysis, black-white sexual intercourse follows naturally from contact and association—it has less to do with class or clan. Southern whites have known this from their own experience, and it is this truth of experience that they express in their opposition to a free and open society. Southern whites knew, as did no other American people, that despite all the legal and other more barbarian efforts to prevent or retard the process of interracial unions, the process was beyond prevention. It is for this reason they have followed the only route their convictions could find—public and private sanction of the legislation against black-white marriage. Black-white unions came to fruition in America accompanied by both upper class and popular opposition and support; it was as natural for some to be for black-white cohabitation as it was for some to be against it. The private behavior of upper class whites did not differ from that of lower class whites; the difference lay in their expression of public sentiments, although eventually upper class, middle class, and lower class whites came by devious routes to the same degradation. Southern whites spread their gospel far and wide—what is sauce for the goose is not sauce for the gander. The peril of the double standard in the South led to paradoxes throughout the land.

It is clear to us as we look back that the fanatic American will to increase legal enactments against black-white marriages did little to inhibit the exploitation of black women by dominant white men and that they were not intended to do so. They did prohibit extensive stable and honest relations which could have led to marriage, and this result was no mere accident.

Given the victimization of blacks, it comes as no surprise to learn that their leaders never advocated black-white marriages. However, the National Association for the Advancement of Colored People opposed from its inception the laws framed to prevent black-white marriages. The N.A.A.C.P. was born about the time antiblack-white marriage legislation was popular among legislators both in the South and in the North. It was in 1913 that W. E. B. Du Bois, then the director of publicity and research for the N.A.A.C.P., led the fight against laws prohibiting marriage in black and white. He held that the laws implied the inherent inferiority of blacks and led to concubinage, illegitimacy, and the degradation of black women; that they promoted what they were supposed to prevent, black-white intercourse; and that they were unnecessary because marriage in black and white was infrequent even where it was legally sanctioned. Du Bois wrote to all Northern legislatures considering antimarital legislation between blacks and whites in 1913 the following statement of position, which was printed in the fourth annual report of the Association:

The National Association for the Advancement of Colored People earnestly protests against the bill forbidding intermarriage between the races, not because the Association advocates intermarriage, which it does not, but primarily because whenever such laws have been enacted they become a menace to the whole institution of matrimony, leading directly to concubinage, bastardy, and the degradation of the negro woman. No man-made law can stop the union of the races. If intermarriage be wrong, its prevention is best left to public opinion and to nature, which wreaks its own fearful punishments on those who transgress its laws and sin against it. We oppose the proposed statute in the language of William Lloyd Garrison in 1843, in his successful campaign for the repeal of a similar law in Massachusetts: "Because it is not the province, and does not belong to the power of any legislative assembly, in a republican government to decide on the complexional affinity of those who choose to be united together in wedlock; and it may as rationally decree that corpulent and lean, tall and short, strong and weak persons shall not be married to each other as that there must be an agreement in the complexion of the parties."

We oppose it for the physical reason that to prohibit such intermarriage would be publicly to acknowledge that black blood is a physical taint, something no self-respecting colored man and woman can be asked to admit. We oppose it for the moral reason that all such laws leave the colored girl absolutely helpless before the lust of the white man, without the power to compel the seducer to marry. The statistics of intermarriage in those states where it is permitted show this happens so infrequently as to make the whole matter of legislation unnecessary. Both races are practically in complete agreement on this question, for colored people marry colored people, and white marry white, the exceptions being few. We earnestly urge upon you an unfavorable report on this bill.[10]

The bills Du Bois and the N.A.A.C.P. opposed in 1913 were being considered by the U.S. Congress and by the state legislatures of California, Colorado, Illinois, Iowa, Kansas, Michigan, Nebraska, New York, Ohio, Pennsylvania, Washington, and Wisconsin. The N.A.A.C.P. was successful in aiding their defeat in all of these states but Nebraska. Despite the N.A.A.C.P.'s successes in 1913, by 1932 there were still thirty states with anti–black-white marriage laws.

The Fourteenth Amendment to the Constitution of the United States was intended to provide blacks, as of course every citizen, with all of the privileges and immunities of United States citizenship and to guarantee blacks equal protection under the law. With the adoption of this amendment the issue immediately arose as to whether blacks were not being denied their equality under the amended constitution in the legislation prohibiting black-white marriage. It appeared to a good many that the state laws prohibiting marriage of a black and a white were a flagrant violation of the Fourteenth Amendment.

Over the years many cases challenging the constitutionality of laws forbidding marriage between blacks and whites were lost and the statutes held to be valid in state courts. Marriage has been the province of state courts since our earliest legal beginnings. In 1819, Mr. Chief Justice John Marshall pointed out that

> all of our marriage and divorce laws . . . are state laws and
> state statutes; the national power with us not having
> legislative or judicial cognizance of the matter within these
> localities.[11]

State control in matters of marriage was virtually unquestioned throughout the first half of this century. In 1887 it was noted by the United States Supreme Court that

> marriage as creating the most important relation in life, as
> having more to do with the morals and civilization of a
> people than any other institution has always been subject to
> the control of state legislatures.[12]

There has been little doubt about the valid control of marital relations by the states, but the control exercised over marriage of blacks and whites has been nameless, unreasoning, and unwarranted. With respect to this unreasoning control, the United States Supreme Court held, in the case of the *American Sugar Refining Company v. Louisiana,* that

> the doctrine of legislative control does not carry with it the
> right to enact race and class legislation. Such legislation may
> not be discriminatory, irrational with no legitimate end, but
> rather, an unreasonable expression of popular prejudice.[13]

There we have in a nutshell the real basis for state after state holding valid its antimarriage laws—the "expression of popular prejudice." When laws prohibiting black-white marriages were tested for validity in the courts, the states generally used variations of the following assumptions to support their contention that their anti-marriage laws were constitutional:

1. Marriage is a social and domestic institution which comes solely within the state powers. Marriage is not a legal or political right which are the only rights of moment in the Fourteenth Amendment.

2. Laws forbidding black-white intermarriage are constitutional because no discrimination is involved. That is, such marriages are forbidden to blacks and whites, and both are equally subject to the same penalties.

3. Intermarriage between blacks and whites is both unnatural and productive of deplorable results. A Georgia Court stated in its decision the following: "Our daily observation shows us that the offspring of these unnatural connections are generally sickly, effeminate, and that they are inferior to the full blooded of either race in physical development and strength." [14]

4. Racial marriages would produce such widespread group feelings "and racial repulsions and antagonisms" that the security and tranquillity of the state would be threatened.

The reality of white males engaging in sexual intercourse with black females at will and the fact that the children of these unions would be attractive to blacks and whites and if allowed to develop naturally would be able to marry whites with as little fanfare as they could marry blacks created a paradox and in order to prevent this natural process, a threat to assumed white superiority, legal definitions of what constitutes a black were deemed necessary. Of course, as we have seen, no legal definition could be agreed upon. The most common assumption was that a black is a person with one-eighth black blood, but why this vaguity does not make one white is, by whatever test of logic it makes one black, il-logical. In the end, no jury could know if a person with one-eighth black blood in him was white or black on the mere test of looking at him, the only test finally available for such cases. The key to whether a black person was black or white simply came down to how the person was viewed by those who knew him. Conse-quently, the imprecise statutory definitions amounted to legal fiction and genetic nonsense which reinforced popular prejudices, and that after all was the entire point.

The legal bases of antimarriage laws were grounded in the same peril as the definitions of a black man, in unreality and pop-ular prejudice. The distinction between cultural and biological human developments finely set forth by scientists were ignored in favor of the old beliefs, as in the Missouri case where it was le-gally held that interracial unions were incapable of procreation. Later courts followed this pseudoscientific precedent, and as late as 1955 a Virginia Court ruled that "we find no requirements that the states shall not legislate to prevent the obliteration of racial pride, but must permit the corruption of blood even though it weaken or destroy the quality of its citizenship." [15] The early Su-preme Court argument that black-white marriages "cannot possi-bly have any progeny," or its modern revision that "the progeny of black-white marriages are inferior," had no basis in fact.

The "equal application" theory was based on an 1883 United States Supreme Court decision, which upheld the original convic-tion of a black man and white woman for fornication even though the penalty was more severe than it would have been had two blacks or two whites been involved, and supported the position of no discrimination between the races with respect to these laws. Of course there is some truth here, but the fact remains that races do not marry, only individuals marry, and if the states treat each group equally, they still fall short of the Fourteenth Amendment, as interpreted by the Supreme Court, which guarantees the right of individuals to marry. States have contended they alone have the right of determination with respect to marriage. From this commonly accepted tradition, those states with antimarriage laws have leaped to the conclusion that marriage in black and white may be banned on the grounds that they provoke the general will to riot. However, the presumption that antiblack feelings can be eliminated through perpetuating in law the popular prejudices that cause the antiblack feelings in the first place is irrational. Anticipation of civil disturbance is no basis upon which to support a law which will deprive persons of their constitutional rights. In fact, this argument suggests that local authorities are either unable or unwilling to maintain order. After all, race riots are nonexistent in areas such as Brazil or Hawaii, where intermarriage is common.

When the anti-intermarriage laws were repealed and defeated in a number of states around 1913, the drive for the legalization of caste in America had to be spent in upholding an unofficial caste system. The underlying intent of the unofficial caste system was the preservation of the racial integrity of citizens and the curbing of any further movements toward "a mongrel breed of citizens." The singular purpose of these laws was the preservation of the purity of the majority of whites in America: "to keep America white"; to maintain "white American culture." If all the states would not agree on the legalization of caste, some states would maintain this officialdom on their behalf until that time in the future when whites everywhere would wish to follow suit. In the meantime, states finally rested their case for the laws prohibiting marriage of a black and a white on their sense of obligation to keep married couples and their children from psychological harm and social maladjustment. On this most sensitive point there remains a national consensus and the states with antimarriage laws have maintained their sway by exciting in the nation as a whole and in their people in particular the prejudice of protecting children of such marriages from *a feeling of inferiority as to their status in the community that may affect their hearts and minds in a way unlikely ever to be undone.*

In 1932 there were thirty states with these laws and in 1951 there were twenty-nine. Most of the states which repealed their laws after 1951 were Western, including Colorado (1957), Nebraska (1963), Nevada (1959), South Dakota (1957), and Utah (1963). It is clear that the decisions of these Western states to abolish their statutes prohibiting marriage in black and white were not made on the basis of a change of heart, nor on the basis

of a change in the popular will, or, even on a general popular indifference to black-white marriages. These states merely agreed
with the Supreme Court ruling of 1940 (*Cantwell v. Connecticut*)
that there were no grounds for "attaining a permissible end"—
such as securing peace and tranquility—by using regulative powers which would "unduly infringe" on a freedom the law should
protect. The Court states that the real danger of civil uprising over
black-white relations results when

> the coercive activities of those who in the delusion of racial
> or religious conceit would incite violence and breaches of the
> peace in order to deprive others of their equal right to the
> exercise of their liberties.[16]

The people of the Western states were law-abiding citizens who
did not want to resort to such means, and the repeal of these laws
was hardly due to a feeling of self-righteousness or to the appearance of a liberal and cosmopolitan and therefore Eastern attitude.
These states simply followed the legal maxim that a law should
cease when the reason for the law has ceased. At the turn of the
century it had been feared that a great many blacks would in-
migrate to these Western states, and the antimarriage laws were
not the least effective instruments for discouraging masses of
blacks from settling in them. Moreover, it seemed certain that the
1954 United States Supreme Court decision would soon be
brought to its logical conclusion and that all statutes based on unreasonable restrictions in areas of intermarriage would be declared void. These states moved ahead of the Supreme Court with
little cost, for blacks remained a negligible part of their popula-
tions, and black-white marriages were so infrequent that they
could easily be ignored.

Arizona repealed its law in 1962 for several reasons, including the expected logical end of the 1954 Supreme Court decision,
the small population of blacks, and the ludicrous history of its
laws which in one period so defined a mulatto that he could not
marry anyone, including another mulatto, and, at another juncture changed the law "so that a mulatto could marry an Indian
but could not marry a Negro, a Caucasian, or another mulatto." [17]

The United States Supreme Court never directly handed down a ruling on the constitutionality of state legislation forbidding black-white marriages until June 12, 1967. There were at that time nineteen states with these laws.

In December 1964, the Supreme Court struck down the Florida statute that made it a crime for blacks and whites to cohabit. Connie Hoffman, a white woman, and Dewey McLaughlin, "a Spanish-speaking merchant seaman from British Honduras," were convicted of violating the Florida criminal law which punished "extramarital cohabitation" only where the offending couple involved one black and one white person. In the opinion of Mr. Justice White,

> we deal here with a racial classification embodied in a criminal statute. In this context, where the power of a state weighs most heavily on the individual or group, we must be especially sensitive to the policies of the Equal Protection Clause, which . . . were intended to . . . subject all persons to "like punishment, pains, penalties, taxes, licenses and exactions of every kind, and to no other." [18]

Justice White based the decision against Florida on the opinion that a law may not make the same act a crime when it is performed by blacks and not a crime when it is performed by whites. Mr. Justice Douglas and Mr. Justice Stewart concurred:

> It is simply not possible for a state law to be valid under our Constitution which makes the criminality of an act depend upon the race of the actor. [19]

The Supreme Court was a long time in coming to so direct an opinion on this singular issue, but its opinion was not conclusive. The Florida law stated that it was illegal for a black person and a white person not married to each other to habitually "occupy in the nighttime the same room." Florida's Assistant Attorney General argued that the law was necessary to prevent intimacy leading to intermarriage. While refusing to express "any views about prohibition of interracial marriage," Justice White replied to the reasoning of the Florida Assistant Attorney General as follows:

> We reject this argument, without reaching the question of the validity of the state's prohibition against interracial marriage or the soundness of the arguments rooted in the history of the amendment.[20]

In this decision, the Court went a long way down the long road of legal evolution on which one finds that marriage is a social relation subject to the state's police powers; that this power of a state to regulate marriage is not unlimited under the Fourteenth Amendment; that the "equal protection" clause of the Fourteenth Amendment includes consideration of discrimination between consenting adults who may choose to marry; that elimination of invidious racial discrimination and restrictions on the freedom to marry is imperative; that marriage is a basic civil right; that the freedom to marry or not to marry a person of a different skin color cannot be infringed upon by a state; and that the central meaning of the Fourteenth Amendment is clear:

> All persons born or naturalized in the United States, and subject to the jurisdiction thereof, are citizens of the United States and of the State wherein they reside. No State shall make or enforce any law which shall abridge the privileges or immunities of citizens of the United States; nor shall any State deprive any person of life, liberty, or property, without due process of law; nor deny to any person within its jurisdiction the equal protection of the laws.

Most of the civil rights laws were pressed by civil rights lawyers of the N.A.A.C.P. Legal Defense Fund. Part of the reason, then, that the United States Supreme Court never addressed the constitutional question of whether these state laws violated the Equal Protection and Due Process clauses of the Fourteenth Amendment was the fact that in recent years the civil rights legal brains did not press this issue. Their reasoning, since the 1954 Supreme Court decision with the maneuvering about "all deliberate speed," was largely that such a decision of unconstitutionality would harm the civil rights movement. The argument that an earlier decision would have been a serious error "misstates the question to ask whether a decision should be deferred because the issue is incendiary to some whites and insignificant to most Negroes." [21] Of course it is the case that legislation cannot end the repulsion for black-white social equality, but it does not follow that laws which foster social inequality should continue to exist. Perhaps a free society can long endure with its antithesis, popular opposition to the union of individuals, one black, one white; yet it is intolerable that a free society should nurture this popular prejudice by allowing its legislation in any state. The spirit which opposes the natural attraction of a black and a white can be broken, but the process is not aided by allowing laws to stand. It is the case that the civil rights lawyers' and leaders' recent lack of concern about antimarriage laws was a tactical strategy, and one which differed remarkably from the initial stand of the N.A.A.C.P. Their public indifference toward black-white marriages for the risk of speeding up advancement of blacks in every other area was a poor one. The actual cost of this compromise was the maintenance of symbolic and psychological forces of repression otherwise "unsupported by reason or morals." It has finally dawned upon us that the civil rights movement to bring about integration with "all deliberate speed," in "all things essential to mutual progress," cannot be sharply delineated from progress "in all things purely social." It may well have been argued that the real crunch of antimarriage laws caught only those who were so foolish as to transgress them. The truth of the matter lies in the fact that such laws cause incalculable injury to all blacks, for these laws designate all blacks inferior, whether or not they contemplate a black-white marriage. The distance that black leaders maintained from support of black-white marriages had the opposite effect of what was intended: the more blacks retreated from this crucial issue, the more racist whites pressed their case. Armed with laws prohibiting marriage in black and white, they appealed to the magnificent American superstition and myth of the innate inferiority of blacks to whites. The result of not gaining an early decision from the Supreme Court led the Supreme Court, by its silence, to demonstrate that the highest law of the land deemed blacks inferior in their rights "to enter into the most private and personal of relationships."

Sixteen states still had antimarriage laws in 1968 when the Supreme Court finally ruled on the constitutionality of this issue in *Loving v. Commonwealth of Virginia.* Mr. Chief Justice Warren set forth the perimeters:

> In June 1958 two residents of Virginia, Mildred Jeter, a Negro woman, and Richard Loving, a white man, were married in the District of Columbia pursuant to its laws. Shortly after their marriage, the Lovings returned to Virginia and established their marital abode in Caroline County. At the October term, 1958, of the Circuit Court of Caroline County, a grand jury issued an indictment charging the Lovings with violating Virginia's ban on interracial marriages. On January 6, 1959, the Lovings pleaded guilty to the charge and were sentenced to one year in jail; however, the trial judge suspended the sentence for a period of 25 years on the condition that the Lovings leave the State and not return to Virginia together for 25 years, stating that:

> > "Almighty God created the races white, black, yellow, malay, and red, and he placed them on separate continents. And but for the interference with his arrangement there would be no cause for such marriages. The fact that he separated the races shows that he did not intend for the races to mix."

> After their convictions, the Lovings took up residence in the District of Columbia. On November 6, 1963, they filed a motion in the state trial court to vacate the judgment and set aside the sentence on the ground that the statutes which they had violated were repugnant to the Fourteenth Amendment. The motion not having been decided by October 28, 1964, the Lovings instituted a class action in the United States District Court for the Eastern District of Virginia requesting that a three-judge court be convened to declare the Virginia antimiscegenation statutes unconstitutional and to enjoin

state officials from enforcing their convictions. On January 22, 1965, the state trial judge denied the motion to vacate the sentences, and the Lovings perfected an appeal to the Supreme Court of Appeals of Virginia. On February 11, 1965, the three-judge District Court continued the case to allow the Lovings to present their constitutional claims to the highest state court.

The Supreme Court of Appeals upheld the constitutionality of the antimiscegenation statutes and, after modifying the sentence, affirmed the convictions. The Lovings appealed this decision, and we noted probable jurisdiction on December 12, 1966.[22]

The State of Virginia advanced the traditional arguments, but in 1968 they were met with this opinion:

There can be no question but that Virginia's miscegenation statutes rest solely upon distinctions drawn according to race. The statutes proscribe generally accepted conduct if engaged in by members of different races. Over the years, this Court has consistently repudiated "distinctions between citizens solely because of their ancestry" as being "odious to a free people whose institutions are founded upon the doctrine of equality.[23]

Chief Justice Warren continued:

The fact that Virginia only prohibits interracial marriages involving white persons demonstrates that the racial classifications must stand on their own justification, as measures designed to maintain White Supremacy. We have consistently denied the constitutionality of measures which restrict the rights of citizens on account of race. There can be no doubt that restricting the freedom to marry solely because of racial classifications violates the central meaning of the Equal Protection Clause.

These statutes also deprive the Lovings of liberty without due process of law in violation of the Due Process

Clause of the Fourteenth Amendment. The freedom to marry
has long been recognized as one of the vital personal rights
essential to the orderly pursuit of happiness by free men.[24]

Upholding marriage as one of the "basic civil rights of man," indispensable for human "existence and survival," Chief Justice
Warren reached the decision:

> To deny this fundamental freedom on so unsupportable a
> basis as the racial classifications embodied in these statutes,
> classifications so directly subversive of the principle of
> equality at the heart of the Fourteenth Amendment, is surely
> to deprive all the State's citizens of liberty without due
> process of law. The Fourteenth Amendment requires that the
> freedom of choice to marry not be restricted by invidious
> racial discriminations. Under our Constitution, the freedom
> to marry or not marry, a person of another race resides with
> the individual and cannot be infringed upon by the State.
>   These convictions must be reversed. It is so ordered.
> Reversed.[25]

Since 1951 fourteen states have repealed their antimarriage
laws (Arizona, California, Colorado, Idaho, Indiana, Maryland,
Montana, Nebraska, Nevada, North Dakota, Oregon, South Dakota, Utah, and Wyoming). Maryland repealed its laws banning
black-white marriages in 1967 when the litigation against Virginia
was initiated. The Virginia decision of 1968 reduced the number
of states with prohibitions against black-white marriages from sixteen to fifteen (Alabama, Arkansas, Delaware, Florida, Georgia,
Kentucky, Louisiana, Mississippi, Missouri, North Carolina,
Oklahoma, South Carolina, Tennessee, Texas, and West Virginia), and it is not altogether clear that the June 12, 1968 unani-
mous Supreme Court ruling voided the laws still on the books of
these states. The ruling of Chief Justice Warren appears sufficiently broad and disapproving to cover these other states even
though the decision was directed specifically at the laws of Virginia. It is the case that Virginia's "racial integrity law" uniquely

defined blacks in order to recognize and protect "the descendants of John Rolfe and Pocahontas":

> Every person in whom there is ascertainable any Negro blood shall be deemed and taken to be a colored person, and every person not a colored person having one fourth or more of American Indian blood shall be deemed an American Indian; except the members of Indian tribes existing in this Commonwealth having one fourth or more of Indian blood and less than one sixteenth of Negro blood shall be deemed tribal Indians. [Virginia Code Annotated, 1966.]

However, despite this quirk in the Virginia laws, the other states with laws prohibiting black-white unions in all probability were not excluded from this 1968 ruling, for in a footnote Chief Justice Warren appeared to make the ruling universally applicable:

> Appellants point out that the State's concern in these statutes, as expressed in the words of the 1924 Act's title, "An Act to Preserve Racial Integrity," extends only to the integrity of the white race. While Virginia prohibits whites from marrying any non-white (subject to the exception for the descendants of Pocahontas), Negroes, Orientals, and any other racial class may intermarry without statutory interference. Appellants contend that this distinction renders Virginia's miscegenation statutes arbitrary and unreasonable even assuming the constitutional validity of an official purpose to preserve "racial integrity." We need not reach this contention because we find the racial classification in these statutes repugnant to the Fourteenth Amendment, even assuming an even-handed state purpose to protect the "integrity" of all races.[26]

The law of the land may not be the operational policy of the general public, for blacks and whites are one in public opposition to the spirit of this ruling. Few there are who would both approve in principle and advise in practice their sons or daughters to enter into marriage with a person of a different skin color. Popular prejudices and opinions remain only as long as they are unchallenged, and the present is a propitious time to begin the long process of eradicating the popular sentiment which in the face of law, reason, morals, and science clings to the belief that blacks are inferior to whites. No enlightened people should accept the sentiment that black-white tensions will be eliminated by perpetuating by popular consent the irrational prejudices which cause the tension.

Chapter Four

"PASSING": MYSTERY, MAGIC, MISCHIEF, AND THE INVISIBLE COLOR LINE

My old man's a White old man,
And my old mother's black,
　If I ever cursed my White old man,
I take my curses back.

　If I ever cursed my black old ma
And wished she were in hell,
　I'm sorry for that evil wish,
And now I wish her well.

　My old man died in a fine White house,
My ma died in a shack,
　I wonder where I'm gonna die,
Being neither White nor Black.*

Langston Hughes's "Cross" has been interpreted by Rabbi Albert Gordon, in his book on *Intermarriage,* as stating "suc-

---

* Langston Hughes, "Cross," in *Selected Poems of Langston Hughes* (New York: Alfred A. Knopf, 1959), p. 158.

cinctly and accurately the problem which the children of interracial marriages so often face." Such an interpretation is a gross
misreading of the poem in order to support the judgment Gordon
wishes to perpetuate. The poem serves as a fitting introduction to
this chapter, which seeks to show that intercourse with black
women by white men created the phenomenon of *passing* which in
turn became a problem conjured up in the white sickness of mind,
body, and soul. Only a superficial reading of this poem would
lead one to hold it up as an illustration of "the problem which the
children of interracial marriages so often face." The personal re-
morse in this poem is but an instrument for expressing the social
tragedy produced by whites who not only fail to accept their children who accept themselves for what they are, "neither white nor
black," but who fail even more in brutalizing their victims
through inflicting increased pain instead of healing the wounds.
Instead of repenting or rethinking whites continue repressing, unable to see that they are *the problem* "which the children of interracial marriages so often face."

The registration of races and legal circumscription of blacks,
consigning them to an unequal status in defiance of the Fourteenth Amendment, had a cumulative effect upon the children of
mixed parentage. The society that once favored blacks *obviously*
endowed with white genes for economic advantage above sentimental reasons had given this body of blacks every reason to believe they were superior to blacks not endowed with white characteristics. Children of masters and slave women were often
provided a running start in life by way of a higher purchase price
and domestic responsibilities as "house niggers," rather than
"field niggers," and the subsequent special training for skills was
often followed by freedom, education, and benefits bequeathed to
them in their master's last will and testimony. This preference for
whites over beiges, beiges over browns, and browns over blacks
was demonstrated in a thousand ways and places until the values
of whites became the values of blacks. But when the economic advantage waned, whites changed the rules of the relationships and
no longer gave some blacks preferential treatment over others. It
is not an astonishing fact to learn that blacks so conditioned to
this pattern of preferential treatment continued to respond in the

manner previously expected by whites and practiced this preferential treatment for a long period among themselves in crude imitation of life in the old days. We shall develop this class hierarchy based upon color caste among blacks presently.

Here it is sufficient to note well that the dependent role of blacks was a far more difficult matter to change than that of whites by whose initiative the black reflexes had been conditioned with great care. For the whites did not bother to deprogram blacks when the old dependent relationship was no longer useful with anything like the care taken to program mixed blacks for a better life than that of pure blacks. For example, the anti-marriage laws were on the books when whites began to treat lighter blacks with higher regard than the darker ones. These laws were most inconsistent and imprecise in their interpretations of the point at which one is no longer black or white but becomes the other. Yet, the laws on the books were one thing, the operational policy another. To marry a black had long been taboo; to have intercourse with a black and thereby gain children for economic value, or, as in some cases, for sentimental value, was not incompatible with the anti-marriage laws. The special production and treatment of these bastards was known to be expected by blacks as well as whites. Antimarriage laws did not prevent the special treatment of light skinned blacks and, indeed, set the stage for the higher value of this special breed in the postbellum as well as antebellum eras. It is understandable that the automatic relationship between light skin and opportunity should be continued between light and dark pigmented blacks to the advantage of the former as if it were biological necessity rather than the result of social conditioning.

Despite their inconsistency, the ubiquitous anti-marriage laws formed a massive base for far more than the relegation of black-white intercourse to the white male's illicit and monstrous disregard for the black female. These laws were the foundation stones for racial integrity, purity of the white race, the press of white supremacy. Following Reconstruction, antimarriage laws (the means by which blacks were legally determined, if not wholly defined) nicely combined with Jim Crow laws to rule blacks out of acceptable bounds for public as well as private intercourse. When the caste casket was finally closed, though not sealed, there were a number of blacks in the South who had greater ambition and higher expectations than those in accord with this seemingly zero status burial. We have previously seen how the kept black women found it difficult to break the habit of white men and the dividends received from this extramarital activity. But of moment is the more affluent, sophisticated, intelligent, and proud group of blacks who found this unexceptional closing of the doors to opportunity and success an unbearable frustration. This group, largely professionals and middle class business men, responded to this struggle for survival in a manner fitting those who affirm the survival of the fittest. We have come to accept E. Franklin Frazier's stereotype "the black bourgeoisie" as generally descriptive of this group.

In the early days the more a child of a black woman and white master resembled the father in skin color, physical features, and hair texture, the more that child received society's benefits. In time, a class of these favorite children emerged which was well bred, who enjoyed the pleasures of good living and cherished a solid family life, education, and culture. Under the regimentation of Jim Crow and the institution of "separate but equal" hyperbole, the separate (if not equal) determination appeared to be guaranteed best by permitting blacks to create their own community and control it to a considerable degree. In practice, in the South, this "separate but equal" philosophy resulted in blacks manning their own schools, businesses, and enterprises of all sorts and conditions. Those who initially took charge of this "separate but equal" profit making system were those in a position to do so by dint of the accidents of history and inheritance. For the most part they were the sons and daughters of families nearest the white image which prepared them for advantage. This privileged position of early advantage was kept within the immediate circle of family and special friends. In time, there was a gradual widening of the exclusive circle because of increased need and opportunity, but this widening was never allowed to blur the exclusiveness of those who were light and included from those who were born unmarked by the white man.

The failure of the white society to acknowledge as they once did the superior status of the lightest blacks did not immediately erase from the minds of whites or blacks the association of light color with economic and cultural superiority among blacks. The direct relation between light color and economic superiority was long viewed in the black community as a biological rather than a cultural factor, a fiction perpetuated by the light skinned blacks who began early to be the profiteers in the black community and were sustained in this hegemony for a long period of time by the support of whites whose vested interest in their success was as unmistakable as their preference for dealing with light complexioned blacks was undeniable.

The long association between color and economic and cultural superiority inevitably led blacks in a segregated society to place high value on light skin color, straight hair, and thin lips. This esteem of the white beauty standard among blacks at the turn of the century can be traced to the pre-emancipation preferences of whites and their continued preference, through the early years of this century, for mulattoes "because they look more like white people." Consequently, blacks developed a class system within the black community which paralleled that between the lightest blacks and whites.

The style of life developed by the light skinned black bourgeoisie was one of inconspicuous living between the lower class black world and the world of whites. There in insulation grew a privileged but frustrated group, unable to break entirely away from the stigma of the lower black world and unable to break into the even more elusive specter of the white world. The fine art of avoidance of both these other worlds was developed to an edge of hair splitting distinction. Y. A. Robertson once described his black society as " 'Color Lines' Among the Colored People":

These mulattoes . . . regard themselves as much the same way as do white Americans whose ancestors came over on the *Mayflower,* setting themselves up as arbiters of things social. They form cliques to which the other two divisions are admitted only by wealth or education. The first will secure the same sort of toleration for its owners in Negrodom as it will in white circles, but the latter will cause the blacks to be

treated as though they were black as the result of some
unfortunate oversight.[1]

A once popular jingle suggests the fascination light skin held for
white-conscious blacks:

I wish I had a nickel,
I wish I had a dime,
I wish I had a yellow gal,
I'd kiss her all the time.

In the first quarter of this century it was rare to have an automo-
bile, but this pleasure with a pretty yellow gal was real living:

The high yaller gals ride in automobiles,
The high-browns ride the trains,
Poor black gals ride old gray mules,
But she gets there just the same.

"Brown skins" was a popular term used to describe a very broad
range of medium color, shading off into "high-browns" on one
side and shades of black on the other:

The social status of the particular browns known as
"high-browns" is scarcely different from that of the
mulattoes. By this term the Negro usually means one whose
hair is straight, but not so coarse-grain as that of the
mulatto. . . .
    In Dixie everyone knows everyone else, or will before
going very far with them socially. Therein is the reason for
the South's social cliques—both white and black.
    In any other part of the country "color lines" would be
something less than silly. Like all indications of caste, they
require some tradition and enough of a leisure class or a class
having genteel employment to entertain itself.[2]

In virtually all respects the style of life of blacks who inherited dominant white marks was indistinguishable from that of the

genteel South: "Like a valet in his master's suit, they thought themselves superior to the aforesaid laborers." [3] The black bourgeoisie did perform some charity and good works, and there was some missionary endeavor among fellow blacks of less fortune on the assumption that lower class blacks could be raised bit by bit from the depths. However there was little respect for lower class blacks, very little participation in their life, and even less appreciation for their values. Those blacks in positions of authority as teachers provided little example at the distance maintained, though, like missionaries, they made every effort to pass on their preferred morals and manners. Of course the relationship between upper class and deprived blacks was largely one based on fear, fear that the upper class minority might be pulled down to the level of the masses.

Dignity without freedom, pride without power, desire without fulfillment, style without opportunity, faith without fight—this twilight existence was comfortable for many, a satisfactory height for some, an achievement for others. Other blacks were excluded because they were neither blue eyed nor white skinned, and when in doubt their status was determined by the pigmentation beneath the finger nails with as much accuracy as whites detected one ounce of black blood. Southern whites had made black-white marriage or social equality a very special province and had denied entrance to those blacks who were as white as many whites by any test of genesis. Stymied by this lack of acceptance in what they believed their rightful heritage, light skinned blacks made up their own game of top-of-the-heap and played it fiercely among their own. Existence on the knife edge with pomp and circumstance was a deadly earnest affair, for if they showed whites they were equal to them in every way the time would come, some ventured to hope, when those who imitated best would be granted their rightful social inheritance. It took a special effort to develop and nurture among a selective people ability with flexibility, the wherewithal to withstand the slings and arrows which inevitably pierced the partitions from either side of the color curtain.

Some of the white skinned Southern blacks who were light and bright enough, but who failed the rigid test of the in-between world because they lacked inheritance or connection or who found the make believe world as unbearable as the naked Jim Crow world, made their own ways as individuals across the color line in parts of the South where they were not known or in the urban North. In the urban areas there resided a substantial host of white skinned blacks produced by white Southerners in massive numbers before the turn of the century, increased by Northern whites in the South and North in the disorderly days of Reconstruction. Caught between a world where light was might if you were right and one where white was might and right, there were those who chose neither horn of the dilemma, but instead rode through the middle, escaping the full impact of either horn. Such persons became chameleons, depending upon the situation. They did not protest for equal rights and opportunity, they simply did not refuse them when they came their way by dint of chance or the accident of mistaken identity. By playing the game of social acceptance in this way, they were no more antiblack than those who chose to create a caste system among blacks. If in the South some blacks took economic and social advantage of their black skinned brothers, other white skinned blacks in the North and South found personal gain in their skin color which took advantage of whites. It is academic at this juncture to ask if this dual identity or totally white identification was immoral or anxiety ridden, or a betrayal of blacks, for it was no more so than that of their fellows who lived the life of avoidance or harassment.

We have reached the crucial juncture in this chapter. When whites created blacks in their own image and sustained in them the belief that they were superior to their unmarked brethren, they also indicated that these children of their wantonness were to be given special treatment as the Brahmins of blacks, if not finally assimilated into white society. When whites changed their minds and determined that all blacks were to be more or less equally unacceptable, the Brahmins could not accept this reversal and continued down the path of exclusion. Whites found this response to be compatible with their wishes and reinforced the Brahmins as the best defense of white supremacy.

Whites created in their own image blacks who for various reasons did not find the Brahmin life to be their own. Whites had made the white society too attractive and too easily accessible to these black souls in white skins, so they took the route called *passing*, a phenomenon that unleashed tremendous anxiety and fear and fascination among whites and disclosed the unreality which envelops so much of our black-white attitudes toward marriage in black and white. We turn now to this phenomenon created by the white society and the desperate ways in which whites sought to conjure up as visible what was by their own design an invisible color line. We shall treat briefly the various forces of law, science, and morality whites brought to bear upon this phenomenon to stop it. If we do not appear to deal too harshly with blacks who *passed* it is because this phenomenon, like white supremacy, carried within it the seeds of its own destruction. *Passing* is an important relic of our past and one which is necessary for understanding our present antimarriage and antisocial equality sentiment, not so much for the insight it gives us into the black mind as for the illumination it gives us of the preconscious color prejudice and irrational white folk religion.[4] We live in an era, now, when silence from blacks is not held to be golden, when compromise is suspect as betrayal, when confrontation and passionate black honesty are cherished. True humanity lies in this direction, engulfed as it is in black consciousness and group pride. It was not always so, though "race consciousness" emerged at about the time the phenomenon of *passing* had peaked. There was a time when the choice for many seemed to be to swallow their pride or lose their hide.

In 1925 there were nineteen states, in addition to the District of Columbia, which did not have anti-marriage laws on the books: Connecticut, Illinois, Iowa, Kansas, Maine, Michigan, Massachusetts, Minnesota, New Hampshire, New Jersey, New Mexico, New York, Ohio, Rhode Island, Pennsylvania, Vermont, Washington, Wisconsin, and Wyoming. This was the year in which the American Public Health Association was addressed by Dr. W. A. Plecker of Virginia, who, in his capacity as State Registrar of Vital Statistics was in charge of seeing that the new "racial integrity" law of the state worked to perfection. His total commitment to this responsibility was reflected in his speech to the Public Health Association on "Virginia's Attempt to Adjust the Color Problem." Dr. Plecker was concerned about the mixing of the races and particularly about the "many instances" where blacks were known to have gained recognition as whites as persons "or groups of persons," a state of affairs he deemed more detrimental to the welfare of whites than "an increase of the death rate from preventable diseases":

> Even in Virginia, where the questions of race and birth receive as much attention as anywhere in the country, the process of amalgamation is nevertheless going on, and in some localities is well advanced. Complete ruin can probably be held off for several centuries longer, but we have no reason to hope that we shall prove the one and only example in the history of the world of two races living together without amalgamation.[5]

Dr. Plecker expressed as candidly as any speaker could the solution to the problem of mulattoes and their tendency toward amalgamation:

> There is but one absolute solution which is acceptable and feasible, and that is the one advocated by Lincoln and other farseeing statesmen of the past—the separation of the races by gradual repatriation of the colored races. This measure is still possible, but the longer it is deferred the greater the task.[6]

There is no doubt that the extraordinary production and number of mulattoes in Virginia coupled with their post-Reconstruction freedom led many whites to have nightmares. They were terrified by the mulattoes high fertility rate and by a misplaced fear that the then twelve million blacks would become twenty, then thirty, and finally one hundred million by the year 2000. There was little hope that the past could be undone by a nation-wide colonization movement which would send repatriated blacks back to Africa. To prevent what seemed the inevitable crowding out of the white population by blacks through such measures as *passing*, Virginia took a radical route:

Virginia has made the first serious attempt to stay or postpone the evil day when this is no longer a white man's country. Her recently enacted law "for preservation of racial integrity" is, in the words of Maj. E. S. Cox, "the most perfect expression of the white ideal, and the most important eugenical effort that has been made during the past four thousand years." Of course this law will not prevent the illegitimate mixture of the races, but it is possible to stop the legal intermixture, and the law defines a white person as one with "no trace whatsoever of blood other than Caucasian," and makes it a felony to make a willfully false statement as to color.[7]

The illicit relations between blacks and whites were not feared by Dr. Plecker or other Virginians because they knew these relations almost always involved white males and black women, and, while some children resulted from them, the laws were expected to place enough fear in the mothers so that they would rear the children of these illicit relations as blacks. This did not always work, but the floodtide of *passing* appeared so monstrous—the genes of whites were seen to be infiltrated by the genes of blacks, quite a different story than the reverse—that every effort was made to prevent further proliferation of *passing*. It is obvious that *passing* was active. It could not be stopped by simply defining a white person as one with "no trace whatsoever of blood other than Caucasian," since the clerks, who were not permitted "to grant licenses allowing white persons to marry those with any trace of colored blood," were unable to make this distinction when it came down to it. The pressure was as much on the clerks and other officials as it was on those who were *passing* because to mistakenly suggest that a white person was a black person brought forth legal suits which were more costly than the situation was embarrassing. It seemed most effective to place the fear in those who might seek to *pass* by making it a felony to willfully falsify a "statement as to color."

The registration of races was an all-out effort to prevent the flow of *passing,* and although the cost in time and additional work proved significant it was rewarding:

We are greatly encouraged by the interest and cooperation of physicians, local registrars, clerks, school authorities, the general public, and even the midwives. Our success during the first four months of the enforcement of this law, in securing more accurate statements as to color on our birth-certificates and in correcting previously existing errors, is far beyond expectation.[8]

It was a truly heroic effort Virginia was making on behalf of the entire white race:

The white race in this land is the foundation upon which rests its civilization, and is responsible for the leading position which we occupy among the nations of the world. Is it not, therefore, just and right that this race decide for itself what its composition shall be and attempt, as Virginia has, to maintain its purity?[9]

But Virginia needed help and appealed for it by demonstrating how vital statistics could be a force in stopping "all further legal and much of the illegitimate" black-white mixture at least until Lincoln's "real remedy can be adopted":

This, however, is but the beginning, and our efforts will be of less avail until every State in the Union joins in the move to secure the best marriage law as possible, and a wholesome public sentiment on this the most important of all questions confronting us as a nation.[10]

Perhaps the majority of whites throughout the land emotionally supported Virginia in what she called the struggle for the "life or death of our civilization." But it was not with whites in general but with those white-skinned blacks in particular that Virginia was having real trouble. They were *passing* despite the laws, and there was nothing that could be done about it except to bring pressure to bear in the hope of smoking out those so engaged, curbing the desire of those who might be thinking about it, and working the odds so that the future racial mixture would not be as extensive as in the past:

> The colored races should be equally zealous in preventing both legal and illegal admixture of the races. We are glad to say that the true negro of Virginia is beginning to appreciate this point and is agreeing to the wisdom of this movement. Our chief trouble is with some of the near-whites who desire to change from the colored to the white class.[11]

In looking back upon the alarmist position which Virginia took, it is impossible to learn how much of the paranoia resulted from actual *passing* and how much of it was the result of an intention to capitalize upon the fears of the present in order to head off any crucial alignments in the future. That there was no basis for the expressed fear of being tinged by the "tar brush," black genes, because of the considerable amount of *passing* there can be no doubt. Of course, in America we have never known with any precision the amount of black and white ancestry possessed by persons of multiple ancestry, nor indeed do we know how many persons of multiple ancestry are or have been dominated by white genes. It is certain that popular opinion fastened on this problem in the early years of this century, and that the problem was subsequently taken up by social scientists, who also became fascinated with it. It may not be too much to say that the guilt suffered by those who had produced so many near-whites, their fear of turnabout as fair play, and their expectations that *passing* might speed up the black-white solution made a mountain out of a mole hill.

The issues centering around miscegenation and its particular form of *passing* led to the first scientific study of crossings between blacks and whites in 1913. In that year, Dr. Charles B. Davenport, Director of the Department of Experimental Evolution of the Carnegie Institution, produced a scholarly paper, "Heredity of Skin Color in Negro-White Crosses." In this study he unwittingly popularized certain terms for mixed blooded blacks which were widely and loosely used. As early as 1854, Frederick Law Olmstead reported that Southern Frenchmen had developed their own classifications of black people:

> *Sacatra*—Griffe and Negro
> *Griffe*—Negro and Mulatto
> *Marabon*—Mulatto and Griffe
> *Mulatto*—White and Negro
> *Quadroon*—White and Mulatto
> *Metif*—White and Quadroon
> *Meamelouc*—White and Metif
> *Quarteron*—White and Meamelouc
> *Sang-mêlé*—White and Quarteron

From the Spanish *mulato,* the diminutive of *mulo,* a mule, comes the word mulatto or a young mule, the result of its hybrid origin. The first cross between pure African and pure North European Caucasians gives a mulatto. A fairly definite prediction of the physical characteristics and skin color can be made from this crossing. A definite prediction cannot be made of all of the characteristics which will result from the crossing between a pure African and the Mediterranean Spanish and Portuguese, since the Spanish and Portuguese have for generations crossed with the Moors. The study by Davenport upgraded the French designation and suggested further classifications, which resulted in the following terminology for mixed blacks:

> *Mulatto*—Black and Caucasian (1/2 each)
> **Quadroon*—Mulatto and Caucasian (1/4 Black)
> **Octoroon*—Quadroon and Caucasian (Less than 1/4 Black)
> *Cascos*—Mulatto and Mulatto (Less than 1/2 Black)
> *Sambo*—Mulatto and Black (3/4 Black)
> *Mango*—Sambo and Black (3/4 Black)
> **Mustifee*—Octoroon and Caucasian (Less than 1/16 Black)
> **Mustifino*—Mustifee and Caucasian (Less than 1/32 Black)

> * Pass for White

As *passing* became a terrifying issue to whites the categorization of blacks took on more and more meaning. Where once differentiation of skin color and features went unnoticed, the classification of blacks into octoroon and quadroon and mulatto became a favorite pastime among whites. In the popular mind, the typology of blacks took on an aura of mystery and black magic. The more white blood a black seemed to have, the more he and his ancestry, especially his black ancestry, were believed to be engaged in mischief. The very existence of mischief making or *passing* intensified the tension between blacks and whites, particularly where there was great fear that the slightest drop of black blood would "contaminate" the white race.

Of course the difficulty with these typologies is evident. For example, the strict definition of a mulatto refers to a person who is a first generation and direct offspring of a fullblooded black and a fullblooded white. A great to do was made by the general public and social scientists about the amount of ancestry particular mulattoes received from blacks and whites. The trouble was that the term "mulatto" became a general category for blacks mixed with any degree of white genes. Further, the accuracy of many reports has to be taken with a bushel of salt when the singular fact is that we do not know how many Africans originally set down on these shores were fullblooded. We do know that a considerable number of Africans were imported here from other slave holding territories, as well as directly from Africa, and that in both cases these Africans were already recipients of white genes. A study of the percentage of black and white mixture to determine whether a mixed black was a mulatto or a casco or a quadroon depended in most instances upon the mixed black tracing his ancestry, and it is highly possible that many did not know whether or not their earliest African ancestors on these shores had been previous victims of hybridization.

The realization of these facts tempered the work of some social scientists, but it made no impact upon the popular mind or on the popular writers who enjoyed a good yarn. We begin to see how a base of some fact becomes the fact for all bases when we read the sensational but inaccurate stories of *passing* printed in the popular journals. The popular interest in *passing* was high earlier in this century and everyone was aware of its reality, if not from their personal lives then from the copyrighted stories:

> No statistics are available, naturally, of the number of
> persons who do not acknowledge their Negro ancestry but

pass for white in their home communities and elsewhere, but it is a large and rapidly increasing number.

Crossing the color line is so common an occurrence that the Negroes have their own well-understood word for it. They call it "passing." It is less and less difficult for the young man or woman of African descent, whose skin, hair and features are not decidedly Negroid, to "pass" without fear of detection.[12]

That the setting forth of such information in the *Outlook and Independent* in 1931 was considered good copy is evidenced by this magazine's reporting of the scientific investigations of the Carnegie Institution which testified that the issue of *passing* was

a matter of great social moment to hundreds of our citizens, namely the possibility of a reversion in the offspring of a white-skinned descendant of a Negro to the brown skin color. There is a current opinion that such an extracted white, married to a pure-bred white, may have a black child. This tradition has been used to create dramatic situations in novels and in newspaper stories; and the dread of this tradition hangs over many a marriage that might otherwise be quite happy. In our studies no clear case of this sort has been found and our fundamental hypothesis leads us not to expect it. . . . It follows from our studies that persons of African descent whose skin color contains ten per cent or less of black pigment will, if mated with a like person, produce only white-skinned children. . . . Such persons constitute "fixed white." [13]

The fear of the results of *passing* was increased by the popular misconception of a person who possessed any sizable amount of both black and white genes. It was held that such mixture produced a hybrid less fecund than the pure black or pure white. This misconception developed into one which contended that all blacks would become mixed with whites and produce a halfbreed race that would eventually die out from infertility caused by the absence of a racial purity. Of course this misconception was based upon a false analogy between the mulatto (*mulo,* or mule, in Spanish) and the mule, the ass-horse hybrid, which is notably sterile.

There were a good many liberals two decades or more ago who, as we pointed out in the first chapter, held with Franz Boas, the Columbia University anthropologist, that the marriage of white men with black women was a good thing, the solution to black-white conflict. With the authority of persons like Franz Boas behind them, popular writers translated the concern and transmitted it to the general public as a service:

> The fear of becoming the parent of a distinctively Negro child is all that keeps many young octoroons of both sexes from crossing the color line matrimonially; the same fear keeps many young white men from marrying young women to whom they are strongly attracted but, who, they have reason to suspect, have a strain of Negro blood. The general realization that such "throwbacks" are biologically impossible when one of the mates is pure white and the other has no more than one-eighth Negro blood will certainly tend to accelerate the process of "passing." [14]

This kind of reporting stirred the adrenalin of whites persuaded by the Virginia "racial integrity" laws and the popular theories. If, indeed, such liberal attitudes were efforts to show the harmlessness of whites' marrying blacks and to promote such marriages—as well as to demonstrate that blacks who *passed* would not give themselves away through biological detection—these efforts were also embedded in the most precarious scientific pretensions. Over and over again *passing* was held to be commonplace, inevitable, large scale, and to be valued on the grounds of stories which claimed to be based on "scientific investigations," or "scientific observation," or "common knowledge":

> In New York, where only one person out of thirty-four is an acknowledged Negro, it is a matter of common repute among the colored folks of Harlem that more than ten thousand of their number have "passed", and are now accepted as white

in their new relations, many of them married to white folks,
all unsuspected. In Chicago, with a Negro population of one
in twenty, and in Philadelphia, where one in thirteen is a
Negro, the proportion of annual "passings" is said to be even
larger.[15]

The myth which condemned *passing* and black-white marriages
on the grounds that a halfbreed race would be sterile and therefore die out was opposed by the equally false myth which promoted *passing* and black-white marriages. Both myths indicate the
extent to which whites were caught up in their own myth making
and the powerful effect *passing* once had upon our populace:

> The results of this scientific investigation indicate that the
> Negro race is not dying out from infertility but is bleaching
> out through admixture with the white race. The white strain
> is the dominant one, and this fact has a direct bearing upon
> the increasing number of Negroes with three-quarters or
> more of white blood who "pass" every year and marry into
> white families.[16]

We have seen the extent to which the repressive forces of our
past were willing to go in order to stamp out *passing*. But to make
clear that *passing* was the white man's problem—a factor of his
own creation and a reaction to a deep guilt that put up a straw
man to knock down—and not a matter of concern to blacks when
they were met by whites who wanted to learn about the black
concern over *passing*, it may be helpful to set forth two stories reported as fact. These stories may be true, but they are more important as illustrations of the white psyche which believed them
as well as many others in the 1930's:

> Quite recently, at a dinner dance at a fashionable New York
> hotel, at which most of the guests were in or near the Social
> Register, one of the men fancied there was something
> familiar in the appearance of one of the young women, an
> especially attractive demi-blonde. When he met her she
> seemed to be greatly agitated, but it was not until she drew

him aside and piteously begged him not to give her away that he recognized her as his mother's former personal maid! Although he knew she had been classed as Negress in his home town, several hundred miles from New York, he promised to say nothing, and kept his promise. She married a wealthy young man.[17]

The second story is longer but so typifies the thousands of others which once were so exciting to white America that it merits retelling:

Somewhere in the United States, if they are still alive, are two persons, a man and a woman, brother and sister, who have always been known as pure white and who do not themselves know that they are not of the oldest and purest New England Puritan strain. They are the son and daughter of two quadroons, the story of whose sacrifice for their children's sake was told me many years ago by an elderly statesman, now dead. This is the story as he told it to me:

In the dark days of Reconstruction, immediately after the war between the states, when the "carpet-bag" governments were running riot in the South, the men who had fought in the Confederate Army were barred from the ballot box and the newly freed Negroes were encouraged to vote, many Negroes were sent to the United States Congress. Among them was Blanche K. Bruce, a highly intelligent quadroon from New Orleans. After his short term in Congress, Bruce was appointed by President Grant to the post which, in Republican administrations, is always occupied by a Negro, and in Democratic administrations by an Indian—the post of Register of the Treasury. He held that position until the first Cleveland administration.

My friend who told me this story had known Bruce in Congress, had great respect for his ability and character, and befriended him in many ways. One day he met Bruce, who seemed distraught. My friend asked him if there was anything he could do for him as he seemed to be in trouble.

"Nothing that anybody can do," replied Bruce. "I

wouldn't tell anybody but you what is worrying me, but I must talk to somebody. My wife is about to become a mother."

"Why that's nothing to worry about," replied my friend, in surprise.

"Not for white folks, nor for black ones," was Bruce's response but "we're both quadroons, and it's something to worry about when you don't know whether your baby is going to be white or black."

"Which do you want?" my friend asked.

"For the baby's sake, we hope it will be white; but for my wife's sake I hope to God it will be black," Bruce answered. "We've had two children, and both were white. We couldn't take them back South with us, for we would have to bring them up as Negroes, so we found a fine white family up in Massachusetts that adopted them when they were so little they didn't know the difference. They have another name and they never will know these white folks aren't their real parents. I've provided for them so they are no burden on their foster parents. But it almost killed my wife each time she had to give her baby away. I think she'll go crazy if this one is white, so I'm praying every night that it will be black, so she can have a baby to keep for her own."

A short time later Bruce lost his position in Washington, and it was years before my friend saw him again and learned the sequel to the story.

"I met Bruce on a steamship, coming from Europe," said my friend. "I reminded him of our last conversation and asked him whether the child was white or black. 'Black, thank God!' Bruce replied. 'We had a boy that we could keep.'

" 'What did you do with him?' I asked.

" 'I sent him and his mother to France,' said Bruce. 'We were both slaves in an old French family in New Orleans, so the language was familiar to us; and over in Paris they don't draw the color line, like they do in America. I've just been over to see him take his degree in medicine at the Sorbonne.' "

That was all that my old friend told me, but it came
back to my memory a few weeks ago when another friend,
just returned from Paris, told me of a Negro physician with a
wonderful practice, whom the French people seemed to take
as a matter of course, as they had taken Alexandre Dumas,
the great novelist, also of Negro descent.[18]

The mixture of truth and fact in these two stories may not
produce fiction, but the fact that these stories come close to
fiction and to that extent tend to make the whole white drama
about *passing* one great fiction is underscored in the following suspect observation. It is suspect because what we have learned earlier about Booker T. Washington's attitude toward marriage in
black and white runs counter to this interpretation of his supposed description of black people and *passing.* Caleb Johnson, in-
terestingly enough, told this story long after Mr. Washington's
death. This story illustrates beautifully the importance of being
white to whites, and, as we shall see, the little importance of *passing* to most blacks who were able to *pass:*

A few years ago I visited Booker T. Washington's famous
school at Tuskegee, Alabama. Watching the fifteen hundred
Negro students, of every shade from coal black through all
the degrees of brown and yellow, as they filed into the
Assembly Hall one morning, my attention was caught by a
boy of eighteen or so in whom I could not detect a single
trace of Negro pedigree. He was a slender, handsome blond,
whose high-bridged nose and distinctive bearing seemed to
hark back to England.

"What is that boy doing here?" I asked Dr. Washington,
whose own blue eyes and saddle-brown skin betokened his
large percentage of white blood.

"Wait until the girls come along and you'll see his
sister," was his reply. And the golden-haired, blue-eyed
beauty of sixteen was well worth waiting to see. She was not
merely pretty. There was high intelligence in her expression
and a poised dignity in her carriage which would have made
her the center of attention even if her companions had been

the pupils of the most fashionable girls' school in the North, instead of the Negroes with whom she was laughing and chatting.

"Who are they?" I asked the principal.

"They are the children of a wealthy planter, who lives not many miles from here," replied Dr. Washington. "He is devoted to their mother, but he cannot legally marry her, for she is a quadroon. These children are the apple of his eye. But being octoroons they cannot enter any white school in the South, and he cannot take them North, to be brought up as white without breaking up his family; for their mother is readily recognizable as of Negro blood. So he brought them here to me, as being the only place where they could receive a good education. He frequently visits them, and is more solicitous for their comfort than most parents are."

"What will become of them when they grow up?" I pursued. "I can't imagine either of them voluntarily choosing to remain in the Negro classification."

"Nor I," he responded, "particularly as it seems to be the highest ambition of most of the people of my race to be as much like white folks as possible. I suppose they will go North, eventually, and 'pass,' as so many do."

Then the famous educator told me of scores of similar cases, of white men, leaders in politics, in business and the professions, whose illegitimate Negro families were often more dear to them than their legitimate white offspring, and whose descendants have "passed" and sometimes won renown as white folks. There were governors and statesmen of national repute among the names he mentioned. There was the story of the grandson of Charles Manley, a famous governor of North Carolina, who "passed" in order to obtain work in Philadelphia, lived for years as a white man, prominent in public affairs, then went back to his own people for love of his Negro wife and children!

"A good many colored folks that try to be white find that it isn't as pleasant as they imagined it would be," said Dr. Washington, chuckling. "White folks don't really have a good time, from the Negro point of view. They lack the laughing, boisterous sociability which the Negro enjoys." [19]

Fabricated myths and popular fiction all attest to the importance of *passing* in the white scheme of things. Some whites were vehemently opposed to *passing*, others found it intriguing, there were a few who believed it to be the destiny of blacks, but all whites used this issue for their own particular purposes. *Passing* had become a white concern in the North as well as in the South. It was at least widespread and significant enough to attract some real scientific research, so it is safe to conclude that *passing* was of real import to whites. It is true that birth records were not kept with accuracy in the early years of this century. This fact and the mobility of people made *passing* on a very large scale very plausible. The feasibility of *passing* and its traumatic impact led to the first scientific research on black-white crossings by Davenport. Poor birth records, mobility, and the illicit beginnings of black-white mixtures led Davenport to Jamaica and Bermuda in search of data for the study of heredity of skin color in such crossings. There he undertook to determine as scientifically as he was able the transmitted black characteristics through several generations of cross breeding.

In order to determine the amount of pigment in the skin of his subjects, members of several hundred cross-bred families, Davenport used an instrument called the Bradley Color Top:

> In this device disks of colored paper are so arranged that any given proportion of the whole circle can be exposed in each color. Then, when the top is rotated rapidly, the blending of colors produces a share in which the exact proportions of each different color can be determined by the proportion of each disk exposed at the time.
>
> In testing the color of a Negro's skin the arm or some other part of the body not usually subjected to the action of the sun was exposed, and the disks of the color top adjusted until the blended color exactly matched that of the subject's skin. This gave a precise percentage of the different pigments in the skin.
>
> It was found that in pure-blooded Negroes the

percentages of pigmentation ran about as follows: Black, 50 to 77 per cent; red, 20 to 40 per cent; yellow, 3 to 12 per cent; white, 3 to 17 per cent. The average proportions of a miscellaneous group of Bermuda Negroes of pure blood was 67 per cent black pigment, 19.5 per cent red, 5 per cent yellow and 8.5 white.

Similar skin-color tests on a miscellaneous group of persons of pure Caucasian descent, none of whom could be suspected of having a trace of Negro blood, and who ranged in tint from dark Portuguese brunette to flaxen-haired English blond, gave an average pigmentation of 5.5 per cent red, 18 per cent yellow and 42 per cent white.[20]

As a result of this year-long study based upon accurately determined subjects, Davenport discovered that after three generations of crossings with Caucasians most of the offspring (octoroons) could pass for white and that their offspring (mustifees) would be "fixed whites." In large measure, all other characteristics were found to follow the pattern of skin color. Davenport concluded:

Certainly the offspring of an octoroon and a white person will, so far as skin color goes, be a "white person." . . . Our studies, then, justify the legal limitation. Indeed, a person of one-eighth blood is completely "across the line"; married to white there is no expectation of dark-skinned offspring.[21]

Davenport made an important contribution to our knowledge about the black-white genetic combinations, but this knowledge was not intended to determine the future of blacks in relation to whites. His scientific study was used as a foil for less scientific speculations and predictions by popular interpreters:

Taken in connection with the rapidly increasing mixture of the races in the North and the steady migration of Negroes from the South to the North, it suggests interesting possibilities as to the future of the Negro in America. There is no new Negro stock coming into the United States, with the trivial exceptions of the part-white Negroes from the

West Indies and occasional Moor, Berber or Abyssinian from North Africa. Will the Negroes already here always remain Negroes, or will they eventually "pass"? With the spreading out of the Negro population into regions where its proportion to the white population is progressively less, the mingling of the races seems to be on the increase, and the proportion of those who will "pass" annually seems likely to become greater, year by year.

It took six hundred years for the Moors to lose their identity in the mass of the Spanish population and to change the complexion of Spain from that of the blond Visigoths to the dark brunette Spaniard of today. Ten per cent of Americans today are recognizably Negroid; and incalculable percentage carry Negro blood in their veins though classed as white. It seems not inconceivable that the American Negro will eventually vanish, completely absorbed into the general body of mixed bloods of all races which will constitute the American people of the future.[22]

The life sciences, especially biology and genetics, in direct response to the public alarm over miscegenation and *passing,* have determined clearly the results of mixtures between blacks and whites of various combinations through several generations. We have known for a number of decades now that when blacks reach the level where they are able and willing to *pass* there is no way of detecting their heritage by their biological fruits. If in some quarters of our country such people are not legally or morally white, they are white because they choose to be so and they are able to so choose because they are dominated by diffused white genes.

Social scientists were much slower in bringing to light the actuality of *passing* and in complementing the life sciences in their findings of what occurs if and when there is *passing.* Understandably, the social scientists have the more difficult time of it, given the surreptitious nature of the process of *passing.* Some social scientists have estimated that two hundred thousand blacks *pass* each year, but in the late 1940's the figure was generally held to be between fifteen and thirty thousand. The disparity of these figures and the general inflation of the situation gave rise to active imagi-

nations which took these estimates, which were at best guesstimates, for scientific fact instead of unscientific guesswork:

> They are based on careful studies by experts of census
> reports, immigration records, vital statistics and information
> from other sources. These studies show very conclusively that
> approximately 20,000 Negroes disappear every year, and that
> their absence from the black population cannot be counted
> otherwise than by passing.[23]

Of course we know today that a substantial proportion of black
males are unaccounted for in the census because of their mobility,
and, if we do not know for how long the failure to include a number of blacks in the census reports has been going on, we are
probably not far off the mark in concluding that it is not a new
phenomenon, even if it is a new discovery. A magazine writer like
Herbert Asbury was unaware of this flaw when he wrote a popular article for *Collier's* in 1946 based upon these guesstimates:

> If the estimates of the number of Negroes who pass annually
> are even approximately correct, they mean that more than
> 2,000,000 persons with colored blood have crossed the line
> since the end of the Civil War. But these figures tell only a
> part of the story. A large majority of the Negroes who pass,
> marry white and raise white families, the members of which
> in turn seek white mates. Thus a constantly widening stream
> of colored blood is introduced into the white population. A
> great deal has also come into the white stream through
> Negro-white intermarriage, which is now legal in eighteen
> states, and even more through illicit Negro-white matings
> which have resulted in children.
>
> It is now estimated that there are at least between
> 5,000,000 and 8,000,000 persons in the United States,
> supposed to be white, who actually possess Negro blood. In
> reality, this is a very conservative estimate. . . .
>
> Hundreds of prominent American men and women who
> live as whites are actually white Negroes. Many believe
> themselves to be pure white, since the original passing in
> their families was done several generations ago. . . .[24]

Historically, being black in America was a biological, social, and legal matter. The biological fact that some blacks had as little as one sixty-fourth, or "any discernible amount" of black genes (or "blood," as it was popularly designated) still made them socially unacceptable and therefore the victims of laws which attempted to define a black. The number of blacks who were indistinguishable from whites made the *passing* of the legal black for white a disturbing presence; but it was not until the 1940's that social scientists ascertained with some degree of accuracy the number of legal blacks who *passed* for white.

The initial study which sought to arrive at an unbiased estimate of the number of legal blacks *passing* for white was made by Hornell Hart in 1921.[25] This work was widely known and un-

---

Table 1[26]

Native Whites of Native Parentage, by Age Groups,
for 1900 and 1910

| Ages | | Population | | Increase |
1900	1910	1900	1910	or Decrease
0–4	10–14	5,464,881	5,324,283	−140,589
5–9	15–19	5,174,220	5,089,055	−85,165
10–14	20–24	4,660,390	4,682,922	+22,532
15–19	25–29	4,234,953	4,049,074	−185,879
20–24	30–34	3,805,609	3,401,601	−404,008

---

doubtedly served Herbert Asbury in his speculative estimates and projections. Hart's method, as Herbert Asbury rightly described it, was to analyze the census return for native whites of native parentage, by breaking it down into age groups. This method was based on the solid assumption that this group cannot increase. Deaths and emigration could decrease it, but there should be no increases. Despite this logical method, Hart found a marked increase, as indicated in Table 1.

As seen in Table 1, Hart discovered that the group which had been between ten and fourteen years of age in 1900 and were twenty to twenty-four years of age in 1910 "had not only lost no one by death or emigration but had actually increased itself

22,500—an absolute impossibility." [27] John H. Burma in reviewing this study commented:

> Hart estimated that actually some 140,000 had died, others
> had emigrated, and that therefore from 165,000 to 170,000
> persons had materialized from the thin air—or elsewhere. His
> own solution to this problem of magic was that a little of the
> increase could be accounted for by the return of previous
> immigrants, more was due to incorrect returns to the Census
> Bureau, but the bulk of the increase was the result of the
> passing of the legal Negro upon reaching maturity.[28]

When Hart compared the migration and emigration statistics of
blacks with those of whites, he concluded that "a quarter of a million
or more persons per decade, born in families classified as
Negro, report themselves as members of the white race." [29]

It is understandable that this work of a competent sociologist
would gain a wide hearing in popular articles and in the lectures
of college professors. His methods were clear, his premises logical,
and the figures of the Census Bureau could readily be checked.
However, Burma found that the 1900–10 decade studied by Hart
was atypical. Burma used Hart's methods and applied them to the
decades of 1920–30 and 1930–40 with surprisingly different results,
as shown on Table 2 (p. 126).

Burma's statistical work disclosed that none of the four
decades was comparable, that the estimated deaths for the
decades 1920–40 bore no relation of significance to the census
count and consequently, that figures from the Census Bureau
could not be construed as revealing the number of legal blacks
passing as white.

Students of population and race have known for decades that
the male : female ratios of blacks and whites were dissimilar. This
difference in sex ratios has led to a general consensus that more
black men *pass* than black women. This consensus was founded
on the casual observation that there is a low ratio of men to
women among mulattoes, which is revealed as well in certain
censuses, but not for the black group. This low sex ratio was
widely interpreted to mean that mulatto men were passing into

Table 2[30]

Total Native White of Native Parentage

Ages In 1910	In 1920	Population Count 1910	1920	Increase or Decrease	Estimated Deaths*
0–4	10–14	6,546,282	6,455,709	−90,573	—
5–9	15–19	5,861,015	5,599,046	−261,969	—
10–14	20–24	5,324,283	5,176,707	−147,576	—
15–19	25–29	5,089,055	4,764,802	−324,253	—
20–24	30–34	4,682,922	4,096,041	−586,881	—

Ages In 1920	In 1930	Population Count 1920	1930	Increase or Decrease	Estimated Deaths*
0–4	10–14	7,366,530	7,528,352	+161,822	−630,750
5–9	15–19	6,977,863	6,932,503	−45,360	−113,601
10–14	20–24	6,455,709	6,355,507	−100,202	−122,147
15–19	25–29	5,599,046	5,509,780	−89,266	−158,283
20–24	30–34	5,176,707	4,016,005	−206,701	−180,625

Ages In 1930	In 1940	Population Count 1930	1940	Increase or Decrease	Estimated Deaths*
0–4	10–14	10,108,160	10,298,744	+190,784	−867,569
5–9	15–19	11,019,290	10,799,262	−220,028	−179,389
10–14	20–24	10,515,890	10,130,640	−385,250	−198,963
15–19	25–29	9,871,673	9,479,994	−391,679	−279,081
20–24	30–34	8,865,481	8,497,387	−368,094	−309,300

* Estimated deaths are on the basis of 1929–31.

the white world in greater numbers than mulatto women. Burma does not break down the sex ratio into mulatto and black groups, but places all variations of blacks in one category to show the dissimilar sex ratios of blacks and whites.

The statistical data, the lower sex ratio for blacks than for whites up to age fifty at which time it is reversed, as shown in Table 3, have been interpreted to prove that black males *pass* more than females, that this occurs around age twenty, and that after age forty they return to the black group. The data have been further interpreted to show that some four per hundred black

Table 3[31]

Ratio of Males to 100 Females of Native-born
Negroes and Whites, by Age Groups

Age	Negro	White	Difference
Under 5	99.09	103.80	+4.71
5–9	98.92	103.49	+4.57
10–14	98.81	103.25	+4.44
15–19	93.42	101.26	+7.84
20–24	85.32	98.02	+12.70
25–29	86.07	88.07	+12.00
30–34	89.19	99.14	+9.95
35–39	88.31	99.46	+11.15
40–44	96.08	100.11	+4.07
45–49	100.43	100.74	+0.31
50–54	105.30	100.86	−4.44
55–59	108.53	100.01	−8.52
60–64	108.46	98.25	−10.21
65–69	105.31	95.76	−9.55
Average	94.92	100.14	+5.22

NOTE: Arranged from *Sixteenth Census Population* (Second Series), *Characteristics of the Population*, U.S. Summary Table 7; and *Sixteenth Census, Population, Characteristics of the Non-White Population by Race*, Table 2.

males semi-permanently *pass*. As Burma made clear, the data reveals nothing of the kind. What actually occurs in this data is that the black male death rate makes an upward turn at age twenty for a variety of reasons. Burma computed on the basis of vital statistics that the white male in the twenty to thirty-four age group dies at the rate of 19.62 per thousand, while the black male death rate in the identical age bracket is 59.01 per thousand.[32] This wide variation led Burma to conclude that there was more than enough margin of error here to account for the discrepancy without assuming the question of *passing*. Moreover, the wide margins of error between Tables 2 and 3 indicate that the discrepancies lie precisely in statistical errors.

In Dr. Caroline Day's study of three hundred forty-six families with black-white genes a different method was used which called into question the large numbers of blacks *passing* as indicated by Hart.[33] Dr. Day found that in these families there were thirty-five blacks who *passed* permanently and twenty-two who *passed* periodically. When Day's figures are projected, the number of blacks who *pass* is far less the number than reported in Hart's study. Over seventy-five per cent of blacks have white genes and they tend to marry each other within this wide range.

Burma estimated that forty per cent of all black families are comparable to those studied by Day. Assuming that the ratio held for all black families as for Day's sample, Burma figured the number of blacks who have *passed* as white and married white equaled about four per cent of black families in the United States. In 1946, the year in which Burma was working, there were some 2,750,000 black families, four per cent of which gives approximately 110,000 legal blacks *passing* as white. This group of 110,000 covered four decades, indicating that between 2,500 and 2,750 legal blacks *pass* for white each year. Burma's 1946 estimates of 2,500 blacks annually *passing* is ten per cent of the 25,000 Hart estimated in 1929.[34]

In 1937, T. T. McKinney estimated there were 10,000 legal blacks annually *passing* as white.[35] In 1946, Herbert Asbury estimated the number as high as 30,000.[36] The reason Burma held to the lower figure as more accurate, though itself only an estimate, was due to the large amount of nonscientific opinion and pseudo-scientific guesswork surrounding the inflated issue of *passing*. E. W. Eckard came to Burma's conclusion via the route of questioning the data and statistical methods employed by those who had arrived at estimates of from 10,000 to 30,000 legal blacks *passing* as white each year. Eckard found that crude birth rates and death rates, along with other improper use of statistics, had led to these incredible results. In cooperation with the chief of the Population Statistics Section, Population Division Bureau of Census, Eckard revealed the effect of sampling errors:

The total population of the United States in 1930 and 1940 was 122,775,046 and 131,669,275, respectively. The respective Negro population for the same years in the United States was 11,891,143 and 12,865,518, with the Negro population being 9.7 per cent of the total in 1930 and 9.8 per cent in 1940. If 30,000 Negroes "pass" the color line each year, they amount to only .023 of 1 per cent of the total population and .25 of 1 per cent of the Negro population in 1940. The attempt to arrive at a number that is such a small part of the total population by approximate methods cannot bring forth an acceptable answer. For example, an error of 1 per cent of the Negro population will amount to 110,000 which is much larger than the alleged number of Negroes "passing" each year.[37]

Eckard worked out a systematic and careful statistical analysis and through this sophisticated procedure concluded that

Negroes "passed" into the white race at the rate of 2,600 per year during the decade from 1930 to 1940. Owing to errors, the author believes that the number was actually much less.

It is possible that in a decade such as the one from 1920 to 1930 there may have been more economic inducement for Negroes to become accepted as whites than from 1930 to 1940. But before 1930 the registration of deaths was too incomplete to achieve a very great degree of accuracy with research on the subject.[38]

Our knowledge of the numbers of legal blacks who *passed* for white in the first four decades of this century is limited by the slow development of vital statistics so imperative for accurate work among social scientists. Another complicating factor was the very inaccurate work of census takers who were ill equipped to fathom the color distribution. In fact, if one relies on the census reports it is not possible to be clear on the amount of white ancestry necessary to *pass*. The confusion is increased when it is recalled that at one time in our history a distinction was made by the Census Bureau between mulattoes and blacks, a distinction which led experts to contend that the amount of black-white mixture was considerably more than ever reported by the census, and often undistinguishable by the census people:

The proportion of the Negro population returned as mulatto in the various censuses as follows: 1850, 11.2 per cent; 1860, 13.2 per cent; 1870, 12.0 per cent; 1890, 15.2 per cent; 1910,

20.9 per cent; and 1920, 15.9 per cent. Considerable uncertainty, however, attaches to this classification since the accuracy of the distinction made depends largely upon the judgment and care of the enumerators. Moreover, the definition of the terms "black" and "mulatto" adopted at different Censuses has not been uniform. At the Censuses of 1850 and 1860 the two terms appear not to have been defined at all. At the Census of 1870 the instructions were to report as "black" all persons who were "evidently full-blood Negroes" and as "mulatto" all other persons having "some proportion or perceptible trace of Negro blood." At the Census of 1890, the term "black" included all persons "having three-fourths or more "black blood," other persons with any other proportion of "black" blood being classified as "mulattoes," "quadroons," or "octoroons." At the Census of 1910 the instructions were substantially the same as at the Census of 1870. Finally, at the Census of 1920 the instructions were to report as "black" all full-blooded Negroes and as "mulatto" all Negroes having some proportion of white blood. It is an interesting sidelight on the variability of these results that the relatively high proportion of mulattoes reported in 1910 is attributed to the greater care exercised that year and the employment of many Negro enumerators who returned a higher proportion of mulattoes than has usually been reported by white census takers.[39]

The divergent accounting of the number of blacks who *pass* was based upon false statistical data and errors and compounded by ill-founded preconceptions. For one thing, as we have previously discovered, the amount of wholesale miscegenation without inter-marriage decreased considerably in this century. That is, while a great amount of black-white intercourse continues, it does not produce children as it did in those more stable relations of previous centuries. The vast number of quadroons, octoroons, and mustifees at the turn of the century caused a considerable amount of upheaval among whites who had forgotten that at the same time they were alarmed about *passing* there began the significant decrease in child producing black-white intercourse that continues to this day. Thus the total number of blacks who could *pass* has been waning in this century in comparison with previous ones. By the time the statistical analyses had caught up with the biological realities the panic over and phenomenon of *passing* had peaked. It took some time, however, for anthropologists to catch up with the biological and statistical facts.

Anthropologists and other social scientists concerned with the black-white conflict could as late as 1947 issue their projections in terms of the erroneous facts surrounding *passing* which we have just considered. They would largely agree with Dr. Ralph Linton, who in 1947 was Sterling Professor of Anthropology at Yale University and President of the American Anthropological Association:

> "What do anthropologists consider to be the long range solution of the Negro problem?" . . . most anthropologists agree there will be no Negro problem in another two hundred years; by then there will not be enough recognizable Negroes left in this country to constitute a problem.[40]

Although Dr. Linton was futuristic in his prediction which held out the year 2147 as the one of "the vanishing American Negro," it is understandable that he would catch the ear of so infamous a crusader against black-white intimacy as Mississippi's Senator Bilbo, who misquoted Dr. Linton approvingly in a campaign speech:

> Dr. Linton . . . stated a few weeks ago that if the present rate of intermingling, intermarriage and interbreeding of whites and blacks in this country goes on . . . within nine generations we will have no whites and no blacks . . . only yellow.
> I had rather see my race destroyed by the noted atomic bomb than to see it gradually destroyed by mongrelization of the white and black races.[41]

Linton based his prophecy upon three considerations which were more demonstrative of his imagination than of the actual

disappearance of blacks. First, Linton held that blacks were vanishing because the "proportion of Negroes to whites is steadily de-
clining." Linton was reflecting upon the fact that since 1790 while
the total number of blacks in the society had continued to increase, the white population had increased even more signifi-
cantly. If one looks at the Census Bureau's figures regarding the
percentage of blacks in the total population, Linton's point seems
substantiated:

1790	19.3
1830	18.1
1860	14.1
1900	11.6
1910	10.7
1920	9.9
1930	9.7
1940	9.8

Of course this comparative diminution, a reduction to nearly one-
half between 1790 and 1930, was due in large measure to the fact
that there were virtually no significant numbers of black immigrants and some 38,000,000 white immigrants between 1820 and
1930. So the smaller net production of blacks when compared
with that of whites over these decades was not the whole story.
More important, however, is the fact that since 1940 blacks have
shown a gain in the total population percentage, in part because
of the decrease in the number of white immigrants. The black
birth rate has always been greater than the white birth rate, but so
has its death rate. With the improvement in the standard of living
for blacks, there appears to be a decrease in the death rate and
thus an increase in the overall proportion of blacks to whites.

The second basis for Linton's prophecy that blacks will eventually disappear from America was the in-migration of blacks
throughout the country. His assumption was that if blacks would
no longer concentrate in the South they would spread "evenly
over the entire country," gradually be lost through marriage with
whites as happened to blacks in England during the seventeenth
and eighteenth centuries. It is a well known axiom that blacks and

whites tend toward marriage where blacks are few in numbers compared with whites. However, it is clear that blacks are concentrating, if not concentrated in Northern and urban ghettos with the same intense density as in the South.

The third and main reason for Linton's case for the vanishing black as a distinct American minority

> is that the Negro population is becoming lighter with each successive generation. This is not a matter of paling out in a northern climate—it takes thousands of years to evolve a new biological type—but of steady infiltration of white blood into the Negro group.[42]

It was Linton's position that ten per cent of blacks are pure African. Regardless of the actual percentage, Linton believed erroneously that the reduction of the number of pure blacks took place after their arrival on these shores and failed to note the considerable amount of black-white reproduction, perhaps as much as fifty per cent, which had taken place on other shores prior to the arrival of blacks here:

> If Negro blood has been diluted to this extent in the past two hundred years, why is it not reasonable to suppose that the continuing dilution of the next two centuries will make those with Negro blood practically indistinguishable from the general population? If there were no physical stigmata to mark the Negro as different, it would be impossible to maintain prejudice and discrimination against him.[43]

Linton was an old-line liberal who believed that the problem of blacks and whites could only be solved by erasing the color line, thus erasing the distinctiveness of being black. This assumption, based on good will, got in his way of being a careful social scientist. He continued the theory that blacks have neither past nor present experiences and culture which contribute uniquely to the Western world. He not only overlooked the fact that American whites have contributed nothing unique to Western culture, but the solid fact that black Americans have singularly contributed through jazz. Linton could not have known that blacks would develop their own consciousness in response to a white society that would not accept them on their own terms, a society that is so vicious as to desire the elimination of blacks rather than to painfully but realistically join with them in a common humanity of diverse richness. There have been no more violent ideas and distorted theories than those of social scientists like Linton who said that there was no black culture and therefore did not bother to make an objective study of this commonplace falsehood:

> The Negroes have no distinct religion or culture to set them apart from the rest of the population. They would be eager to accept the mores of the white group whenever it became possible for them to do so without arousing antagonism.[44]

Linton understood that miscegenation was on the decline; that is, that the relations between blacks and whites which lead to fertility were fewer than in previous centuries, although those which did not produce children were not. Yet in the face of noting the decline of miscegenation, Linton insisted that blacks were becoming lighter in color. Linton held with other anthropologists that this increasing lighter hue was due to a "developed caste system" among blacks which he believed was dominant and determinative among black people. Linton was a casual observer of the dynamic relations between blacks in the 1940's as well as of those of preceding decades. He was quick to note that preferential mating took place, whereby light-skinned blacks were "the most admired and sought-after" for their Caucasian features:

> The result is that the lighter members of the race are increasing and prospering, while the darker ones tend to die out. The mulatto man who marries an octoroon girl will have offspring lighter than himself; they will in turn seek light partners, so that even without black-white crosses, there is a constant dilution of Negro blood. The Negro artists, educators and professional men I have met have almost invariably been married to women much lighter than themselves.[45]

In 1947, Linton was describing a situation that had peaked. In the twenty or thirty years prior a "race consciousness" had developed whereby blacks had become aware of the fact that their light skins made them no more acceptable to whites, and in some cases a good deal more suspect than if they were of pure black hue. It is obvious today that "instant black" is preferable among whites and blacks. What is of moment here, however, is Linton's biological and sociological assumption that in two hundred years the "Negro problem" will have resolved itself biologically through preferential mating among blacks. Only conjecture is possible now as to the biological possibilities of the vanishing blacks, for the sociological situation has altered—to be black today is to be beautiful. Where once blacks preferred the lighter hue and the lighter-hue blacks were relatively more successful than the darker ones, it is no longer the case that "the darker ones tend to die out." Linton's theory was that the preferential mating of mulattoes, octoroons, and quadroons would genetically produce a lighter and lighter black population until all blacks *passed:*

> As the Negro becomes lighter and lighter, passing is bound to become more prevalent, since the Negro knows that he has a better chance to make something of himself, both socially and economically, if he steps over the line into a white world.[46]

While the popular forces of the society were developing all kinds of instruments to deter black-white marriages and *passing,* Linton was highly conjecturable in his promotion of *passing.* William M. Kephart criticized Linton's perspective as inconceivable from the standpoint of present day genetics, specifically regarding what is known of the "gametic factors for black in Negro skin pigmentation," and concluded that "the comparatively few Negroes, moreover, who do "pass" each year usually marry whites, hence add little in the way of white genes to their forsaken race."[47] If *passing* had been an important issue, instead of a fixation whites were once immobilized by, the kinds of questions John T. Blue enumerated would have been answered for the purposes of prediction:

1. What are the physiological factors (melanin, melanoid, etc.) causing a given skin color which are hereditary?

2. How many genetic factors are involved in the transmission of the physiological color factors to offspring?

3. How frequently does genetic segregation result in persons of white or Negro appearance, and what is the genetic character of their offspring?

4. What is the genetic composition of a representative sample of the Negro population?

5. What is the representative pattern of crossings for the various genetic categories of Negro, mixed Negro, and white?

6. How frequently does genetic segregation result in persons of white or Negro appearance, and what is their genetic character?

7. What is the net reproduction rate for several genetic categories of Negro, mixed Negro, and white persons?

8. What is the proportion rate for Negro-white crossings, and the trend?

9. What is the rate of Negro passing, and the trend? [48]

Blue held that there were four aspects of the question of blacks becoming lighter which needed clarification for there to be an adequate handling of the issue:

1. Genetic types of Negroes based on what genes a particular Negro carries.

2. Ethnological types of Negroes based on physical traits resulting from genetic processes.

3. Negro as a social type based on social status and stereotype traits.

4. Negro as a social type based on legal status and the legal definitions of Negro.[49]

It is obvious that these four aspects are so interrelated and under-going such dynamic change that geneticists, population experts, and social psychologists would need to collaborate to answer the question of whether blacks are becoming lighter and therefore moving toward eventual disappearance. It was the absence of this collaboration which made the speculations vis-à-vis *passing* of white racists pitiful and the conjectures of Linton little more than white vanity:

> What will be the effect on the nation if the Negroes are absorbed into the general population within the next two centuries? Contrary to Senator Bilbo's dire warnings, there will be very little effect. Barring some now unforeseen flood of immigrants, the nature of the population two hundred years from now will be determined by the genes carried by the present American population. Less than 10 per cent of this population is classified as Negro. Of these, not more than one-fifth (and most scientists believe not more than one-tenth) are pure Negroes. The balance represents all Negroes of mixture from almost pure white to almost pure black. It is safe to assume that not more than half the genes carried by this mixed group come from the Negro side. Adding these to the genes of the pure Negro group we get three-fifths as the generic equivalent of the Negro population. Since this population forms only 10 per cent of the present whole, it follows that the Negro genes to be absorbed come to only 6 per cent, while, for the reasons given above, even this percentage will be progressively reduced. It may even be doubted whether the final absorption of the Negroes will even cause a significant increase in the proportion of brunettes to blonds or injure the beauty parlor business by giving more Americans naturally curly hair.[50]

The anthropological argument that the *passing* of blacks will lead to their ultimate absorption into the white gene pool without producing a noticeable effect upon the dominant population, and the opposing white racist argument that *passing* will contaminate the purity of white people, both deny blackness as a positive value and underscore *passing* as a problem for whites. In fact, Linton portrays how the discussions about *passing* and black-white intercourse never seriously took blacks into account; they were ignored while only whites engaged in debate with one another as to the relative merits of the phenomenon:

> For the benefit of those concerned with the purity of the white race, it should be noted that when miscegenation does occur, the infiltration is almost entirely in one direction. There is very little Negro blood going into the white race because the offspring of a white person and one with Negro blood, even if the latter is an octoroon and the children are blond, is classed as Negro. Alarmists shout that the Negroes will infiltrate the white race, but it is exactly the opposite which is taking place. White women generally have children only of their own race because mostly they mate with white men. Consequently there is no direct infiltration of blood from the "lower" race to the "higher." However, a certain number of Negro women do have children by white men. These white men may also have children by white women, but every half-breed child born to a Negress takes the place of a full-blood child she might otherwise have borne. Thus the half-breeds increase at the expense of the Negro rather than the white race. By the laws of race mixture, the dominant race inevitably tends to swamp the lower and eventually eliminate it.[51]

But Linton was far from alone in his thinking although he may have projected common assumptions to their logical conclusion. Dr. Edward M. East, the late Harvard University geneticist, predicted that the pure black group would eventually die out, for

> the colored population in the United States . . . is rapidly changing from a fairly distinct Negro group to a mixed-blood group, owing to the greater net fertility stamina, virility which the latter type exhibits.[52]

G. O. Ferguson clung to the belief that the absorption of blacks would be caused by black-white miscegenation and predicted that

> in the course of generations, if the present or a similar rate of white admixture continues, there will be few if any pure negroes remaining in the United States. The whole of our colored population will be mulatto, and as time passes the proportion of white blood will increase.[53]

In response to these predictions of a new race created out of black and white, Dr. Caroline Day stated:

> The grim joke of the whole matter is that for 150 years and more he has been absorbed, and his descendants are constantly rubbing elbows with some of the very ones who are discussing them.[54]

If social scientists became visionary with respect to the future of blacks in America through being too impressed by *passing* they nevertheless commonly assumed that more black males *passed* than females. Although the knowledge of the sex distribution of blacks who *passed* was even less adequate than the knowledge of the color distribution, the sexual patterns of America made this consensus a fairly safe one. It is the male who is the aggressor in sex relations as well as in mobility and job securement. This tendency for the black male to *pass* more than the female is more or less adequately described by Reuter:

> The Negro man of the near-white type is far more likely to leave the Negro group and align himself with the white than is the near-white Negro girl. His opportunities to do so are somewhat better. He is more free in his choice of residence and associates. The near-white Negro girl may, and frequently does, work in an office or store and pass there as a white girl. But her friends and associates are most likely in the Negro group. Rather rarely does she sever entirely all connections with her Negro relatives and friends. Her marriage is pretty sure to be into the Negro group rather than

out of it. In this case her connection with the white world is over unless, as occasionally happens, both man and wife are of the near-white type and together leave the Negro for the white world.[55]

It need only be added that the "near-white" female belonged to a preferred marital group and given the preference for light-skinned girls that once prevailed, her opportunities for marriage for social status as well as for the chance of being chosen were better in the black than in the white community.

The fact of blacks' *passing* led whites to seek knowledge from them about the psychological effects of *passing* upon those who *passed* and on the black group as a whole. The motivation for *passing*, whether it was segmental *passing* as in the case of most women who lived two distinct lives, one occupational and one social, or permanent *passing* was quite obvious. Some writers on the subject viewed *passing* as a psychically dangerous and radical step, as in this description of a man who supposedly *passed* for the first time on a Mississippi River boat:

At first he said he could hardly restrain his exultation, but after a time, although he said he talked and smoked with the white men, he began to be lonesome.

"It grew colder and colder," he said.

In the evening he sat on the upper deck and as he looked over the railing he could see, down below, the Negro passengers and deckhands talking and laughing. After a time, when it grew darker, they began to sing the inimitable Negro songs.

"That finished me," he said, "I got up and went downstairs and took my place among them. I've been a Negro ever since." [56]

This description of alienation testifies more to the individual's lack of familiarity with white folks and to his recent departure from the black world than it does to a common restraint experienced by blacks who *passed*. There is every indication, too, that this is a case of a man who was well along in age before he made the leap over the color line. If a lack of familiarity with the white culture were the only psychological deterrent, blacks would require only a bit more education and cultural sophistication to overcome it. Perhaps the most that can be said about the frame of mind developed by blacks who *passed* was stated by Louis Wirth and Herbert Goldhamer:

> The person who aspires toward the white world and identifies himself with it or who refuses at least to identify himself with the Negro masses may be an unhappy individual, but he may have a greater sense of security and greater personal stability than the individual who has "crossed the line" and is troubled by his conscience and constant anxieties concerning his security of status. Those who have described persons who pass emphasize again and again the tension under which such persons live, a tension which frequently drives them back to the Negro world. It is entirely possible, however, that this aspect of passing has been exaggerated and that numerous individuals pass into the white world with sufficient ease and subsequent success so that no psychic difficulties ensue. It seems likely from the very nature of the case that the individuals who have suffered most when they have undertaken to pass are the ones who would be vocal about their experiences and most accessible to study. The successful and well-adjusted person who passes is not likely to be heard from.[57]

The fixation or fascination with *passing* led social scientists and popular writers to delve beyond the social and economic motivations into the psychological justifications of those who *passed*. While permanent *passing* was perceived as a disloyalty to blacks and a deception of whites, it became clear that segmental *passing* was easily justified

> on the ground that they are not trying to intermarry and intrude upon the white man's more intimate and personal life, but have merely discovered a mechanism for getting around the white man's policy of "total exclusion." Another

justification is made on the ground that this policy of exclusion, based on sheer prejudice, is unjust and immoral; hence, no evil is really being done by "passing." [58]

The gain for the individual who *passed* was clear. As for the black people as a whole, some writers argued that *passing* was a deceptive way of mediating white culture to black people from which all blacks benefited:

> It is sometimes claimed that such [who pass] are able to mediate to the Negroes what they, by stealth, gain from the white groups they enter. This, however, may be questioned. No near-white may hope to pass for white and, at the same time, retain his place with the Negro . . . group. The purpose of such persons is usually not the uplift of the Negro but rather to achieve escape from it. . . . Persons of [this] class are consciously practicing deception, and such deception as much influence, adversely, moral character, as well as racial self-respect.[59]

Of course contact with whites could provide new stimuli which would send the black back to his people with the hope of improving their lot without this hope being a conscious missionary spirit. Nevertheless, it is clear that whites caught up in this phenomenon of their own doing also felt constrained to eliminate the beam from the other fellow's eye.

We can be sure that *passing* was of far less concern to blacks than to whites. Blacks who were able to *pass* in large numbers did not refrain from *passing* in large numbers because they feared the consequences from whites, if they did fear being informed on by blacks, although "Colored people themselves, or rather a certain envious few of them, are ever the quickest to reveal the identity of those who seek to 'pass.' " [60] For one thing, persons who have taken on their white identity

> have seldom been known to rise high in their new world which they have adopted by stealth. . . . They seem to prefer an inconspicuous place in the white world to a position of considerable prominence in the society of Negroes.[61]

For another thing, blacks have not been overly anxious to become white in any great numbers. Robert Moton put it this way:

That the Negro is not actually desirous of being white or of being considered white is evidenced by the fact that relatively few indeed of those members of the race who could under no circumstances be identified by physical marks with the Negro race ever take advantage of this fact to cut off entirely from their people.[62]

Walter White put it similarly: "Large as is the number of those who have crossed the line, they form but a small percentage of those who might follow such an example but who do not." [63] Writing on "The Paradox of Color," Walter White summarized succinctly the black response to *passing,* a possibility which most blacks who could have *passed* refrained from because of their identification with blackness, their desire to openly alleviate the problems of blackness, their sense of comradeship with those who were less fortunate than they, and their family ties:

Negroes naturally resent the loss of some of the brilliant minds which would be an asset to them in their grim struggle for survival. But if any Negro believes he will be happier living as white and thereby escape the barbs and handicaps of prejudices, or if he believes he can use his ability and training to greater advantage on the other side of the racial line, most Negroes wish him well.

There are, of course, individuals who resent passing, particularly if they themselves are relatively few in number. Most colored Americans do not attempt to interfere with the lives of those who are successfully passing. Fundamentally, most Negroes get a sort of grim pleasure out of white Negroes passing and thus fooling the allegedly superior race.[64]

Walter White was the Executive Secretary of the N.A.A.C.P. He identified as a black man, though his skin was white, his eyes were blue, his hair was blond, and no trace of blackness was visi-

ble in any of his characteristics. In those darkest days of segregation, the 1930's and 1940's, he was particularly effective since he
was taken for a white man and was therefore able to investigate
civil injustices on the spot. His second wife was white. In his life
and work and marriage he exemplified the feeling blacks had
toward *passing* and marriage of blacks and whites, a spirit which
rejected the former, embraced the latter, and affirmed blackness:

> I am not white. There is nothing within my mind and heart
> which tempts me to think I am. Yet I realize acutely that the
> only characteristic which matters to either the white or the
> colored race—the appearance of whiteness—is mine. White
> is the rejection of all color; black is the absorption of every
> shade. There is magic in a white skin; there is tragedy,
> loneliness, exile, in a black skin. Why then do I insist that I
> am a Negro, when nothing compels me to do so but
> myself ? [65]

The son of an Atlanta mail carrier whose prosperity was resented
by whites and whose white skin and ethical standards were resented by blacks, Walter White openly presented the paradox of
color:

> It is I, with my insistence, day after day, year in and year out,
> that I am a Negro, who provokes the reactions to which now
> I am accustomed: the sudden intake of breath, the
> bewildered expression of the face, the confusion of the eyes,
> the muddled fragmentary remarks—"But you do not look
> . . . I mean I would never have known . . . of course if you
> didn't want to admit. . . ." Sometimes the eyes blink rapidly
> and the tongue, out of control, says, "Are you sure?" [66]

What made White sure of his blackness was "a thousand
lynchings and a million nights in shacks," but most of all that
night when five thousand whites moved through "nigger town" in
Atlanta to the White house on its edge. For the first time guns
were brought into the Whites' home to protect the family from the
rambling mob of whites who had given every indication that they

were out to burn down the black section. As the mob approached, Walter White's father said, "Don't shoot until the first man puts his foot on the lawn; and then don't miss." Young Walter recalled a voice crying out, "Let's burn the house of the nigger mail carrier! It's too nice a house for a nigger to live in!" As the mob moved toward their home, Walter froze, but suddenly a volley of shots from their neighbors stopped the mob and they retreated:

> In the quiet that followed I put my gun aside and tried to relax. But a tension different from anything I had ever known possessed me. I was gripped by the knowledge of my identity, and in the depths of my soul I was vaguely aware that I was glad of it. I was sick with loathing for the hatred which had flared before me that night and come so close to making me a killer; but I was glad I was not one of those who hated; I was glad I was not one of those made sick and murderous by pride. I was glad I was not one of those whose story is in the history of the world, a record of bloodshed, rapine, and pillage. I was glad my mind and spirit were part of the races that had not fully awakened, and who therefore had still before them the opportunity to write a record of virtue as a memorandum to Armageddon.[67]

It was neither fear nor lack of opportunity which led blacks who could have *passed* in large numbers to do so in such small ones, and then more often segmentally than permanently. Walter White, who was in a position to know a good deal about *passing*, probably estimated a far larger number of blacks *passing* than was actually the case. He characterized this group as follows:

> Every year approximately 12,000 white-skinned Negroes disappear—people whose absence cannot be explained by death or emigration. Nearly every one of the 14 million discernible Negroes in the United States knows at least one member of his race who is "passing"—the magic word which means that some Negroes can get by as whites, men and women who have decided that they will be happier and more successful if they flee from the proscription and humiliation

which the American color line imposes on them. Often these emigrants achieve success in business, the professions, the arts and sciences. Many of them have married white people, lived happily with them, and produced families. Sometimes they tell their husbands or wives of their Negro blood, sometimes not. Who are they? Mostly people of not great importance, but some of them prominent figures, including a few members of Congress, certain writers, and several organizers of movements to "keep the Negroes and other minorities in their places." Some of the most vehement public haters of Negroes are themselves secretly Negroes.[68]

What drove Walter White and many other blacks who could have *passed* but decided against it, to real humanity, to a determination to be both black and fully human, was an understanding of the white frame of reference:

> I have tried to imagine what it is like to have me presented to a white person as a Negro, by supposing a Negro were suddenly to say to me, "I am white." But the reversal does not work, for whites can see no reason for a white man ever wanting to be black; there is only one reason for a black man wanting to be white. That is the way whites think; that is the way their values are set up. It is the startling removal of the blackness which upsets people. Looking at me without knowing whom I am, they disassociate me from all the characteristics of the Negro. Informed that I am a Negro they find it impossible suddenly to endow me with the skin, the odor, the dialect, the shuffle, the imbecile good nature. Instantly they are aware that these things are not part of me. Then they grope for the positive values of the race—genius at song, easy laughter, great strength, humility, manners. Alexander Percy said that the most polite people in the world are the American Negroes.[69]

Whites in our society were once deadly earnest about *passing,* and in this white trauma blacks discovered a refining fire out of which was wrought an insistence upon the value of blackness as an indispensable one for the enrichment of common humanity. Walter White was singular in the gametic and genetic inheritance he received from his white ancestry; in his militant fighting, as a black, for the rights of blacks; and in his continuance of his identity and fight through his marriage to white Poppy Cannon. In his person we see the passing of *passing* as a threat both to blacks and to whites: in the life of Walter White we see that it is possible to be both black and white, to be free enough to choose whom one will live with without denying who one is. Sociological, psychological, anthropological, and biological studies pale into irrelevance in the face of the determination to be human. We can best sum up this chapter on *passing* with Walter White's words on the subject for he subtly discloses that marriage in black and white is a human venture into the depths of humanity and not as in the case with *passing,* a manipulation of human dignity, either by the desire to absorb or deny blackness:

> I am one of the two in the color of my skin; I am the other in my spirit and my heart. It is only a love of both which binds the two together in me, and it is only love for each other which will join them in the common aims of civilization that lie before us. I love one for the sins she has committed and the fight she has made to conquer them—and conquer them, in great degree, she has. I love the other for her patience and her sorrows, for the soft sound of her singing, and for the great dawn which is coming upon her, in which her vigor and her faith will serve the world.
>
> Some of the members of the black race are passing over to the white race. It may be that I am one of these; that I am a member of a vanguard that in the millennium to come will transmute the great potentialities of the colored races into the civilizations which are to follow. I pray that those civilizations will be better and more virtuous than ours, and that the bridge which I and others are building will grow strong and be a highway for good.
>
> . . . As the social pattern of the Negro evolves, will his color

change? Is it changing now? We do not know, and I, for one,
am sure that it does not matter. I am white and I am black,
and know that there is no difference. Each one casts a
shadow, and all shadows are dark.[70]

Chapter Five

PERSPECTIVES OF CONTEMPORARY SOCIAL
SCIENTISTS ON BLACK-WHITE MARRIAGES

The obvious fact about black-white marriages is the very limited and sparse research in the field by social scientists. It is not difficult to determine that the poverty of research on black-white marriages is due in some measure to the indifference of social scientists, an indifference which reflects that of society. Careful research in this area is as difficult as it is expensive, and the limited amount of research which has been done reflects in part the limited number of research grants which in turn indicates the low priority given to research on marriages in black and white by persons responsible for resources. There is also a growing concern that black-white marriages are a strictly private affair with precious little public sanction needed, though there is awareness that such marriages are not supported by the public will. The shift in emphasis from changing attitudes to changing behavior patterns has engulfed social scientists who should know better than to conclude that emphasis upon one or the other and not both is futile. It may be that social scientists conclude there is no solution to the black-white problem; the best one can do is work at its economic, educational, legal, housing, and political manifestations. At bottom, then, social scientific research on marriages in black and white which could lead to significant acceptance of these persons in a changed society is not sufficient in its findings to develop an instrument for a social solution to this social problem. Perhaps the barrier is due to an unbecoming awe for the general will in opposition to black-white marriages which social scientists do not deem it their prerogative to change, though they are far less reticent to induce change in creative and manipulative ways in many other folkways. Even where social scientists focus on intimate and permanent relations between blacks and whites they describe them as *intermarriage,* rather than *marriage,* and until learned men use terminology which is not loaded to describe that which is natural, little more can be expected of them by way of healthy interest in private and public attitudes and behavior for the common good than from those who are even more the victims of American myths, prejudice, and racism.

There may be something to the argument that contemporary social scientists shy away from marriage in black and white because they are not as under fire from blacks in this area as they are in others. Yet a few decades ago, social scientists were strong and vehement in their support of marriage between blacks and whites as the solution to our American schizophrenia. Though these older social scientists were wrong in their prognostication that the issue between blacks and whites would be overcome in two centuries or so through marriage, they were right in their estimate that the solution had a great deal to do with marriage. The old school of social scientists did not see the possibility of creating a society with a new spirit where marriage in black and white would become a free choice whereby blacks and whites would be free enough to freely choose or not choose a white or black partner in a society where either choice would find social support. Contemporary social scientists do not see this possibility either, or have not set about producing the conditions wherein it can take root. Though the old school of social scientists believed in the elimination of blacks through social force or eugenics or evolution, they were mistaken in their strategy and tactics; but they were concerned with a solution to the black-white conflict, as well as its manifest symptoms. There was a total concern in the old school of social scientists that is missing among contemporary experts, who tend to work in more narrow spheres. However much social scientists of the past lacked realism or pragmatism, they did possess a total concern. Contemporary social scientists may have learned from their predecessors what not to stress—visionary idealism, for example—but they have not learned as successors what to do about this pivotal concern of marriage in black and white.

The emphasis of the old school of social scientists was in the face of opposition from whites who either considered themselves the friends of blacks or knew what was in their best interest, or both. The most vocal opponents were Southerners who mouthed the sentiments of millions of whites and found allies in Northern writers and professors. Southern whites were formidable foes. They could bury the fact that America was rooted in a soil drenched in the blood of ten million Indians and built on the backs of forty million slaves—a fact which we are beginning to rediscover at a very painful price, a fact we can no longer escape try as we may, by special pleading:

> By what authority do I speak on this vexed subject of race relationship in the South? For more than two centuries my people have lived in the South, and I myself am a Southern man. My father was a Whig, a thoroughgoing Union man and opposed to secession. He followed Mr. Webster and not Mr. Calhoun. In 1861, when one year of age, I became the owner by will of a three-fourths interest in five negro slaves. I sucked the breast of a negro woman, listened to the wonderful tales of my father's slaves, rode "horse" on their backs, swam and fished with them, and ate their ash cake in the cabin. The negro, I think, is my friend; I know I am his. Thus I ought to be impartial.[1]

These words were written in 1923 by Robert Watson Winston, a native of North Carolina, a leading lawyer in his state, and a judge of the Superior Court of North Carolina. His was one of the minority of respectable voices which social scientists encountered:

> Why do we of the South refuse to admit the facts, and when some blunt fellow, like the late Senator Tillman, blurts out

the truth, why do we straightway fall to denying and
disclaiming? On the other hand, why do few people outside
the South seem to understand or care what consequences will
follow the destruction of the caste system upheld by a color
line so rigidly drawn?

A certain inexorable race law should be kept in mind if
one would understand the magnitude of the issue involved:
No two homogeneous races will long continue to exist side
by side in the same country on terms of perfect equality
without race blending.[2]

There was no doubt in the mind of Winston that blacks and
whites were compatible and homogeneous—"Are the two races
homogeneous? They are, undoubtedly":

But bloody revolutions, much legislation forbidding race
intercourse of any kind, innumerable race riots, lynchings
and burnings in the "Black Belt," together with the white
womanhood of the South—all these were required to
separate the two homogeneous races.[3]

The rational bigot who admitted his prejudices appeared to
be a foe whom social scientists could challenge or disarm with the
strategy of reason. But the Southern voice of seeming reason had
behind it a different solution from that assumed by rational scientists, and one just as solid:

Were I a negro, facing the future, concerned about children
and children's children, I would cease to fight against white
prejudice, but raising the banner of "Pan-Africa," I would
herald that "Unity of the Colored Races sense by far-seeing
negroes," as Dr. Burghardt Du Bois phrases it, until my latest
breath. And why shall not the National Government sponsor
negro exodus, making ready a suitable home for the race?
President Lincoln recommended colonization "in some place
or places of suitable climate"; President Grant recommended
to Congress colonization on the Island of Santo Domingo.
Why may not French Guiana and Sierra Leone be added to

> Liberia, creating an ample fatherland for such
> Afro-Americans as choose to go? [4]

Lurking behind the voice of the moderate or the voice of the ex-
tremist was the bad scene of black-white marriage or any form of
"race blending":

> It is not possible to place Southern whites and blacks on
> terms of social and political equality as soon as the blacks are
> fitted for citizenship, as many philanthropic organizations
> are now insisting, because the Southern white man is
> tenacious of his rights and on this subject is adamant
> regardless of consequences. With him a white man's
> government means a white man's government. If Congress
> should pass a Force Bill and undertake to put it into
> operation, the Irish upheaval would be a mild affair in
> comparison with conditions in the Southern States. Either
> the white man would exterminate the negro, or the negro
> would exterminate the white man. The white man will brook
> no peer. It is not a question of whether the negro is a good
> citizen or a bad citizen; it is deeper than this; it has to do
> with race integrity, race autonomy. [5]

Social scientists and those who opposed marriage between blacks
and whites came to the same ultimate conclusion: "We must conclude, therefore, that eventually the two races in America will
blend if they be placed on social and political equality, and if they
are in fact homogeneous." [6] But they differed in their basic assumptions about civil rights, as those opposed to equal opportunity now conclude with the statement, "The negro desires to be
free and he is right. The white man claims that the South is his
rule and control, and he, too, is right." [7] Thus in the end
reasonable Southerners and unreasonable ones were of one mind:

> Why is the negro not right? Self-determination is of God, not
> of man. But the black race must not underrate the task. They
> are lined up against descendants of men who fought a four
> years' war against the world without salt, shoes or powder,

and whose courage and endurance no man questions. Men of the South place race integrity above politics, property, religion, or life itself. The South alone among nations is today making a fight against a universal ethnological law of race-blending. The mistake is in not boldly admitting the facts, flinging defiance to the future, spurring representation based on negro population in the electoral college.[8]

Southerners and Northerners alike knew precisely what they were doing in their opposition to black-white marriages; as it was not a matter of ignorance, they suffered no guilt. The voices of the moderates who admitted blacks and whites were so homogenous that, left to themselves, without lynchings, riots, beatings, or other disruptive tactics they would relate naturally and intimately, were few and far between. In proposing marriage as the solution, or at least demonstrating its lack of fatal effect upon whites, social scientists challenged those popular myths which claimed scientific proof for the supposed inferiority of blacks. They not only took on the popular myths, they took on the entire society and challenged it to eliminate all the forced barriers between blacks and whites and to allow all people to relate naturally. These old-line social scientists were concerned about blacks and whites; they cared about solving the conflict. Their proposal was of marriage of white males and black women for the purpose of eventually paling out the blacks as the ultimate solution, by way of the American Creed of justice and equality for all. The old liberal and humanistically oriented social scientists were dead right in what they affirmed—the American Creed, and dead wrong in what they denied—the acceptance of blackness as a firm and rich experience to be cherished. Equality for the black male was not within their vision, but that blacks could become white culturally as well as biologically, possessed them so completely that the necessity of whites becoming black in thinking and feeling, though not in genetic composition, never crossed their grid. This blindness (from which we still suffer) that blacks are without a worthy past and therefore have neither a present nor a future of value, cannot be dismissed as profoundly affecting this particular generation of Americans. Yet the great courage and vision, even if misguided, of these old liberals and humanistically oriented social scientists cannot be ignored for it was born of courage and of the right but misplaced emphasis. If the general white American public suffered from a denial of the American Creed and put in its place reinforced varieties of white supremacy through naked and illegitimate power manipulations, the liberal elite social scientists suffered from an affirmation of the American Creed which took form as a paternalistic and beneficent white supremacy that would bury blacks in the sea of white gametic and genetic sperm. Both paths led to the denial or extermination of blackness as a positive force. Both denied the American Creed in the name of white superiority: one through repression and the other through subtle genocide.

A singular example of an exception to the pattern of old-line social scientists who saw the blackness of blacks as a special problem to be solved through absorption was Melville J. Herskovits. In his writings he used the social science methods of his colleagues with the same amount of skill and understanding as they set forth in their findings. Herskovits's first publication on the black man was a 1928 book entitled *The American Negro.* From that writing, through *The Myth of the Negro Past,* which he undertook as a basic monograph for Gunnar Myrdal's epic *An American Dilemma,* he was accused and attacked for not being coldly objective. For example, he held that blacks had a past which was worthy of noting and underlining, and he set out to make this past a viable one which the blacks could use in the present. His colleagues said that his work was not scientific because he created a myth of the black past out of fragments gained from his studies. He knew that his work was not entirely "scientific" in the sense of being unassailably objective, but in this he knew far more than his colleagues: they did not know that their work was not purely objective. The claim that blacks had no past meant that blacks had no future, and Herskovits challenged this assumption made by scientists in the name of objectivity by attempting to get them to do basic field research on blacks, instead of spinning out their theories on the basis of unproved assumptions. Because of the early presumption that there was no black past, social scientists in the American present were led to assume that one did not exist without even looking for one. With this assumption they claimed to be scientific in their conclusion that blacks were to be ultimately absorbed as the solution to the conflict. By using the same methods of social science to prove blacks had a past, and affirming that past as a healthy and even necessary element if blacks were to be influential in the present, Herskovits stressed intersubjectivity as the direction and meaning for such fields as social science. But then Herskovits was not only an able social scientist who knew all the tricks and how not to be trapped by them, he was also a Jew. As a Jew he knew from a long history the importance of a past for a people, especially a dominated people. When the supposedly objective scientists finished spelling out the myth of blacks without a past and passing it on from one generation to another, they were forced to the unscientific projection that the only solution was the elimination of blackness through sperm extermination or genocide. Having sized up the problem and given their solution, to be acted upon in centuries hence, the tension between blacks and whites no longer appeared to be a problem worthy of investigation and resolution through the methods and influence of a socially conscious social science.

Herskovits outlined the myth of the lack of a black past which made the unshakable idea of black inferiority valid even for social scientists:

1. *Negroes are naturally of a childlike character, and adjust easily to the most unsatisfactory social situations, which they accept readily and even happily, in contrast to the American Indians, who preferred extinction to slavery;*

2. *Only the poorer stock of Africa was enslaved, the more intelligent members of the African communities raided having been clever enough to elude the slavers' nets;*

3. *Since the Negroes were brought from all parts of the African continent, spoke diverse languages, represented greatly differing bodies of custom, and, as a matter of policy, were distributed in the New World so as to lose tribal identity, no least common denominator of understanding or behavior could have possibly been worked out by them;*

> 4. *Even granting enough Negroes of a given tribe had the opportunity to live together, and that they had the will and ability to continue their customary modes of behavior, the cultures of Africa were so savage and relatively so low in the scale of human civilization that the apparent superiority of European customs as observed in the behavior of their masters, would have caused and actually did cause them to give up such aboriginal traditions as they may otherwise have desired to preserve;*
>
> 5. *The Negro is thus a man without a past.*[9]

Social scientists who perpetuated this myth were black scholars as well as white ones. Of course behind the perpetuation of the myth was the good hope that blacks would blend readily into the society; and this process would be made all the more easy if the only preventing force was skin color, for which a solution had been worked out. If white America could be sold on the scientific fact that amalgamation or miscegenation would not be harmful to whites, the effort put forth in repressing the African past would be worth the effort. Thus the distinguished social scientist Charles S. Johnson, while president of Fisk University and still an active scholar, could write that

> the Negro of the plantation came into the picture with a completely broken heritage. . . . There had been for him no preparation for, and no organized exposure to, the dominant and approved patterns of American culture.[10]

E. Franklin Frazier put it this way:

> Probably never before in history has a people been so nearly stripped of its social heritage as the Negroes who were brought to America. Other conquered races have continued to worship their household gods within the intimate circle of their kinsmen. But American slavery destroyed household gods and dissolved the bonds of sympathy and affection between men of the same blood and household.[11]

Building upon these presuppositions, which were not questioned, white social scientists thought of blacks as imitative and childlike:

> The characteristic of self-abasement, involving as it does a lack of self-respect, explains the Negro's extraordinary imitativeness.[12]

> The mind of the Negro can best be understood by likening it to that of a child. For instance, the Negro lives in the present, his interests are objective, and his actions are governed by his emotions.[13]

These social scientific assumptions in the name of objectivity, revealed for their most unscientific biases by Herskovits, became popularized. While social scientists were out to prove that blacks were readily assimilable, their studies reinforced popular prejudices that blacks were inferior and a threat to the white race. Social scientists were looking forward with real expectation to the day when blacks would become white and dissolve into the white sea, while the popular mind was fearful of the miscegenation societies organized by abolitionists after the Civil War and the advocation of marriage between blacks and whites by such notorious Americans as Wendell Phillips and Theodore Tilton. The popular mind was not ready to accept as inevitable what was believed to be a new race resulting from the marriage of blacks and whites. Theodore Roosevelt returned from Central America and wrote about the new race acoming, a new race of mulattoes born of the fusion of blacks and whites in Central America, a process which appeared to be occurring in Brazil, Cuba, Mexico, and Portugal. The implication of all this to the popular mind was that race blending would take place in America if the color line and segregation were not maintained, and such a measure of race mixture was believed to be negative rather than positive:

> Schults in "Race or Mongrel" declares that "if conditions that now exist continue nothing need be done with the negro; the problem will solve itself. The immigration of Southern mongrels is in-grafting more and more negro blood in our

veins." To the same effect is Hoffman's "Racial Traits and Tendencies": "The process is now rapidly going on and the black race will be absorbed; a condition which, though unpopular, is not unwelcome to many thinkers." Document 188 of the Carnegie Foundation has valuable data showing universal race blending in Jamaica and Bermuda. Sir Sidney Olivier, Governor of Jamaica, advocates the blending of whites with blacks "as a buffer to prevent race conflict." In Volume 79 of the Popular Science Monthly he takes the ground that "we must make our account for a legitimate and honorable interblending between whites and blacks, and must look upon it not as an evil but as an advantage," adding that "the black race is everywhere eager to mix with the white race." [14]

The widespread fear of "the yellow peril," a new race of mulattoes, seemed confirmed by social scientists and by what laymen perceived in South America and other colonies of former slave masters throughout the world. Such paranoia, the creeping demise of the color line, took special root in the South and branched throughout the North:

If it were possible at the present time to blend the races, Southern people would have more than one-third colored blood in their veins and less than two-thirds white blood, and Northern people would have about 3 per cent colored blood and 97 per cent white. Moreover, if amalgamation were to take place now, the whole of South Carolina and Mississippi and half of Georgia, Florida, Alabama and Louisiana would grade about 50 per cent negro blood and 50 per cent white. The North, on the other hand, would grade about 3 per cent colored blood and 97 per cent white, a mixture well within the rule of "fixed white"; whereas the Southern mixture would not reach the grade of "passing for white," the offspring of such persons being subject to the law of reversion to color. [15]

Armed with the conviction that marriage between blacks and whites was the only solution to the conflict, secure in the knowledge that this would not occur for several centuries, social scientists safely brought their intellectual and scientific guns to bear upon "the yellow peril" paranoia.

In April 1928, Dr. C. B. Davenport, Director of the Department of Genetics of the Carnegie Institution of Washington, D.C., addressed the Institution on his findings with regard to "Race Crossing in Jamaica." After tracing the intermingling of races throughout the world and comparing this world-wide natural process with the American experience, Davenport came quickly to the question at issue:

> Those who look to the future are naturally concerned with the question: What is to be the consequence of this racial intermingling? Especially we of the white race, proud of its achievement in the past, are eagerly questioning the consequences of mixing our blood with that of other races who have made less advancement in science and the arts. Is it possible to predict the consequences of such racial intermingling? Is there any reason for thinking that hybridization, such as is going on even among the races of Europe, leads to an inferiority of the offspring? [16]

Though not a social scientist, Davenport was a geneticist particularly concerned about the hybrid result of pure black and pure white crossings. He closely studied the genetical traits with respect to the nose, the hair, and twenty-seven other traits among pure blacks and whites and their crossings of brown or hybrid. He gave the selected members of the three groups intelligence tests, psychological tests, physiological tests, musical tests, the Knox moron test, and the Army Alpha tests. His conclusion was that "physically there is little to choose between the three groups":

> But in regard to intellectual traits the conclusions are different. The browns show great variability in performance. They comprise an exceptionally large number of persons who are poorer than the poorest Negroes or the poorest of the

whites. On the other hand, they show some individuals of a high intellectual quality. The average of performance of the browns is generally somewhat better than that of the Negroes. It is, however, this burden of ineffectiveness which is the heavy price that is paid for hybridization. A population of hybrids will be a population carrying an excessively large number of intellectually incompetent persons. On the other hand, a population composed of hybrids between whites and Negroes will contain persons better endowed in appreciation of music and in simple arithmetical or mental computations, as well as more resistant to certain groups of diseases, than a pure white population. If only society had the force to eliminate the lower half of a hybrid population, then the remaining upper half of the hybrid population might be a clear advantage to the population as a whole, at least so far as physical and sensory accomplishments go.[17]

Davenport was convinced that racial crossings which were not "controlled by selective breeding" led to "undesired traits." Since eugenics was not a live option for human beings, he concluded that racial mixtures were not either:

There exists in mankind a strong instinct for homogeneity. Even children tend to mock at the cripple or deformed person. A homogeneous group of white people will always be led by its instincts to segregate itself from Negroes, Chinese and other groups that are morphologically dissimilar from themselves. We should consider the psychological, instinctive basis of this feeling. It is not sufficient merely to denounce it. It probably has a deep biological meaning and so long as it exists, so long we should be led to follow it as a guide if we are to seek to establish a commonwealth characterized by peace and unity of ideals.[18]

This less than scientific conclusion from a scientific paper gave support to the popular mind and a call to refutation by social scientists.

In 1930, E. B. Reuter, an expert social scientist in the field of black-white relations and Professor at the University of Iowa, reflected upon the increasing intermixture of races throughout the world and its impact upon America:

> This wholesale and indiscriminate intermixture of biological strains is, in extent at least, unlike anything before known in the contact of peoples. The conditions of the miscegenation have in many cases violated conventional and formal standards and expressed, or given rise to, serious social disorganization and personal demoralization. The facts as well as the apparent immediate consequences have aroused active and violent emotional condemnation. The general public as well as many social students impute great significance to this amalgamation of the races. The prevailing note in the sociopolitical discussion is one of pessimism: there is fear of racial degeneracy, moral decadence and culture decline; an uneasy and unanalyzed sense of impending racial and cultural disaster. In some cases this emotional attitude has been expressed in formal and legal as well as in popular efforts to check the movement already accomplished or beyond control.[19]

Reuter attacked the belief that the inbreeding among whites was beneficial, while outbreeding was detrimental to the race. He pointed out that studies in genetics proved that neither inbreeding nor cross-breeding produce characteristics not latent in the ancestral strains. In fact, cross-breeding decreases the likelihood of recessive traits perpetuated in inbreeding. Since it was not generally understood that race crossing and cultural crossing are not antithetical, Reuter set out to explain the opposing doctrines of the value of race crossing and the decline in cultural value due to race crossing.

In the late nineteenth century and early part of the twentieth century the notion was widespread that racial stocks are unequal in the degree of native capacity for cultural achievement. The major premise of this doctrine was that there exists a mental hierarchy between racial stocks and that the existence of a superior racial stock is a precondition for the use and maintenance of complex forms of culture and social organization, so that creative men can be produced only by a superior race. The conclusion of this argument is that any addition of the unequally endowed to the superior group deletes the capacity of one and raises the capacity of the other. Thus through the cross-breeding or amalgamation of races there results a decadence in the superior stock and a decline in its cultural status.

This argument, a self-fulfilling prophecy that demonstrated to the satisfaction of those who believed it that racial groups are unequally endowed, found support in history, biology, and psychology. A proof of the superiority of the white racial stock was attempted by Herbert Spencer, a British evolutionist philosopher (1820–1903). Spencer created the phrase the "survival of the fittest," a phrase which Charles Darwin took over and added to his theory of natural selection. Darwin defined nature as the "aggregate action and product of many natural laws," and laws as "the sequence of events ascertained by us." From this definition resulted the doctrine that in nature there is a struggle for existence resulting from the universal tendency of organisms to produce more offspring than can survive; and that those who do survive are able to do so because of some superior fitness. The Spencerian doctrine stated that it was possible to show that the present development of racial stocks represents stages in the evolutionary process. Whites are more sharply in contrast with apes with respect to brain weight and size (though Spencer did not bother with the fact that in many other respects whites are more like apes than are other racial groups). Spencer and his followers assumed a correlation between the size of the brain and the efficiency of its functioning and concluded that the white racial stock excels colored races and that the North European white stock is superior to other subdivisions of the white stock. This doctrine led its supporters to hold concurrently that the same correlation was true with respect to sex and class differences within the society: women are inferior to men in size of brain and hence in efficiency of performance; the aristocratic, educated, leisure, professional groups outproduce the socially inferior groups because of the size of their brain and its weight. The biological arguments were supported by various tests and historical exegesis as proof that cultural advancement was due to biological endowments. The conclusion of the Spencerian argument was that racial groups differ widely in mental ability and cultural capacity, and therefore miscegenation leads to racial disaster.

This Spencerian theory was refuted by an opposing doctrine which held that racial amalgamation results wherever divergent groups come into association, and in such situations the parent stocks are enriched. Superior stocks result from this mixture of stocks and every great people rests upon a mixed racial base. Evidence for this position was put forth in the superior cultural achievement of the mulattoes over pure blacks in the United States as well as in South Africa, Brazil, and the West Indies.

Reuter pointed out that the presupposition of these two contending doctrines is that culture is a function of race, that a causal relationship exists between race and civilization. Both positions hold that culture facts are in some direct way determined by biological facts. This assumption originated from and persisted on a common sense explanation:

[T]he spontaneous tendency of the popular mind is to assume a direct cause and effect relation between coincident phenomena and between phenomena that stand to each other in temporal sequence. It is a matter of proverbial wisdom that the naïve person transfers his emotional reaction from a bit of unwelcome news to the carrier of the information.[20]

This tendency to assume causality because of coexistence or sequence is particularly acute in matters of biology and society:

The facts of human culture do not appear or persist apart from the facts of human biology; there are no human beings without culture; there is no culture without human beings. Moreover, the differences between the various racial groups and various culture complexes are gross and notorious.[21]

In this way the poverty and ignorance of blacks in America could be easily accounted for and there was no need to take on the responsibility for their deprivation:

Moreover, the doctrine puts the ineffective classes and retarded races somewhere outside the strictly human groups to which the ethical imperative applies and so affords a basis and justification for the urge to use and exploit them.[22]

Reuter further explained that the absence of a definitive analysis with respect to the interdependence of organic and social reality was an important factor in the perpetuation of the assumption that a causal relationship exists between race and civilization. Reuter pointed out that race is a product of variation followed by long periods of isolation

and close inbreeding of the variant forms. The heritable racial marks are fixed by inbreeding; they are lost in cross-breeding. Without a long period of isolation, whether it be maintained by spacial separation or by conventional barriers, distinctive racial marks are lost and purity of race is non-existent. The only human groups of even relative racial purity are those that have been separated from foreign contacts and inbred through long periods of time.[23]

Cultural development, Reuter maintained, results from association with other groups. With respect to culture, isolation leads to fixity of standards and suppression through law and order, to traditional behavior and stagnation. Through social interaction new values and ideas and methods are introduced. Contact with divergent groups is the precondition for growth.

Reuter was satisfied to explain the errors of the two doctrines centering around the question of the amalgamation of races in the United States, by simply indicating as he did that race and culture are independent facts and processes:

Either purity of race or mixture of race may go with either a superior or a retarded culture. Neither racial amalgamation nor racial purity is a causal factor in civilization; neither offers any explanation of cultural decadence.[24]

He had a concern for the issue of black-white unions, an issue that was exploding across his world of the 1920's. Yet he stopped after analyzing moral problems. He was influenced by Davenport and took to heart his admonition:

> The person who seeks to secure the racial improvement of any species has only two courses open to him: Either to await new mutations in the race which he wishes to improve, or else to cross it with some other race that already has the quality he desires.
>
> Thus the English race, which is poorly endowed with musical capacity, could get that capacity by mingling with the Negro.
>
> The difficulty in waiting for the desired mutation to arise in the race is that it is a slow method. The method of hybridization has the difficulty that it introduced other, undesired traits into the complex. Of course, by controlled selective breeding the undesired traits can be bred out, while the desired traits are retained.
>
> But we have no such control of human matings as is demanded if success is to follow the method of improvement by race crossing. It seems hardly applicable to mankind.[25]

Though Reuter was not able to discover an effective action whereby cross-breeding between blacks and whites could occur, he could not go all the way with Davenport and hold to the notion of a "strong instinct for homogeneity" in mankind which has "deep biological meaning" that must be respected, for Davenport's conservative conclusion opposed natural as well as systematic cross-breeding or marriage between blacks and whites and tended to support the position Reuter refuted—that decadence occurs when supposedly superior stocks cross with inferior stocks. Reuter did not commit himself to action in the practical order because he did not believe that it is the scholarly duty to do what he can, as a man and as a thinker, to help solve the burning questions of his time. Reuter took the middle ground between opposition to and affirmation of black-white marriages and held firmly to the position that such unions, if not desirable, were at least not detrimental and might even be instrumental to profound social change:

> It is, however, an extreme position to assert that racial amalgamation has no cultural significance. In an indirect way the crossing of races is conducive to social change. In its earlier stages, at least, the intermixture of races takes place for the most part on the outskirts of the civilization. It is in general contrary to the tradition and in violation of the mores; it is usually extramatrimonial and shocking to the conventional moral standards; it is condemned, opposed, forbidden. Racial miscegenation in these early stages is an evidence and form of social disorganization. It contributes to social disorder, disintegration and confusion of standards at the same time that it makes them evident. It is of course from social disorganization that progress must proceed; change is not possible without it. On the other hand, the social disorder incident to the contact of varian standards and practices is conducive to the violation of the traditional sex tabus, hence is favorable to racial miscegenation.[26]

It is apparent that the social scientists who challenged the myths of the inferiority of blacks and their unacceptability as marriage partners for whites reasoned in the face of scholarly colleagues who took the opposite position in support of popular sentiments. U. G. Weatherly, a professor of social science at Indiana University, was a renowned writer on "problems of the American Negro" who was much quoted in magazines and lecture notes. In 1911, Weatherly wrote a widely circulated article in which he supported "a world-wide color line" and took a tack which polarized his position with respect to Reuter's:

> In the last analysis color prejudice is based on cultural difference more than on the degree of pigmentation. Because extremes of physical difference do actually in large measure accompany difference in culture rank, the most radical race antagonisms are those between the extreme whites and the extreme blacks. A black skin is everywhere associated in

thought with cultural inferiority. Back of this may lie a subconscious suggestion of the historical fact that the negroid races have achieved few of the cultural values that are to the white man the marks of superior mental and social efficiency. To the extent that the blacks live down this stigma of cultural inefficiency prejudice against them will lose its force. There are abundant evidences of color aversion on the part of the white towards the yellow, brown and red races, but it nowhere reaches the intensity of that directed against the blacks, nor is it of sufficient depth to constitute a fundamental social problem.[27]

In the midst of the controversy over the value and disvalue of black-white marriages, Professor Ulysses Weatherly took the position that race was a causal factor in the development of culture and that with the narrowing of the gap "between the actual cultural status of the races" the worst aspects of racial antagonisms would be eliminated. While opponents were lining up on one side or the other with some in the middle on the value of black-white marriages, Weatherly came forth as a strong cultural pluralist or conservative. He did not oppose black-white marriages, nor did he find it advantageous for whites to make up their deficiencies through miscegenation and thus promote a universal type of humanity made up of all races:

Scientific breeders have long ago demonstrated that the most desirable results are secured by specializing types rather than by merging types. The perfection of individual qualities insures a high degree of general efficiency in case those qualities can be coordinated in a systematic organization. This is particularly true of human types. The doctrine of Darwinism no longer implies a struggle in which the defeated is exterminated. Under conditions prevailing in modern civilized association it implies rather an application of the selective principle through a combination of competition and cooperation, by which the superior qualities of each race are sifted out and brought to efficiency. It implies a rough sort of interracial division of labor.[28]

Weatherly was one cut above many of his peers, including Reuter, in not alluding to blacks as members of the "lower" or "inferior" race and whites as members of the "higher" or "superior" race, but though he appealed to the self-interest of both, Weatherly claimed for whites a "higher efficiency." In this and in his instinctive support for his cultural and therefore racial pluralism he was a cut below a number of his colleagues:

> The color line is evidence of an attempt, based on instinctive choice, to preserve those distinctive values which a racial group has come to regard as of the highest moment to itself. Although sometimes based on a blind prejudice surviving from the primal instincts of periods of isolated savagery, it invariably, in its better phases, has in it the core of a sound scientific truth, which is that specialization is the law of efficiency. The fact that it is always the lighter race that puts the taboo on the colored, and that the latter is everywhere eager to mix with the whites, is only an evidence of the general trend of choice towards the higher efficiency of the white race.[29]

Though Weatherly was a cultural pluralist, he was no less possessed of racial imperialism. Thus as a pluralist he was as suspect in his time as pluralists are today, for the call to pluralism is an appeal to self-interest to keep the race line clean for the maintenance of "the higher efficiency of the white race":

> A culture people will do more useful service for civilization by following the lines of its own natural capacities. A backward group will advance more securely and will be more likely to attain a stable culture if it retains its own fundamental type, accepting by assimilation whatever of advantage it can profitably adopt from without. Co-operation in the work of civilization can be realized without the mongrelization of the world's peoples. Preservation of distinct racial types means the saving of characteristic traits and capacities which are as stimulating and beneficent for the world community as are varied individual traits for smaller social units.[30]

His failure to distinguish between race and culture as Reuter did makes Weatherly's opposition to black-white marriages clear:

> The concept of race, in the widest sense, both a physical and a psychic unit implies group choices and group standards. When a choice, whether one of adaptation or one of conscious volition, becomes instinctive it is embedded in the ethnic sense. In this manner instinctive prejudices and preferences become hereditary. Herein lies the power of custom. That to which the group has not accommodated itself comes to be regarded as not good and a thing to be avoided. That which has been found by experience to be beneficent or pleasurable, whether such experience be one of sensation or observation, is stamped with the group approval.[31]

By mixing race and culture and coming out with custom, which he not only sanctions but holds to be inviolable, Weatherly states the classic position against black-white marriages in particular and interracial-interethnic-interreligious marriages in general: races have the right to be and therefore should be supported in group customs antagonistic to mixed marriage. Weatherly does not allow for the dynamics of change and indeed the necessity of change in group customs as a means to growth rather than stagnation. Whatever the group determines is held to be valuable and unchallengeable, and all efforts to break up the "cake of custom" are written off as doomed. This is a position which leads not only to a self-fulfilling prophecy but a self-perpetuating one as well:

> Sentiment perpetually cuts across the lines of established usage unless restrained by a power stronger than the individual. Moreover, contrast and novelty furnish an additional element of sexual attraction which particularly appeals to the youthful imagination. If, then, present individual satisfaction were the determining factor, mixed marriages would not necessarily be unsuccessful. But marriage as an institution also pertains to the welfare of the group. For this reason, in societies where individual interests

are definitely subordinated to group interests, choice of mates is always in some degree regulated by parents or by social convention.

However potent may be the influence of sentiment and sex-attraction in temporarily breaking down the barriers or race prejudice, it rarely proves sufficiently enduring to render mixed marriages successful in cases of pronounced diversity of type. With the decay of sentimental attraction the inexorable need of co-operation in the practical business of living together in society asserts itself. Actual or virtual separation is the only alternative where this proves impossible.[32]

Weatherly's basic opposition to black-white marriages may be covered by his appeal to pluralism and the cooperation of races, but his intention is not based on the best interest of blacks so much as it is on the best interests of whites, for he sees this group as superior. In a word, Weatherly's position comes down to being pragmatic, and in his pragmatism he not only opposes black-white marriages but supports the status quo and in so doing makes clear the unchallenged or undisturbed presuppositions which belie any claim to objectivity:

The gospel of race amalgamation which was preached with passionate earnestness in the North during and after the Civil War was in the main an exaggerated outcome of the humanitarian social philosophy which underlay the abolition movement, but it had a quasi-scientific basis in the belief in physical advantages to be gained by race crossing. Wendell Phillips and the authors of the "Miscegenation" collection held that, since intermixture of nearly homogeneous types in numerous historical instances had proved beneficial, intermixture must again prove so with races so far apart as the whites and negroes. It was contended that an infusion of the blood of a tropical race would augment the versatility and vitality of whites. Such views, it need hardly be pointed out, were developed and survive, in so far as they still exist, in communities where the negro never has been found in sufficient numbers to have been the cause of an aroused race consciousness. In the South, where the question has perforce always been a practical rather than an academic one by reason of the presence of large masses of colored population in every community, opposition to mongrelization has been consistently grounded on the principle of culture preservation as determined strictly by race lines. Rigid insistence on the color line is, indeed, often the outgrowth of prejudice and passion rather than of scientific analysis, and as such may itself become a serious social danger. But for certain societies and for limited periods it can hardly be disputed that the practical identification of race solidarity with culture solidarity furnishes a wise principle of social action.[33]

The philosopher Josiah Royce believed that the black-white conflict was merely caused by antipathies, and since antipathies are learned, they therefore can be unlearned:

Train a man first to give names to his antipathies, and then to regard the antipathies thus named as sacred merely because they have a name, and then you get the phenomena of racial hatred, or religious hatred, or class hatred, and so on indefinitely.[34]

Weatherly believed the black-white issue to be more positively rooted than Royce claimed:

But whatever be the facts about other antipathies, aversion to intermarriage with supposedly lower ethnic types is based on mental processes which lie deeper than mere names. It is the expression of a normal ethnic instinct of self-preservation. Cross-breeding is something more than a union of individual lives of the parties. It generally involves a change of the culture status for the present and succeeding generations. It means a modification of the self-conscious ethnic personality which whether good or bad, efficient or inefficient, is at least a settled reality that would be lost by blending with an alien type.[35]

In the end, Weatherly opposed black-white marriages or what he called "physical amelioration" because the gain would represent a loss at the expense of other fundamental elements of civilization. Not only is it the case that

> behind physical aversion to alien types there lurks an instinctive recognition of racial standards as a social capital that must not be dissipated by surrendering race purity,[36]

but the loss in the present via black-white marriage means an even greater loss in the future:

> Now for the future of mankind nothing is more vital than that some races should be maintained at the highest level of efficiency because the work they can do for thought and art and letters, for scientific discovery and for raising the standard of conduct, will determine the general progress of humanity. If therefore we were to suppose the blood of the races which are now most advanced to be diluted, so to speak, by that of those most backward, not only would more be lost to the former than would be gained to the latter, but there would be a loss, possibly an irreparable loss, to the world at large.[37]

Here in a brief form is the white hope for mankind, the ultimate case for western imperialism, the call to erect every conceivable unnatural barrier to guard against the natural affinity of blacks and whites.

Given these widespread pseudoscientific rationalizations for public sentiment against black-white marriages, one can appreciate the extraordinary efforts made by social scientists who sought to combat their peers and the general will. Anthropologists like Franz Boas of Columbia University, Ralph Linton of Yale University, and Melville J. Herskovits of Northwestern University were scholars who thought and wrote against the mainstream of white racial and cultural chauvinism. Herskovits was unique in that he alone believed in the value of being black as the necessary precondition for the unity of a people and their mobilization for power and respect. These three anthropologists, though they differed in their objectives, were foremost among their colleagues in attacking the fallacies of racial inferiority as a stumbling block to race crossings. Though they were brilliant and sincere in their broad approach to black-white marriages, which they saw as inherently valuable, their inability to perfect an instrument for action in this sphere of the impossible possibility led later social scientists to deal with black-white marriages as a phenomenon to be investigated as a matter of personal interest rather than as a force for change vis-à-vis the social issue of our society.

Because of the deep-seated American tradition that holds over the head of a person with any degree of black blood the threat of having a "black baby" as offspring, even if the amount of blood is only one sixty-fourth black, Herskovits was led to study the findings with respect to human heredity and race crossing for verification of this black babies myth. Herskovits pointed out that peoples of racially mixed origin, irrespective of how diverse their background or ancestral stocks, after a long enough period of inbreeding beyond the initial period of different stocks crossing develop a homogeneous combination of the characteristics of both races. The variability in numerous physical traits of blacks in America, isolated socially rather than geographically from whites, is lower than that of the general white population:

> In terms of the principles of heredity, this would seem to make less valid the concept of the "throw-back" that has occupied such a large place in our thinking on the subject. There seems to be some principle at work—call it multiple Mendelianism if you wish—that causes the members of these mixed populations to merge the characteristics of both parental types, so that somewhere between the ancestral extremes a combination of those types is achieved. While it is true that the limits between which the physical traits of a given person may conceivably vary are set by his total ancestry, the mathematical chances of his having any but the traits of relatively recent forebears seems to be so small as to be negligible. This is why the "throw-back" is heard of more in literature than in life, and why it is possible to combine

people of two extremely different races into a homogeneous folk.[38]

Lurking behind the black babies myth was the inferiority attributed to being black and fear that the intimated involvement of blacks and whites at any level might lead to exposure and therefore social ostracism to the tenth generation:

> The meaning of this, in terms of the tales of "black babies" born to seemingly white parents, is clear; it means that there is no foundation for such stories. Every tale of this kind which, to my knowledge, has been traced to its source has resulted in the discovery that there is not only the possibility, but often the strong probability, of more Negroid parentage of the "black" child than would be assumed on the face of the report. All scientific evidence goes to indicate that even where both parents have a slight degree of Negroid ancestry, the chance of the appearance of such a child is highly remote.[39]

With respect to Weatherly's position, Herskovits came to a different conclusion:

> What of the claims that race-crossing leads to a loss of vitality, to degeneracy? Or, on the other hand, that mixture gives new vigor to the offspring? There is not enough scientific evidence to support either position; in the main, it appears that it is the ancestral stuff that has gone into a person, rather than the racial types from which he has descended, that makes him what he is, and the same would appear to hold true for entire peoples.[40]

Franz Boas largely agreed with Herskovits that individuals differ with respect to their biological constitution, although he did not feel the same could be said of races. Boas held with Reuter that biological and cultural constitutions are distinct forces, but went on to hold that emotional reactions are no more clearly the result of biological conditioning than they are of cultural conditioning, a position which disagreed sharply with Weatherly's:

> I believe the present state of our knowledge justifies us in saying, that while individuals differ, the logical differences between races are small. There is no reason to believe that one race is by nature much more intelligent, endowed with great will power or emotionally more stable than another, that the difference would materially influence its culture. Why is there any good reason to believe that the differences between races are so great, that the descendants of mixed marriages would be inferior to their parents? Biologically there is neither good reason to object to fairly close inbreeding in healthy groups, nor to intermingling of the principal races.[41]

Herskovits was mainly concerned with demonstrating the viability of the African heritage and the value of blacks becoming conscious of their past as a means to shaping their future and that of the American society as a whole. Boas placed primary emphasis upon the individual worth of individual blacks; that blacks must be seen and respected as individuals and not prejudged as a group. Boas recognized the desire of racial groups to be exclusive and seek "racial exogamy in order to maintain racial purity":

> On this subject I take issue with Sir Arthur Keith, who . . . is reported to have said that "race antipathy and race prejudice nature has implanted in you for her own end—the improvement of mankind through racial differentiation." I challenge him to prove that race antipathy is "implanted by nature" and not the effect of social causes which are active in every closed social group, no matter whether it is racially heterogeneous or homogeneous.[42]

But Boas was fundamentally convinced that the real problem between blacks and whites existed because blacks were treated as members of a class instead of as individuals. Nevertheless, Boas held firmly to the belief that "the greatest hope for the immediate future lies in a lessening of the contrast between negroes and whites, which will bring about a lessening of class consciousness." [43]

Thus, Boas moved from the position of objective scholar to that of strategist and problem solver. To reduce the differences between blacks and whites, Boas called for racial interbreeding between blacks and whites:

> In a race of octoroons, living among whites, the color question would probably disappear.
>
> There is absolutely no biological evidence which would countenance the assumption that race mixture of itself would have unfavorable results, that the children of white fathers and of mulatto or quadroon mothers would be inferior to their negro ancestors. [44]

In his call for miscegenation, Boas was concerned to eliminate the black-white problem in the most expeditious manner he could conceive. He must be credited for going beyond mere analysis of the problem. Yet in his solution he fell far short of the call to miscegenation made by the abolitionist Wendell Phillips, who did not restrict marriage between blacks and whites to black women and white men as did Boas. Boas was unconsciously bent on genocide and illustrates classically how the most evil policies are created by good men in the name of goodness. Here was a man who saw the value of a black as an individual but contended that the values of blacks as a group, while not inferior in biological or cultural constitutions, were so socially unacceptable that blackness must be eliminated so that the black problem will disappear in America via dilution of black blood to a point "that it will no longer be recognized":

> It would seem, therefore, to be in the interest of society to permit rather than to restrain marriages between white men and negro women. It would be futile to expect that our people would tolerate intermarriages in the opposite direction, although no scientific reason can be given that would prove them to be detrimental to the individual. [45]

Boas was sure that "no matter how rigid the laws that prevent intermarriage between various groups of a population they cannot ultimately prevent a gradual intermixture." [46]

Ralph Linton joined Boas in the belief that blackness would be exterminated, or at least be eliminated, through the genetic process. Linton was less bold in his affirmation of black genocide but just as deadly in his objective. Linton held that blacks would become lighter in color through *passing*, "since the Negro knows that he has a better chance to make something of himself, both socially and economically, if he steps over the line into the white world." [47] The difference between Linton's and Boas's theories of absorption of blacks is that Linton believed blacks would commit genocide out of individual self-interest while Boas believed whites would accept black woman-white man marriages out of a desire to take the path of least resistance.

These grandiose ideas about ending the black-white struggle in America through marriage of the two racial groups failed because they were ideas without grounding in strategy and tactics. The attempt to develop a universal type of humanity or an "American type" composed of all groups proved a dehumanizing ideal—an attempt to alleviate a problem by eliminating differences, as opposed to becoming enriched through them. Contemporary anthropologists and other social scientists, looking back at the failure of earlier humanists in the field to deal effectively with black-white marriages as the keystone in the American dilemma, have resolved to view such unions as peripheral. Since 1918, sociologists and demographers have evidenced some anxiety regarding black-white marriages; they have urged "each other to engage in research on a neglected aspect of human relations—intermarriage." [48] By and large, however, their interest has been much narrower than that of their predecessors. In the 1940's and 1950's, sociologists and demographers were far more precise in their studies than previous generations, but far more frivolous in their findings and far more irrelevant in their conclusions. For the most part their research has been so confining (usually limited to a single city studied at different times by different investigators) that no generalizations or general principles are warranted.

Contemporary research and analysis of black-white marriages is usually undertaken for the following reasons by social scientists:

> In a multigroup society like the United States, they have maintained, the study of intermarriage may provide a precise, quantitative measurement of such vital and related sociological questions as the process of assimilation, the degree of internal cohesion in individual racial, religious, and ethnic groups, and the extent of social distance between groups of these types.[49]

As we have seen, earlier social scientists saw in black-white marriages the solution to the American Dilemma. Among such, in addition to those previously cited, was Israel Zangwill, who in 1909 wrote *The Melting-Pot.* It is the failure of his vision (and those of like mind) to become dominant that leads some contemporary scholars to carefully analyze, without exposing their values or suggesting any resolution, the issue of black-white tensions through the medium of marriage:

> Of interest to them [social scientists] is the considerable number of American people who have not adopted Zangwill's romantic notion that America is God's crucible, that the new society's complex ingredients should blend eventually by intermarriage into a race of supermen, combining the virtues of all races, creeds, and nationalities. Indeed, many Americans today look upon the practice of intermarriage as a threat to their social values and way of life rather than as a panacea for their tensions in intergroup relations. For example, Gunnar Myrdal found that most southern whites place the taboo on racial intermarriage in the highest rank among the various parts of their concern about the maintenance of the status quo between themselves and Negroes.[50]

If contemporary sociologists, unlike their intellectual forebears, have determined that black-white marriages are not the solution to the problem, they have not shared with us their findings or their conclusions and this silence may just be because they have not asked themselves deeply enough why so many Americans hold black-white marriages to be *the* social problem rather than *the* solution to it. Social scientist Milton Leon Barron has concluded that marriage in black and white is perceived as a social problem because its practice is a "grave threat to the people's values of identity, homogeneity, and survival." Barron so concludes because this position is precisely that of many Jews—Jews being foremost among those who hold to intermarriage as a menace, a fact which Barron implies when he quotes for corroboration the following reference by a Jewish writer:

> The one great factor, making for group survival, is the ability to keep offspring within the group. As between two or more groups, intermarriage is forever a source of danger to the less favorably situated group, since the younger generation is usually anxious to escape the inherited hardship. The severance of relations favorable to exogamous marriage thus becomes the desideratum of every minority.[51]

Barron comes very close to seeing the need for social scientists to challenge and change the "people's values of identity, homogeneity, and survival." In fact, he sees that clergymen are in the forefront of those "resistant to the practice" of intermarriage and so express themselves by imitating social scientists in naming such marriages as instances of "culture conflict," by which they mean something to be avoided, an implication social scientists ought not to infer in their use of this concept if indeed they do mean to use it in this way. The fact is, that by pretending to be objective, social scientists have really been subjective and in so doing have developed concepts that are so vacuous they can be used by any novice to support the status quo or the "people's values." Social scientists may not have intended their work to be applied in this field or in others, but by sitting on the fence as the thinkers of the objective middle, their descriptive thoughts have been taken as normative actions by people in general, and clergymen in particular, who are not neutral nor concerned with intersubjectivity:

Intermarriage, it is maintained, should be avoided because conflict almost invariably results between culturally disparate mates and harmfully affects their children. The validity of this claim will be weighed in a subsequent section of this article. At this point it is appropriate to suggest that there are two flaws in such a rationalization for resistance. First, there are occasionally only nominal differences at the most between intermarrying mates. Second, important cultural differences often stratify husbands and wives, let us say, of the very same religious affiliation. Yet few priests, ministers, and rabbis preach caution or refuse to officiate at such technically nonmixed marriages.[52]

We have viewed the position of the older social scientists. We need now to look systematically at the admittedly limited research and findings among contemporary American sociologists and demographers vis-à-vis black-white marriages. Their findings may be organized and summarized under causal factors, patterns of incidence and selection, and consequences of black-white marriages.

CAUSAL FACTORS PROHIBITING BLACK-WHITE MARRIAGES

The attitudes and concepts we use shape and influence our behavior with respect to them. The careful delimitation of the concept of intermarriage by social scientists becomes a loaded and negative term when used by the general public. The negative connotation of intermarriage in the mind and heart of the average American finds reinforcement in the concepts developed by experts on human relations, which the laymen use in support of their unquestioned presuppositions without bothering to read or interpret the fine print of the footnotes of the scholars advancing the concept. If we lived only in the world of conceptual truth, this would not be a significant issue. But the advancement of conceptual tools has as its purpose the clarifying and purifying of social truth, social reality. Scientific, logical, or intellectual concepts, theories, and hypotheses bearing on the social condition of human beings need not be in conflict with an increased health of the human condition, but if a conflict arises, responsibility demands that concepts which block progress give way.

The connotation of intermarriage, a descriptive term for social scientists, carries a negative meaning for the average American. Consciously in some cases, unconsciously in others, social scientists use the concept of intermarriage in multiple ways which provide the bridge whereby laymen naturally believe they are justified in seeing intermarriage as a deviation from a rule, and they are of course not led by social scientists to see that all rules are made by human beings and that some of them must be unmade and others remade. The fact of a rule is too often assumed by both social scientists and laymen to be sacrosanct, always to be revered and respected. Some rules are so embedded in a society that they can be changed only as the fundamental structures and fabric of the society are changed. Some rules are so detrimental to a society that the society needs to be changed before the rules can be changed. Social scientists are so establishment oriented (for the good though not sufficient reason that the establishment underwrites research grants) that they seldom proscribe, preferring in the name of objectivity to describe.

The watershed in the relations between blacks and whites is social acceptance, or marriage. This ultimate social acceptance is so important and so overriding that the continued use of the term "intermarriage" is unwarranted. The simple fact is that blacks and whites in our society are technically not "endogamous groups." By reason of biological inheritance, mutual ancestors, geographical proximity, religious affiliation, and commitment to America—blacks and whites are an *endogamous people,* one diverse people in which all are members one of another, though they may belong to different classes within the one group. It is only the perpetuation of the self-fulfilling prophecy which holds that blacks and whites are separate or exogamous people. Between blacks and whites, as between blacks and blacks and whites and whites, there is only marriage—and *not* intermarriage. One may hold to intermarriage in America between religious groups and ethnic groups, but it is sheer folly to reduce the black-white development in this country to that artificial level. The radical distinction between blacks and whites has been blurred beyond recall or any ultimate meaningfulness. The experiences and consciousness of being black or of being white are important and need to be preserved for the enrichment of us all, but that is quite another matter from the racial distinctions which are artificial figments of the social ill-imagination of our society. It is for these reasons that I contend the necessity and even imperative of speaking in terms of marriage where a black and a white person are involved, and I am quite aware that this call to cease and desist with respect to the concept of intermarriage counters the position of so distinguished a social scientist as Kingsley Davis:

> If intermarriage be taken simply in the sense of marriage between two persons who are members of different groups, then every marriage is intermarriage (between male and female, if nothing else) and the word is redundant. Therefore, intermarriage must be viewed as a violation of or deviation from an endogamous rule. Above all, it must not be confused with exogamy. Whereas intermarriage is a deviation from an endogamous rule, exogamy is not a deviation at all but a rule in itself. There is no general term indicating a deviation from an exogamous rule, although *incest* has in some cases been broadened from its strictly kinship meaning for this purpose.[53]

It is my contention that we must change the endogamous rule rather than define or refine it, or resign ourselves to it, or be confined by it.

With respect to black-white marriages, we do not have a pure caste society, but rather an operational system of caste, which is generally and politely referred to as class differentiation:

> In *caste* structures the dominant principle is twofold: inheritance of the parental status at birth, and fixity of this status through life. In *class* structures there is a similar inheritance of the parental status at birth, but it does not necessarily remain fixed, achieved status being possible.[54]

Social stratification in the American system takes the extreme form of caste stratification which is based upon caste endogamy vis-à-vis black-white marriages, and yet black-white marriages occur as unsanctioned intercaste unions. The cardinal principle of our stratified social order is that "the majority of those marrying shall marry equals." Kingsley Davis, influenced by Ralph Linton, Robert K. Merton, and George E. Simpson, singular American anthropologists, calls this rule with respect to black-white marriages caste endogamy. Empirical evidence makes clear that stratification and endogamy develop concomitantly, and that since black-white marriages underscore the most rigid stratification in American social structures, it is here in America that we find the most stringent endogamy. The connection between stratification and marriage is set forth by Davis in two propositions:

(1) We know, empirically, that marriage usually implies equality of caste or class status between the parties, as shown by the symbolic identification of the mates (common name, common living quarters, common offspring); by the element of reciprocal exchange (cross-cousin marriage, sister exchange, gift exchange); by the anxiety of families to marry their children into families having at least as high a status as their own; by the use of marriage, like friendship, as an alliance mechanism and as a means of vertical mobility (the party marrying up would gain nothing if marriage did not imply equality); and by the role of marriage as both a criterion and an agency of assimilation (e.g., assimilation of the Dutch burghers and French Huguenots in South Africa). When we ask why this implication of equality is present, part of our answer lies in the kind of relation marriage is—above all, its intimate character. It is incompatible with the mechanisms of social distance ordinarily insulating members of different castes from one another. If some persons are "untouchable," they must also be unmarriageable, and if food which they cook is "uneatable," they must also be "unusable" in the kitchen. Not only does a primary or *Gemeinschaft* relation always tend to be equalitarian, but it is precisely the more intimate relations that a caste system

publicly bans between strata. Conversely, when intimate relations do arise, they tend to mitigate the caste inequality, as seen for example in the better treatment of house slaves as against field slaves.

(2) Since marriage is an institutional mechanism for procreating and rearing children, the requirements of status ascription in caste order practically require the marriage of equals. A wife reared in a social stratum widely different from her husband's is apt to inculcate ideas and behavior incompatible with the position the children will inherit from their father, thus creating a hiatus between their status and their role. The family structure itself depends upon certain mutual attitudes, e.g., filial respect and parental authority; if the children follow the status of the upper-caste parent, their attitudes toward the other parent will be those of the higher caste toward the lower and therefore incompatible with the proper familial sentiments. Hence it can be seen that the integrity of the child's personality, of the family structure, and of the caste organization requires that the parents be roughly matched in social position—that, in short, there be caste endogamy. Through endogamy the caste system so regulates its reproductive and status-ascriptive institution (the family) that caste distinctions remain clear rather than become blurred in the next generation. This is why in unsanctioned intercaste unions the offspring are illegitimate and either follow the status of the lower spouse or receive an intermediate position, while in sanctioned intercaste unions the mates are usually *made* equal at the time of marriage, the lower spouse and the subsequent offspring acquiring the status of the higher spouse.[55]

With regard to black-white marriages in the United States, we do not have an inflexible racial caste system. It is the case that our caste operational policy differs from the non-racial caste system of the Hindu where "the criterion of caste status is primarily descent, symbolized in purely socio-economic terms," and thus the Hindu system sanctions intercaste unions. Black-white marriages take place in our society but these "intercaste unions" are not sanctioned by the society because its stratification is based on race by which the offspring will inevitably bear the mark of the lower caste, and it is impossible to automatically transfer the status of the black husband to the white wife since she too will bear the indelible stamp of the lower caste:

> Actually the racial and the descent bases are close together, but their results somewhat divergent. The reason that race serves as an excellent basis of caste is that one gets one's racial traits by birth from parents having those traits, and one cannot change these traits during the rest of one's life. But it must be borne in mind that between parent and child there can be no hiatus in descent, by definition; whereas there can be such hiatus in racial traits. . . . Race thus adds another dimension to descent as a basis of caste. This dimension is biological, with its own mode of variation. The hypothesis that the Hindu system began on a racial basis is unproven. Even if true, however, it does not alter the fact that today this system is for the most part purely a matter of descent rather than race, symbolized *only* in socio-economic terms.[56]

We have seen earlier that concubinage was a sporadically developed happening in our society and that it was perfectly compatible with the racial caste system. Its compatibility was based on the fact that concubinage "does not imply equality between the mates or between the upper-caste parent and his natural child." Old line social scientists knew that

> concubinage itself will ultimately break down a racial caste system by the simple process of distributing the racial traits of the upper caste so lavishly among the lower that there remains no actual difference of race on which to base caste distinctions.[57]

But in this society interracial concubinage did not become a fixed institution and therefore a racial caste system developed; whereas in those societies

which subsequently failed to develop such a system in spite
of the juxtaposition of diverse racial elements (e.g., Brazil,
Hawaii, Mexico) interracial concubinage and/or marriage
took place freely at an early date.[58]

The old liberal socially conscious radicals like Wendell Phillips
and social scientists like Franz Boas believed that the principle of
breaking down the racial caste system at work in concubinage
would be no less operationally effective by the deliberate encouragement of black-white marriages. Franz Boas's underlying assumption was that the white male would marry the black female,
exchanging his "higher" status of birth or caste for beauty, intelligence, youth, wealth, sex, and the advancement of the society as a
whole over the generations. Old liberals believed the dominant
philosophy of egalitarian democracy could override caste in
America. The old liberal ideal failed because neither the strategy
nor the motivation needed to induce white males to such noble
obligation was sufficiently developed. Contemporary social scientists put their finger on the force of custom which prohibited
white males from marrying black females, though they do not feel
the obligation to induce changes in the custom. Further, contemporary social scientists perceived that black males more often
married white females, a situation which differed completely from
that of concubinage and the ideal of older social engineers,
though their assumption that black males always marry lower
class white females was one which was not questioned:

> Instead of an upper-caste male marrying a lower-caste
> female, as we would expect, we find the Negro male usually
> espousing a white woman. The reason apparently is that in a
> racio-caste system where the dominant philosophy is not of
> caste but of equalitarian democracy, the class achievement of
> certain Negro males enables them to bargain for females of
> the white caste who stand low in the class hierarchy. Such
> females can gain more by marrying a well-off or superior
> Negro than by marrying a white man of their own class. One
> could object that a similar advantage accrues to a low-class
> white man marrying a superior Negro woman, but in our

culture it is not men (but women) who marry for economic support, so that a white man marrying a Negro woman, is damaged precisely in his own sphere, i.e., economically, without receiving a compensatory advantage. Furthermore, if sex is the motive, caste inequality makes it easy for the white man to take sexual advantage of Negro women without marrying them; also, there is no shortage of white women for sexual satisfaction. Finally, because of the *racial* barrier, it is impossible for a Negro wife to acquire at marriage her white husband's caste status; instead her white husband tends to acquire *her* status in such cases—thus violating not only the caste but also the patrilineal principle. If a white wife takes the caste of her Negro husband, that at least fits the patrilineal principle. Consequently, it is mainly white women who trade their caste status for class advantage by marrying Negroes.[58]

In the United States black-white marriages are inhibited—if not completely prohibited—by a racio-caste stratification system,

first, . . . [by] the institutional mechanism through which descent and socialization are regulated, second, . . . [by] the genetic mechanism through which biological identity is maintained.[59]

But despite the prohibitive and inhibitive pressures of social status, socialization, and "biological identity," black-white marriages take place. They are not all between black men and white women, and it is certainly false to conclude that in the white female-black male marriages the former is predominantly of a lower class and seeking a higher class at the expense of caste. The dynamics of an urban and electric society in constant change amidst the black revolution and the search for real humanity makes the theme of "America divided" expressed by most writers on intergroup relations dated. We do not sanction unions of blacks and whites as yet in this society, but it is no longer the case that we can eliminate sanction of such unions as a live option. The walls may not be tumbling down, but bricks removed make the barrier less formidable and indicates an increasing consciousness of the necessity. Contemporary sociologists are instructive in their acknowledgment that marriage between blacks and whites is the key to the formation and deformation of our "racio-caste system," even if they are not especially helpful in giving us direction: "In making or avoiding a potential caste order, intermarriage played a determining role. It is, indeed, a crucial factor in caste structure of whatever type." [60]

The fact that sociologists perceive color to be a "crucial factor" in our "caste structure," specifically as regards the crucial sphere of black-white marriages, would seem to call for diagnosticians to provide the prescription. It is not that social scientists are immobilized in the face of the crucial issue of the society; it is more likely that they hold to the belief that a society should not be tampered with extensively. Just when and where they make this judgment is as suspect as it is mysterious, since "scientific" tampering is their ultimate objective and peripheral tampering is their daily business. The classic debate between many sociologists and psychologists, or at least those who follow their various professional methods and models, is whether basic changes in social conditions come through changes in social structures which bring about changes in individual behavior or through attitudinal changes of individuals which bring about changes in the social structures. In some respects, sociologists and psychologists are moving closer to one another. Sociologists of the old liberal vintage underscored years ago that change comes through crisis in the social structure, that crisis is necessary for growth. Psychologists have held two basic theories about the personality which have not been consistent. For some psychologists hold at one and the same time that the personality of different individuals grows and is healthy or wholesome either through inflexible stability or through persistent flexibility in multileveled experiments and experiences, depending upon the particular personality. The inconsistency of the role of conflict in these two theories leads some psychologists to perceive that growth for the personality of the individual as for the customs of the society comes through crisis, whether the individual be unalterably stable or more or less a totally flexible personality. In either case, with sociologists or psychologists, crisis is fundamental for growth, but neither breed of social science is willing to induce that amount of crisis necessary for the growth of the society as a whole and of individuals in particular with respect to the crucial issue of black-white marriages.

In the opinion of Freudian-oriented psychoanalysis, the prohibition of black-white marriages in the form of taboos or unsanctioned intercaste unions is reinforced by the belief among white men that black men are everywhere and always out to get white women. This belief is called projection and is caused by the introjection of the great burden white men have carried for their historic free ranging attack upon black women. The fear of retaliation is not to be ignored:

> One source of this fear is the treatment that the Negro has received at the hands of the whites. The slavery of the Negro, his economic and industrial exploitation, his moral degradation, and other historic facts of the modern situation are fundamentally repugnant to civilized moral standards. The members of the dominant racial group are more or less conscious of the injustice that the Negro has suffered at their hands. There is in consequence an uneasy sense of moral guilt, as may be seen reflected in the rationalized justifications of the historic treatment and of the existing social situation as well as in naive apologies for behavior not defensible on accepted moral standards. By a familiar psychological process, sentiments and attitudes that non-socially trained persons imagine that they would have had they been subjected to similar treatment, are imputed to the Negro: the Negro thereby becomes possessed of behavior tendencies menacing to the white man, to his domination of the social situation, and to the culture he represents. This fear complex . . . functions to create an external image which objectifies the psychological state; the Negro becomes the objective symbol of that subjective state rather than an objective reality.[61]

In his *Caste and Class in a Southern Town,* John Dollard has given the most influential psychoanalytical interpretation of this white condition. White men who have deviously used their power to manipulate powerless black women for their own sexual experimentations and gratifications have wondered what they would do were they in the position of defenseless black men. What they have imagined in most cases has led them to the fanatical conclusion that white womenfolk are in perpetual danger of attack by black men. Thus, when a black man and a white woman are intimately involved, it is assumed the black man is the violent aggressor who must be violently disposed of. The interesting twist to this situation, as Dollard notes, is that in black-white sexual relations in the South, white men have ready access to black and white women, a condition which makes for a very strange relation between the black woman and the white man since the black woman, though the object of rather than the initiator of the relationship, has a comparable access to black and white men. While the idealization of white women in the South does not usually work out in actual behavior, it does, however, affect the sexual behavior between white men and white women since white men have the feeling that white women are

> untouchable, that sexual sentiments are unbecoming in relation to them, and that sexual behavior toward white women must take place, though, of course it does take place, only against a personal sense of guilt.[62]

The black woman is viewed as a "seducing, accessible person dominated by sexual feeling." This split image model of Dollard's creation explains

> the luxury of preserving the image of the untouchable white woman and at the same time having available on easy terms the Negro woman as a target for the withdrawn affect.[63]

Although Dollard did not follow through this psychoanalytic interpretation vis-à-vis white women and black men, since black men in the South had less ready access to white women, it is most difficult not to believe that at least on the clandestine level the theory works out for black men and white women. Calvin Hernton, in *Sex and Racism in America*, follows Dollard to his ultimate conclusion—what is sauce for the goose is sauce for the gander.

Contemporary social scientists have listed a number of other well-known social controls preventing black-white marriages:

> The two groups are separated, particularly in the South, by a system of segregation which affects most areas of living—employment, family life, residence, recreation, even transportation. Whether or not this system of segregated living is expressed in legislation, it is public sentiment which gives meaning to, and which enforces, the system. The structure is significant since it allows few opportunities for men and women of the two races to meet at all, fewer opportunities for them to engage in sexual contact, and even fewer for the kind of equalitarian contacts which lead to marriage.[64]

We have dealt at length in another chapter with the legal restrictions. We shall return at other points to the function of the family, but it is well to indicate here that where marriage in black and white is not illegal, the family becomes "the official agency or institution to uphold the mores of racial endogamy." Joseph Golden, who conducted extensive interviews with black-white couples, revealed in his studies how these marriages of persons with strong family ties were frustrated in the beginning by advice from the immediate and extended family members who pointed out the dangers of prejudice or appealed to the individual's loyalty not to bring shame on the relatives. An example Golden uses is instructive:

> The wedding of the Thayers (Negro husband–white wife) was preceded by discussions between the parties and their families and friends. Everyone advised against it. Her family seemed to be mainly concerned with the effect on them. Her sisters believed that if the community in St. Louis heard about this, they and their children would be completely ostracized. His children were concerned about what the marriage would do to his business, but told him to go ahead if that was what he wanted.[65]

In pointing out what couples who have decided to go ahead face within their own families we gain a clue as to why only the strong hearted marry:

> The parents of Mrs. Brown, a German-Jewish refugee, objected to the marriage, although they had no objection to her dates with Negroes. Her father was afraid that the marriage would hurt her career, while her mother feared that her father's jewelry-repair business would be injured when news of the marriage became known in the neighborhood. Mr. Brown feels that they were not "prejudiced," but were really concerned about her welfare.
>
> Few of these persons met their in-laws before marriage. One couple tried it. "We engineered several occasions. They were impressed. Mom thought Jim was very intelligent, quite a speaker, etc., until they found him to be their future son-in-law. Then all hell broke loose. Pop was going to shoot us, shoot Jim, have us arrested and all kinds of things. Nothing ever happened. During the time that we were going together, I wanted to bring him home and say 'This is it.' Jim said, 'No, try to get them used to interracial company and then go ahead.' But it didn't happen. I doubt if it would have, for Pop brought home a picture of an interracial dance in England and during a lull in any conversation, when company was about, would whip it out and say, 'Look at those niggers, etc.' " [66]

While there is no way of accounting statistically for the number of potential black-white marriages broken up by parental pressure, the number is no doubt considerable. We take note here of the fact that the attitudes and the social structure in America are co-primary prohibiting mechanisms:

> Perhaps just as important are the attitudes which buttress the system of segregation, and the myths whose function it is to strengthen the prohibition against interracial marriage.

Along with these attitudes goes the belief that interracial marriage is doomed to fail, that successful marriage is impossible for a Negro-white couple. Whether the belief is based on reality or not is, for the purpose of discussion, irrelevant. The belief itself is a factor in keeping the number of interracial marriages so small that they do not represent a threat to the existing sex mores.[67]

What is important for us to note at this point is the role which social scientists play in reinforcing and perpetuating the belief in the necessary failure of black-white marriages. On examination of texts written for marriage and the family courses we find that many of the leading authorities, under the guise of being objective, are but propagandists for dominant attitudes and social structures. Marriages are doomed in black and white because many social scientists intend them to be failures. Writing in *Marriage for Moderns,* Henry A. Bowman is positive that a black-white marriage "presents unusually difficult problems, which in some cases are hopelessly insoluble." [68] Harold T. Christensen has no doubts but that black-white marriages "are usually inadvisable on social and cultural grounds." [69] Evelyn Duvall and Reuben Hill reflect upon American black-white marriage research conclusions and categorically state that "without exception the findings from this research argue against intermarriage." [70] The social controls which function to inhibit black-white marriages are strong, widespread, and multifold, including

the segregated social structure of our culture; the system of attitudes, beliefs, and myths which grow out of the social system and which serve to strengthen it; the laws which express the sex and marriage customs of the culture; institutional functionaries, such as clergymen, army officers, and governmental employees who attempt to discourage interracial marriage even in those states which have not legislated on the subject; the family, especially the immediate family, which uses affectional ties to prevent intermarriage.[71]

CAUSAL FACTORS INDUCING
BLACK-WHITE MARRIAGES

The fantastic number and variety of artificial social controls ar-
rayed against black-white marriages are necessary because the
lack of social sanction for intercaste unions is unnatural. What is
natural is the tremendous fascination black men hold for white
women and the strong attraction white women are for black men.
Marriages in black and white take place in the face of relentless
institutional and moral opposition because healthy personalities
can develop in unwholesome social environments. Of course the
simple psychological dictum that that which is held to be taboo
becomes the irresistible goes a long way in explaining unhealthy
black-white marriages in an unhealthy society, and the only answer to this situation is to create a healthy society. When we ask
for specific reasons why black-white marriages take place in this
society it is imperative to begin with straight sexual desire. The
sexual motive is not sufficient in itself to explain such volitive and
flagrant violation of general custom any more than it explains
why white men debase blacks and become intimate with black
women, or why black women tangle with white men when it
implies debasement. In this latter instance we must look for more
than crude sexual motives, and the same holds for marriages in
black and white:

> Also to be taken into account, both in transitory and in
> permanent relations, are the element of mastery; the attempt
> to show the racial inferiority of the Negro by the wanton use
> of Negro women; an irresponsible relationship free of cares,
> threats, and duties; and the fact that Negro women cannot
> be protected by Negro men.
>
> A complementary question asks why Negro women are
> accessible to such sex relations with white men outside of
> marriage. The answer seems to lie in sexual pleasure wishes;
> money given to low-paid or low-income women; the prestige
> of the white man; the wish, often unconscious, for light
> children; an element of revenge on the domineering or
> conceited white woman; and the looseness of the marriage
> ties in the lower-class Negro group with its mother-centered
> family and the economic independence of the woman.[72]

Beyond straight sexual attraction and desire, the multiple other factors which cause the public acceptance of a black or white marriage partner by a member of the opposite race are not the same as those which cause black-white intimacy without commitment. We would be remiss to assume without question the popular belief that people who marry in black and white can be placed into a social typology, for the following categories of social psychological types usually cast as the social types who so marry are too broad and interrelated to be meaningful:

> The Intellectuals and "Bohemians"
> The Religious and Political Radicals
> The "Sporting World"
> The Stable Middle Class
> The Emancipated Person
> The Rebellious Person
> The Detached Person
> The Adventurous Person
> The Unorganized or Demoralized Person
> The Promiscuous Person
> The Marginal Person
> The Acculturated Person
> The Desperately Lonely Person
> The Uniformed Person

In addition to simple sexual motivation, the individuals' attitudes are facilitating factors in black-white marriages, and their attitudes are modified by other factors such as opportunity in general and sex ratios and ecological forces in particular. Attitudes or tendencies and preferences that take priority among some individuals over the existing social conditions include the affirmation that neither religion nor nationality nor race is as important as belief in a physical and social diversity for personal welfare and that of one's children, a genuine feeling for the equality of races, a certain physical attraction, an indifference to white status, and the prospect of an exciting married life. These attitudes are formed out of cultural similarity, favorable impressions formed in friendships, liberal teachings in the home and church and school, and the positive experiences of friends and relatives married in black and white.

In the research done on immigrants and war brides it was generally concluded that such persons married blacks because they were ignorant of American prejudices. Joseph Golden makes this point in his "The Negro-White Intermarried in Philadelphia." [73] Sister Annella Lynn in her unpublished Ph.D. thesis at Catholic University on "Interracial Marriages in Washington, D.C., 1940-47," as well as in her Master's thesis on "Fifteen Negro-White Marriages in New York City and the Metropolitan Area," concluded that attitudes were all important in facilitating black-white marriages but that emotions were the key:

> It seems to this writer that when referring to the foreign-born white women who intermarried with the Negro, one of the factors which facilitated intermarriage was in the area of emotions rather than a lack of knowledge of the American disapproval. . . . That is, the foreign-born white are free from an adverse emotional reaction to intermarriage with the Negro. This interpretation is drawn only from my own limited contacts with foreign-born whites who have intermarried with the Negro, all of whom are women. It might be noted that two of the foreign-born whites married to Negroes who were married in Washington, D.C. between 1940-47, have established residence in Philadelphia and both of these were likewise aware of American disapproval of interracial marriages at the time of their marriage. [74]

Attitudes are very important factors leading to black-white marriages in spite of the inhibiting sociological factors. Attitudes are not always or even generally followed by practice, but attitudes do influence the sociological factors as well as being influenced by them. Attitudes alone do not cause black-white marriages, but they are extraordinarily influential among the multiple causative factors.

Some social scientists have held that demographic factors like sex ratios and numerical size are the one "cause" of black-white marriages. Constantine Panunzio located the cause of black-white marriages in the fact of uneven sex ratios:

> Our hypothesis is, first, that sex distribution is a primary factor in producing or preventing intermarriage; that is, whenever a people in proximity to other peoples has an unbalanced sex ratio, they will tend to intermarry; whereas, if they have a relatively well-balanced distribution of the sexes, they will tend to marry within their own people.[75]

John H. Burma researched black-white marriages in Los Angeles as Panunzio had done before him. Burma took the approach of examining the marriage license records of Los Angeles County for the years 1948–59. His statistical approach allowed him to cover over 375,000 total marriages and over 3,200 "mixed marriages" in an eleven-year span and thus he suffered less from the difficulties encountered by most researchers:

> Various meritorious attempts have been made to study interracial marriages on the mainland of the United States, but with a few brilliant exceptions they usually have resulted in reports valid only for a particular group in a particular city or county at a particular date. Because of the difficulty of securing data, most researchers have had to content themselves with a few years and a few dozen or a few hundred cases. Examples include studies by Baber, Barron, Catapusen, Davis and Gardner, Drake and Cayton, Golden, Klineberg, Lawrence, Risdon, McWilliams, Rogers, Schuyler, and Smith.[76]

Burma produced a table (Table 4)[77] bearing on Panunzio's hypothesis that sex distribution is a primary factor producing or preventing marriage in black and white.

If Panunzio's hypothesis were correct, it would be reflected in the following table where the white and black groups contain more women than men:

> If nothing more than sheer numbers were involved, and if all men and women in each group would marry within that

Table 4

Population of Los Angeles County, by Races, by Sex
with Sex Ratios and Sex Differentials, 1960

Race	Male	Female	Excess		Sex Ratio
White	2,656,627	2,797,239	F+	140,612	95
Negro	222,731	238,815	F+	16,084	93
Japanese	38,998	38,316	M+	682	102
Chinese	10,836	8,450	M+	2,386	128
Filipino	7,696	4,426	M+	3,270	174
Indian	4,139	3,970	M+	169	104
Other	3,620	2,908	M+	712	128

group if it were physically possible to do so, then white men would marry only white women and Negro men would marry only Negro women. There would be an excess of both white and Negro women, however, available to marry into other groups. All Japanese, Chinese, Filipino, Indian and Other women would marry within their respective groups, although there would be excess males in each group to marry the excess white and Negro women. According to this hypothesis the largest number of intermarriages would be Filipino-white, then Chinese-white, Other-white, Japanese-white, and Indian-white in that order. There would be no intermarriages involving white or Negro females; they would intermarry like white females except on a one to nine ratio.[78]

As seen in Table 5,[79] Burma discloses "that sex ratios are not very significant causal factors" in black-white marriages.

The following table indicates how fallacious is Panunzio's theory and how obvious is the fact that sheer numbers do not explain black-white marriages:

Negro males, despite having the largest proportion of excess females, out-marry by three and three-quarter times their populational expectancy. White males, despite the excess of white females, make up over one-third of all out-marrying males.[80]

Table 5

Percentage of Males and Females of Selected Groups, Los Angeles County, 1960; Percentage of Males and Females Intermarrying, 1948–59, and Index of Proportion of Each in the Population and Intermarriages

	Males		Females	
	Percent of Total Population	*Percent of Total Population Intermarrying*	*Percent of Total Population*	*Percent of Total Population Intermarrying*
Group				
White	87.51	35.98	90.61	63.98
Negro	7.33	27.60	7.73	10.12
Japanese	1.29	7.02	1.24	13.42
Chinese	.36	5.83	.27	4.94
Filipino	.31	23.95	.14	7.50

With respect to demographic factors, sex ratios, and numerical size, most social scientists do not agree with Panunzio that these factors are primary nor with Burma that they are insignificant vis-à-vis black-white marriages, but instead contend that they "influence the practice in part." [81] Studies in New York City, Los Angeles, Burlington, Woonsocket, New Haven, and Derby "have shown that an unbalanced sex ratio and numerically small representation lead some groups into considerable incidences of intermarriage." [82] Considerable out-marriages occur among the Filipinos in California, the Jews in Stamford, Connecticut, and the Italians in New Haven, Connecticut, but "generally speaking, intermarriage varies indirectly and breadth of selection varies directly with the relative size of the minority group." [83]

Straight sexual attraction, attitudes, and demographic factors would be less enabling factors in black-white marriages were it not for the more important "propinquitous factors," place of residence, place of work, place of recreation, and place of education:

Even more important, in contrast to the theme of "America divided" expressed by most writers on intergroup relations, is that in this immigrant-receiving society our heterogeneous groups have developed cultural and social proximity to a surprising extent. For example, residential propinquity, a well-known factor in courtship, not only because of the premarital contacts facilitated but also because of the economic and cultural similarities implied, is found to be an important correlate of intermarriages as well as in-marriages. Our communities' ecological areas are not homogeneous with regard to race, religion, and nationality.[84]

A large and isolated black group sealed in the ghetto will marry blacks on the whole, while a small and dispersed black minority will tend to marry whites to a greater extent. This latter tendency, however, results more from opportunity than from lack of prejudice in the society.

All other factors being equal, cultural similarity is the most important influence leading to black-white marriages. Cultural similarity includes

European background, length of residence in the United States, occupational and economic class, amount and type of education, church affiliation or lack of it, and linguistic similarity.[85]

In this category there is still a great deal of intellectual imperialism, if not racist and cultural imperialism, among social scientists. Milton Leon Barron reveals this imperialism when he refers to the complementary character of the propinquitous educational and economic factors in black-white marriages:

This is true in many Jewish-Gentile and Negro-White intermarriages in which socially dominant but economically or educationally inferior Gentiles and whites mate with socially inferior but economically or educationally superior Negroes and Jews.[86]

By and large, studies indicate that young people

of diverse groups are led into marital ties through economic propinquity and similarity, both occupational and spatial; by close association and common experiences in the amount, type, and locale of education; and by recreational contacts. Indeed, the high degree of similarity in economic and educational status of those who intermarry lends support to the prediction of the ultimate emergence of clearly defined in-groups and "unconsciousness of kind" along these lines.[87]

The importance of propinquitous factors in the minds of social scientists is clear:

All other factors being equal, the greater the economic propinquity and similarity between people of the same racial, ethnic, or religious group or between people of different groups, the more likely it is that they will inmarry or intermarry. Conversely, the greater the economic distance between them, the less likely it is that they will marry.[88]

Educational propinquity and similarity are also twofold: similarity in amount and type of education, and propinquity in place of education. All other factors being equal, the greater the propinquity and similarity in amount, type, and place of education between people of the same racial, ethnic, or religious groups or between two groups, the more likely it is that they will marry. Conversely, the greater the educational distance and dissimilarity between them, the less likely is their marriage.[89]

A final point to be made about the influence of propinquity and similarity is that the more numerous they are in the relations of two or more groups, the more likely they are to intermarry. Conversely, the fewer the factors of propinquity and similarity and the greater the social distance and more numerous the dissimilarities, the less likely is intermarriage.[90]

In addition to the causal factors (sexual attraction, attitudes, demography, propinquity, cultural similarity) inducing black-white marriages, we have mentioned in passing some peremptory forces which are partially influential because of the authority attributed to them: clerical, parental, moral, and legal factors. Given all of these factors we know that when black-white marriages occur, "culture homogeneity in the main determines the selection," [91] and that the dynamics of the situation may include the fact that

> while social distance between whites and other groups is decreasing in all cases, it is decreasing more rapidly between whites and Negroes. . . .[92]

Social scientists finally conclude that black-white marriages occur

> because of the inefficacy of institutional control by church and state. Historical as well as contemporary evidence demonstrate that churches and synagogues cannot effectively curb religious intermarriage in societies where church and state are separate and civil marriage, accordingly, is an alternative to clerical ceremony. As far as racial intermarriage is concerned, the point is perhaps best made by way of illustration. There were cases of such marriages in California long before October 1, 1948, the date when the state's law prohibiting the practice was ruled unconstitutional by a decision of the State Supreme Court [the winning argument came when two Catholics, one Negro and one white, declared that their religious freedom was hampered by the law; they could receive all the sacraments except that of marriage, which was being unconstitutionally denied them by the law]. In short, easy social contact and a cultural common denominator negate much of the prohibitive impact of institutional control.[93]

To these multiple factors which induce black-white marriages today, we must add the contemporary social conditions of "political emancipation, intermingling of culture, and the spread of tolerance and growth of fellowship" in America.[94] In black-white relations, we can trace this general trend from the Sit-ins in the early 1960's through the university reform movements of the present. In addition, with the rise of black consciousness and the demand for equal opportunity in all spheres, blacks have enhanced their image. Thus, we should expect that whites engaged with blacks in common struggles would rebel against their parents' oppressive values which forbid black-white marriages and express their transcendence of these repressive values through their affirmation of individualistic choice, a value rooted in the "romantic complex" of our culture, and through such marriages. Thus, we should expect future sociological studies to show the wholesome and positive effect of this rebellion against old values and this insistence on freedom of choice rather than what have been traditionally cited as the negative forces in black-white marriages:

> It is proposed that post-adolescence and the premarital years constitute an age of rebellion against the more conservative values of parents, which, coupled with the conflict between generations and the emancipation from family control brought on by extramural and secular experiences in education and the economy, are conducive to intermarriage. For many young Americans the cultural relativity with which they are indoctrinated in public school systems and the psychological association which they develop between the intermarriage taboo and "backwardness" are also conceivably significant in this context. A likely explanation is to be had too in the individualistic choice of a marriage partner imbedded in the "romantic complex" of American culture.[95]

The increase in black consciousness and in black-white marriages cannot be seen as other than a healthy development inducing human rights and freedom over black or white superiority. Thus, if social scientists generally assume that black-white marriages occur because of black self-hatred or "the drive toward upward social mobility," they will miss the fact that these marriages increasingly occur among the young because they have transcended self-hatred and social status qua social status.

PATTERNS OF INCIDENCE AND SELECTION
IN BLACK-WHITE MARRIAGES

The fundamental forces of social change in the values and mores of the American society in the 1960's are a direct challenge to established anti-black-white marriage values. We have not previously known in our history such a sustained attack on traditional attitudinal and behavioral patterns. It will be years before we realize the outcome of the quest for a human society beyond caste, if not beyond class. It should not be surprising to find social scientists in the future reinforcing basic changes and inducing public sanction of black-white mutual acceptance, instead of reinforcing traditional values under the disguise of neutrality and objectivity. It is not too much to state, in light of the pervasive attack upon custom, that past and present research activity on trends of incidence and selection is dated. Sociologists concerned with these issues have naturally found "that intermarriage occurs most often between ethnic groups, less often between religious groups, and least between racially defined groups." [96] This information is useful in terms of evaluating the unacceptance of blacks at the intimate level of our society and in "evaluating the relative cohesive strength" of blacks and whites, but it is not suggestive of "possible realignments in the structure of American society." We shall examine briefly some of the findings of social scientists with respect to the incidence and selection in black-white marriages.

Perhaps the most valuable sociological study in this sphere was made by Ruby Jo Reeves Kennedy in New Haven. Dr. Kennedy analyzed marriage records in New Haven for the years 1870, 1900, 1930, and 1940.[97] She found that black-white marriages were practically nonexistent in New Haven and that ethnic groups married out at a very high rate within the confines of religious affiliation; i.e., Catholics of various national origins married a variety of other Catholics, etc. While her findings indicated a "triple melting pot," other social scientists, such as Barron, have set her results in the following perspective:

The need for further research on this aspect of intermarriage is obvious. The communities studied so far have been few in number, mostly concentrated on the eastern seaboard. It is important that we get a more adequate regional coverage. Second, many more studies are needed on the dynamics of intermarriage. Are second- and third-generation Americans intermarrying more than their first-generation parents and grandparents elsewhere than New Haven? Third, studies of intermarriage incidence and selection must keep within reasonable distance of the changing calendar. It is absurd in terms of time as well as place to assert that "Americans intermarry" according to a pattern of a triple melting pot when all we really know is that residents of one community, New Haven, were demonstrating such a pattern ten years ago.[98]

With respect to black-white marriages, the telling index is the strong communal separation which makes their rate very small:

While no overall national rates are available, such studies of Negro-white marriages as have been made in particular communities where their legality is unquestioned indicate that their rates vary from none to, at the most, three or four per cent out of every hundred marriages involving Negroes. The percentage of whites involved in such marriages becomes, of course, insignificant.[99]

Louis Wirth and Herbert Goldhamer studied the rates of black-white marriage in Boston. The high rate of such marriages in Boston during the nineteenth century was found to be due to the concentration there of abolitionist spirits responsive to the human demands of blacks and to the abolitionist's espousal of the individual's right to a black-white marriage. With the large influx of immigrants who were not tuned in to the tradition of abolition and did not carry forward its sentiments, Boston has come to be like other Northern cities. In the latter half of the nineteenth century, the impact of the agitation for black-white marriages by persons like Wendell Phillips is seen in the following statistics:[100]

	Average per Year
1862–66	9.0
1867–71	17.6
1873–77	34.4
1878–82	24.2
1883–87	24.8

These statistics are insignificant, but Wirth and Goldhamer found that in the middle 1940's there were only approximately nine black-white marriages per year. In the years 1914–1938, 390 out of every 10,000 blacks who married, married whites, while only 13 out of every 10,000 whites who married, married blacks. Wirth and Goldhamer view the change in the social conditions—that is, the large influx of immigrants who were not influenced by abolitionists and did not support their sentiments—as the cause of the decline of black-white marriages. The decline of black-white marriages in Boston contradicts the general assumption that a small minority group will increase instead of decrease the number of intercaste unions. Though they did not indicate it, the fact is that even historically liberal Boston developed a very tight ghetto which served to insulate and segregate blacks from whites, and thus black-white marriages took place on the periphery of the ghetto and not as a part of its inner dynamics:

> The marked decrease in intermarriage which has taken place in Boston cannot be explained by the hypothesis for which there is evidence from a number of multiracial societies, namely, that the smaller the ratio of a minority race to the rest of the population the greater will be the amount of outmarriage. Where a minority racial group constitutes a very small percentage of the total population, the amount of interracial contact appears to be greater. Under such conditions there is less tendency toward strict segregation and less opportunity for the small minority group to develop an autonomous society within the larger society.[101]

Wirth and Goldhamer described a pattern of black-white marriages in which the light-black male sought out such a relationship to enhance his esteem. Here we have clear evidence of their dated work and some suspicion about their technique, for while more light-blacks may have married white women than have dark-blacks, the high incidence of this type of marriage in Boston would seem to be due to the interplay of the cultural similarity plus propinquitous factors (more available to light-blacks) than to their desire to achieve greater self-esteem:

> The much greater frequency with which Negro men marry white women as compared with Negro women marrying white men is probably related to the fact that the lighter Negro male may derive some degree of self-esteem if he is able to marry a white woman, whereas the light and attractive Negro female appears to be more likely to utilize her attractions by marrying into the economically superior stratum of Negro society.[102]

Table 6

Skin Color	Groom	Bride
Dark Brown	26	4
Light Brown	14	0
Light	2	2
White	2	0
Total	44	6

Hair Form		
Kinky	30	4
Curly	10	0
Straight	4	2
Total	44	6

In Philadelphia, Joseph Golden found that the lighter-blacks were not the ones who married whites. His study was based on black-white marriages that occurred during every fifth year over the twenty-five-year period, from 1922 to 1947.[103] In the years studied (1922, 1927, 1932, 1937, 1942, 1947), there were one hundred forty-one black-white marriages and Golden interviewed fifty of these couples. Of the fifty couples interviewed, forty-four of the grooms were black, leading Golden to state that with respect to the above table it is obvious "that the majority of the Negro spouses, both men and women, of the group studied are Negroid in appearance." [104]

There is little evidence today to support Wirth and Gold-hamer's conclusion that light-blacks marry whites with more frequency than dark-blacks do. More important than color is cultural similarity which now knows no color line within the black color spectrum, and black identity is now cherished even in black-white unions. Further, over the long haul other factors have entered to break the pattern described by Wirth and Goldhamer. As Horace Mann Bond points out:

In the process of miscegenation, of course, the members of the dominant group never anticipate social acceptance while engaged in giving their physical traits to their bastard offspring. That problem, unfortunately, always arises when individuals are found with mixed blood who clamor for social acceptance. The usual result has been that the dominant group, after destroying the purity of both parent-stocks, blandly hoists the bars against these left-handed children in the sacred name of racial purity. The Anglo-Saxon Purity League, and other creations of the "Nordic delusion," are instances of this untimely attention to the barn door after the horse has fled. . . .

In our own United States, the land of perfect liberty, where all men are created equal, the situation assuredly gives pause in the application of the formula. There is no ripple of amusement or disbelief from an audience when a speaker who looks like the latest edition of Wendell Phillips' "blue-eyed Anglo-Saxon" passionately declaims upon "the necessity that all of us black men in America and the world stand together!" For the speaker means a very definite thing, if not exactly what he says, and his audience knows it. Time was when there were blue-vein societies and other organizations of like ilk among Negroes in this country, but they seem largely to have disintegrated, owing to two happy chances of fortune. The first has been that those who were so much like the dominant group as to demand and desire full fellowship to the extent of seclusion from the subordinate group have in great part folded their tents and crept quietly into the ranks of the whites, with no more flurry about it. The other fortunate thing has been the unyielding refusal of the dominant group to accept any of its hybrid progeny, if known as such, no matter how highly infused with the superior strain, into its domestic councils. In this country the public acceptance of the dictum of the sheriff in *Show Boat*—"One drop of nigger blood makes you a nigger!"—has done countless good for the Negro, as it has served to focus his energies and that of all his potential leaders upon the immediate task of racial survival. There is here no widespread wasting of energies or efforts on the creation and maintenance of an intermediate group.[105]

The absence of a middle group or "mulatto class" accepted by both blacks and whites did not eliminate altogether the tendency of light-blacks in the immediate past to foster an "upper class" elitism. It was this elitism which Wirth and Goldhamer interpreted to mean that "the lighter Negro male may derive some degree of self-esteem if he is able to marry a white woman."

Wirth and Goldhamer labored under the rhetoric that for a black man to marry a white woman "he is marrying 'upward' " and for a white man to marry a black woman, "he is marrying 'downward.' " The assumption of class distinctions, once firm among blacks and expressed in their marriage patterns, is underscored by Golden:

Ten of the 44 Negro men were either passable or almost passable. In marrying white women, they chose spouses who were more similar than dissimilar to them in the matter of skin color. Some of the remaining 34 Negro men may be said to have followed the practice on the part of upper class Negro men of marrying women lighter than they. Insofar as these men belonged to the Negro upper class, their choice of a wife reflected their class standards.[106]

Yet this once dominant pattern must be seen in another light. As Robert E. Park states:

While it is true that the mulatto in the United States, as is the case of the mixed blood generally, has been disposed to escape from the racial coil in which his origin and his history have involved him by separating himself from the masses of the Negro race, the vigor with which the racial line has been drawn against him has compelled him to take another course.

More and more in the course of his struggle for position and status in the white man's world the brown man has chosen to throw his fortunes with the black and make the Negro's cause his own. He has made himself not merely the leader but the teacher, the interpreter, and in some sense the emancipator of the race. In this struggle the black man, as education has been more widely diffused, has begun to play a more important role.[107]

Wirth and Goldhamer also deal with the fact that black men marry white women with more frequency than black women marry white men in Boston, and they attribute the high incidence of black-groom marriages to the fact that the black man in an urban center has "more opportunities to acquire the occupation and status that would enhance his chances of marrying a white woman." To this explanation they add these cogent remarks:

The greater outmarriage rate of the urban Negroes is almost entirely due to the Negro urban males. The Negro rural females have an outmarriage rate almost as high as the Negro urban females (0.72 as compared with 0.82), and in two of the six 3-year periods exceed the urban Negro female rate. . . .

That more favorable economic opportunities exist for the Negro woman in the city is also probably true, but since the woman, unlike the man, is not so frequently married because of the degree of economic security she can provide, this factor would be of less significance in her case. Consequently, as far as this factor is concerned the chances of a white marriage would tend to be equivalent for the rural and urban Negro woman. . . .

If one assumes that at least the formal initiative in contracting marriage rests with the male in racial intermarriages as well as in racially homogeneous marriages, then in all probability it would be true that facilities and opportunities for interracial contact that exist in urban centers would tend to increase the chances of a Negro man marrying a white woman more than it would increase the chances of a Negro woman marrying a white man; for the increased opportunities for interracial contact in urban centers would be readily utilized by the Negro man. A further factor that may be of considerable importance in this connection is the concentration in the cities of the politically more radical members of the Negro (and white) group. It appears from the results of a study conducted in Chicago by Roberts that an appreciable portion of the parties in Negro-white intermarriages are of a "left" political orientation.[108]

Robert K. Merton holds that lower class white females and upper class black males will marry most often because such marriages involve "a reciprocal compensatory situation in which the Negro male 'exchanges' his higher economic position for the white female's higher status." [109] This position does not hold up from a black point of view since the expected status does not come from the dominant white elements of the society, and there is little evidence that an upper class black society gives status to such marriages. It may be more to the point to hold that black men and white women are more attracted than their opposites because of the repression and taboo which traditionally keep them apart. It may be to the point that black men are more honest in their relations than white men and that the special relation which white men have had with black women over the years may be continuing in clandestine patterns. In the urban and electric centers, shaped by anonymity, there is now no more risk for the white male to marry a black woman than for the black male to marry a white woman. Golden stated that in Philadelphia twenty years ago

no instance was found of a white spouse with a prominent position in the community. Several of the Negro spouses were persons well known in the community. . . .

Contrary to the situation in New York City and in Chicago, the Negro-white couples did not tend to aggregate. Each couple was acquainted with only one or two other mixed couples, and apparently did not feel a need for psychological reinforcement. In Chicago, the Manasseh Club existed from around the beginning of the century until it disintegrated in the late Twenties. They engaged in social and mutual help activities. A similar organization, the Penguin Club, was formed in New York in 1936 to combat social ostracism. "Its members are selected after a character investigation. Prospective candidates had to have at least one child to attest to the stability of the relationship."

Several white spouses reported that they had lost jobs when their intermarriage was discovered. Others were careful not to let the act of the intermarriage become known at their place of employment. . . . Negro spouses seem less subject to economic sanctions. . . . A sizable proportion of both Negro and white husbands were self-employed and, therefore, less subject to economic reprisals. So far as could be judged, the Negro professionals interviewed had made a successful economic adjustment, with a large clientele and high income. They included highly successful doctors, lawyers, and other professional persons. Apparently the situation is otherwise in Chicago, where "Negro professional men are likely to have fewer clients if they marry a white woman." [110]

In Philadelphia, Golden found that black-white marriages were not restricted to any particular occupation.[111] In their study on Boston, however, Wirth and Goldhamer anticipated that

since he is marrying "upward," the Negro groom in Negro-white marriages would be of superior social and economic status within the Negro group; and that the white groom in Negro-white marriages would be of inferior social and economic status within the white group, since he is marrying "downward." Striking confirmation of this is found: Comparison of the occupational distribution of Negro grooms and of gainfully employed Negro males in

Boston clearly demonstrates that the Negro grooms occupy superior occupational positions as compared with all gainfully employed Negro males. Slightly over 60 per cent of the latter were unskilled workers as compared with slightly over 40 per cent of the Negro grooms contracting mixed marriages.[112]

In Philadelphia, Golden discovered that

the majority of Negro husbands were either on an equal or higher level than their white wives, and most of the white husbands outranked or equaled their Negro wives in occupational status.

It would seem, then, that the situation in Philadelphia differs from that in Boston, where "all Negro men marrying white women tend to marry white women with low occupational status, and that to the extent there is any deviation from this rule it is in the direction of the marriage partners marrying within their own occupational rank." The Philadelphia situation seems, rather, to be one of a tendency toward homogamy in the occupational area.[113]

Wirth and Goldhamer found that foreign-born white males married black women "to a greater extent than their representation in the general population," and that compared with the general population of New York and Boston there was an overrepresentation of native-born white females in black-white marriages:

The overrepresentation of the foreign-born white males is consistent with the explanation offered above for the fact that relatively fewer white males marry Negro women compared with white females who marry Negro men, namely, that the formal opportunities for marriage are much greater for the male than for the female since the male can more readily take the initiative. Consequently, one would expect those white males who do marry Negro women to derive from lower status and economic groups within the white population.

An additional explanation may lie in the fact that the foreign-born white males not only occupy the economically inferior positions in the society, but are also, owing to greater male migration, likely to find a dearth of women within their own nationality groups. Consequently, they may marry Negro women, to whom lower economic and social status would not represent a serious handicap.[114]

Their study also indicated a higher rate of black-white marriages among black "servant women" and black chauffeurs than among blacks of other occupations:

Half the Negro women in the "servant classes" marrying white husbands were engaged in housework. It would appear, then, that the Negro brides are predominantly made up of women whose daily work is likely to lead to close contact with whites.

The largest single occupation among the Negro grooms in mixed marriages was that of chauffeur, of whom there were 24, almost 11 per cent of the Negro grooms. It is possible that this occupation also gives the Negro special opportunities for contact with whites, although the prestige derived from acting as chauffeur to socially prominent white families may be of greater importance.

It is possible also that Negroes who act as chauffeurs to prominent white families may "look down" on the "ordinary" Negro and be especially anxious to marry white women.[115]

Golden found neither of these trends (reported by Wirth and Goldhamer in terms of complex and subtle exchanges of economic position for status and vice versa) operative in Philadelphia. He states, briefly, that the "educational matching of the group studied shows that this group does not conform to the prevailing opinion that well-educated Negro men marry ignorant white women."[116]

In his study of Los Angeles, Burma revealed that the probability that any given member of smaller groups will intermarry is much greater than that of any member of the white group:

> For any group the formula of percent of intermarriages divided by the percent of population gives the measure of probability of intermarriage for a person within that group.[117]

Table 7

Percentage of Males and Females in the Total Population, 1960, and Percentage in Total Intermarriages, for Selected Groups, Los Angeles County, 1948–59

Group	Percent in Total Pop.		Percent in Intermarriage		Index	
White	90.2	*90.4*	42.0	*58.0*	.47	*.64*
Negro	7.6	*7.7*	21.5	*6.5*	2.83	*.84*
Japanese	1.3	*1.2*	7.4	*12.6*	5.70	*10.50*
Chinese	.4	*.3*	4.2	*4.4*	10.50	*14.66*
Filipino	.3	*.1*	13.7	*8.1*	45.67	*81.00*
Indian	.1	*.1*	3.8	*4.0*	38.00	*40.00*
Other	.1	*.1*	7.4	*6.4*	74.00	*64.00*

NOTE: Roman figures represent males, italics females.

For white females this index is only .64, for black females .84, for white males .47, and for black males 2.83.[118] Proportionately, white males, though they constitute the largest group, are the least likely to marry other than whites, while white women and then black women form the next largest groups least likely to out-marry. Burma further found that white males who married black females were among the oldest group of males who married. He summed up his findings as follows:

> In summary, this study indicates that in Los Angeles intermarriages are increasing significantly: the largest number of marriages include whites and Negroes, but proportionately the smaller groups intermarry tremendously more than the larger groups; some evidence of intermarriage

by cultural homogamy exists; intermarried couples are on the average somewhat older than persons intramarrying, except if they themselves are the products of intermarriage; and, except for whites, in most cases there was a greater likelihood that one party had been divorced previously than in comparable intramarriages.[119]

The incidence of black-white marriages is low and if increasing does not account for a significant number of marriages.

CONSEQUENCES OF BLACK-WHITE MARRIAGES

The fact that black-white marriages do not have a high rate of incidence is partially responsible for the limited amount of knowledge contemporary social scientists possess with respect to the success or failure of such marriages, measured by the "criteria of divorce, desertion, and separation," as well as by the welfare of the children. While there is only fragmentary information available (as evidenced by our previous discussion of studies on the incidence of black-white marriages), a great deal of speculation has been based on little knowledge. Barron pointed out "there are numerous people who insist on a consequence of overwhelming doom for those who intermarry in social and cultural matters." [120] An example of this doom prophecy is that of Rabbi Israel Tabak of Baltimore, president of the Rabbinical Council of America, who contended at its annual meeting in 1950 that such marriages are 90 per cent unsuccessful and that they

> undermine the stability of the home, increase the number of unhappy marriages and bring children into the world with a rift in their souls which can never be healed.[121]

Rabbi Albert I. Gordon was more psychologically positive in his classic work *Intermarriage,* but no less a prophet of doom:

> Even though we may decry the unreasoning and highly emotional basis for opposition to Negro-white marriages, we must, nevertheless, in all truth, remind those who are contemplating such a marriage, that, in the present state of

American society, they will be placing an unwarranted burden upon their children as well as upon themselves. Opportunities for cultural, economic, political and social advancement may, for some time to come, remain closed to these children because of their color alone. Should prospective parents readily take such a responsibility upon themselves without careful consideration of the implications of their mixed marriage for children yet unborn? I believe that young people definitely have this grave responsibility and that they must meet it.[122]

Another rabbi is more helpful in pointing out our limited knowledge:

There are many Jews who . . . deprecate mixed marriage on simple practical grounds. Marriage, they argue, involves at best many problems and difficulties. Why complicate it still more? Why enter on a union with a reduced chance of success? This would be an impressive argument if we could show that a majority, or even a dangerously high percentage, of intermarriages are failures. We do not, in fact, have reliable statistics; nor do we have a satisfactory way of measuring success in marriage. . . . Everyone knows of successful intermarriages, and they are not so rare as to be labeled startling exceptions.[123]

Sociologists, psychologists, and other experts on the family and marriage have not questioned their basic theory that extreme differences in background foster marital stresses and strains rather than creative tension. For example, Rabbi Gordon states:

I believe that parents who attempt to dissuade their children from intermarrying are not selfish, intolerant people, as their children and others are wont to say. They know, by their own experience, the experiences of others, and even intuitively as well, that opposites in color or religion are far less likely to be as successful in their marriage as are persons of the same color and religion. Ethnic differences were greater sources of friction in an earlier day than they are today because the memories associated with life in other countries were far greater when there were comparatively few native-born Americans.[124]

Specialists in marriage and the family maintain that a black and white couple have a built-in focal point for conflict in that racial differences become "the scapegoat for tensions which originate elsewhere in the marital relationship" and a substitute explanation for a couple's lack of fortitude. Sometimes specialists set an extraordinarily high level for success in marriage:

> On the basis of the evidence presently available it is clear, too, that the chances of happiness in marriage are greatest for those who are culturally, socially, educationally, temperamentally, ethnically, nationally, racially, and religiously more alike than they are different from each other.[125]

On the other hand, specialists maintain that the success or failure of any marriage depends upon the total situation and not merely upon the fact that one partner is black and the other partner is white. The inner solidarity of marriage is affected by the external forces such as the influences of friends and parents:

> Alert and intelligent though they may be, marriage involves not only the man and woman who are the primary parties to the marriage but their parents, kindred and society as well. Their views are generally opposed to such marriages, and the pressures that result have their effect upon the married couple.[126]

Yet, as Milton Barron put it,

> theoretically, no type of marriage contains within itself the germs of its own inevitable failure. Success or failure depends upon total adjustment rather than upon the mere elements of difference.[127]

We shall deal at length in another chapter with the position which holds that marriages in black and white are a threat to the survival of the group, a threat to society, a threat to the children, and a threat to the religious way of life. Here it is important to point out that theorists on marriage and the family hold that the consequences for children of black-white marriages are that they lack adequate identification and must bear, along with other burdens, the status of outcasts:

> I believe that intermarriage is also a threat to the children of such a marriage, in that it may tend to make them marginal in their relationships to parents, their faiths or their races. When we make it difficult and sometimes quite impossible for children to identify with us and our way of life, or our people, we have created a threat to their welfare and to the welfare of society as well because highly charged emotional experiences often leave such children disturbed, frustrated and unable to believe that they can live normal, happy lives.[128]

A great many statistics have been worked out by specialists to support their belief that black-white marriages are a high risk, that they lead to separation and divorce at a higher rate than do other unmixed marriages. The truth is that the samples of black-white marriages studied are far too small to allow for even an educated guess, let alone a significant prediction, of their probable success or failure. On the other hand, Golden found that the fifty black-white marriages in Philadelphia had a very good chance for survival and growth.[129]

In the face of the opposition to black-white marriages and simultaneous expectation that they will increase, for example in the classic work of Albert I. Gordon, it is well to recall here Barron's admonition:

> One final task confronts American sociologists. It is to bring to the attention of laymen the inconsistency of their

conservative attitudes toward intermarriage, on the one hand, with their activities, on the other hand, in creating social and cultural conditions favoring intermarriage. Sending children to public schools and to centers of higher education away from home; the struggle against restrictive covenants, job discrimination, and quota systems; and participation in interfaith activity are but a few of the practices which lead inevitably to intergroup contacts that sometimes become love and intermarriage. The recognition of this dilemma is a fundamental beginning to an intelligent approach to the problem.[130]

Chapter Six

PARIETAL, PEREMPTORY, AND
PERMISSIVE RELIGIOUS FORCES

I n his account of "racial intermarriage" in the New England industrial community of Derby in 1929–30 and 1940, Milton Leon Barron reported in 1946 that

> there are no ecclesiastical laws prohibiting racial
> intermarriage. Nevertheless, clergymen have refused to
> marry couples because the parties differed racially, even in
> states where racial intermarriage is legal. A notorious case
> occurred in Rockville, Connecticut, early in 1928 when a
> Mayflower descendant, granddaughter of a Confederate
> general, and a Negro laborer took out a marriage license. All
> the Christian clergy in the community refused to marry the
> couple, compelling them to have a civil ceremony.[1]

Albert I. Gordon reinforced Barron's reportage and increased its general applicability:

> Religions that stress their universalism do not officially, at
> least, oppose interracial marriages. The Congregational
> Christian Church's declaration: "Race is relevant to
> marriage only insofar as our un-Christian color distinctions

make an interracial marriage more difficult than marriage within a given racial group," while recognizing the difficulties associated with interracial marriage also makes clear its conviction that racial difference ought really not to prevent otherwise good marriages.

    Other church and synagogue groups while recognizing the many problems associated with interracial marriage, make clear their official belief that the factor of difference in race is not an impediment to marriage.[2]

Opposition to black-white marriages does not necessarily prove prejudice where religious groups are involved, nevertheless

> religion, although it is said to be color-blind, is not always so. Despite its insistence upon equality of all men and the Biblical doctrines of the brotherhood of man and the fatherhood of God, persons who call themselves "religious" are not always free from racial prejudice. In theory, all the great religions see no inherent objection to racial intermarriage. In practice, however, they act as if they see many.[3]

The discrepancy between the Judeo-Christian unqualified affirmation of the equality of all men and the individual interpretations of some religious leaders is found even among clergymen who serve institutions of higher learning, where one would expect to find the most liberal religious leaders. In a survey of twenty-five Hillel directors and counselors who minister to Jewish students at twenty-eight different American colleges and universities, Gordon disclosed the following:

> Insofar as interracial marriages are concerned, 12 Hillel directors believe that they cannot work out successfully, while 3 state that *under certain conditions* they believe that they may be successful. Ten of the directors express no opinion on the matter.[4]

Thirty priests serving thirty-seven different colleges and universities presented their personal attitudes in response to a questionnaire:

> In the case of their attitude toward interracial marriages, 19 of the priests were "friendly" to them; 5 of these Newman Club directors expressed opposition to the idea, while 4 declared themselves "unconcerned." One priest declared that, although he was unopposed to such marriages in principle, he might not favor it in particular circumstances. One priest did not reply to this question.[5]

Forty-two Protestant ministers of major denominations (Presbyterian, Episcopal, Methodist, Church of God, United Church of Christ, Lutheran, Reformed Church in America, and Baptist) were polled and all were

> opposed to interracial marriages and give a variety of reasons therefor. They seem to agree that if interfaith intermarriage is likely to be difficult, marriages involving persons of different colors would be even more difficult. Yet, they venture the guess that interracial marriages, too, will increase within the next decade. They speak of the problems that the children of interracially married people might have. They express the hope that such marriages are not entered into as means of demonstrating rebellion against parents. In no case do they decry such marriages as "contrary to the will of God."[6]

The gap between the creed and practice of religious leaders is not entirely surprising, given the fact that ministers see themselves as enforcers of the mores of the people as well as seekers after the will of God. The general assumption that the dominant religious bodies in the United States officially proclaim brotherhood and therefore marriage in black and white merits consideration since there is such a gap between the declaration of the denominations and the will of religious laity and clergy.

In order to understand whether the credibility gap—declaring one thing and acting out another, vis-à-vis religion and black-white marriages—was a reflection of official policy and official folkways or unofficial policy and folkways, I wrote in June of 1966 to the denominational headquarters of every distinguishable religious body in the United States, requesting their policy statement. Some correspondents were shocked by my request, some were pleased to provide me with interpretational information, some were apologetic for not having an official statement, and most did not bother to respond. Those responses I received may or may not prove statistically representative, but their diversity considerably illuminates the importance of distinguishing between official and operational policy and mores. I shall draw upon this and other material here with the clear understanding that in many instances there is no official policy, but that resolutions of official bodies or statements by representative officials or publications of the denominations provide significant revelations.

The Roman Catholic position on black-white marriages is officially permissive. In order to be clear on this matter, I requested information from the former Bishop of Pittsburgh, Bishop Wright, recently elevated to Cardinal, who asked his Tribunal, the Right Reverend Msgr. Jacob C. Shinar, to reply:

> The Catholic Church has enacted no special legislation
> respecting interracial marriages. For the Catholic Church in
> her global perspective this is not a new situation. Yet she has
> always, and does continue to consider an interracial marriage
> by the same law and standard that she applies to any other
> marriage.

Without going into details respecting the historical stance of the Catholic Church, I find that the position stated by Tribunal Shinar is amplified by the Reverend Joseph F. Doherty in his doctoral dissertation at the Catholic University of America on *Moral Problems of Interracial Marriage:*

> Although interracial marriages have certain undesirable
> features, especially where they involve a white person in this
> country at the present time, nevertheless the fact that the
> Church will allow this type of marriage to her qualified

subjects indicates her great respect for the exercise of natural rights and her appreciation of the exalted worth of the benefits of marriage to the individual and to society. For this reason, it would be somewhat incautious to brand interracial marriage in general as something morally reproachable. There is little in the official documents of the Catholic Church bearing on interracial marriage, but where there is even an indirect reference the Church does not seem to indicate any displeasure.

The right to marry interracially and the individual of one's choice is a corollary of the natural right to marry in general. Since the exercise of natural rights is highly beneficial in itself, the same beneficial nature of exercising the right to marry interracially demands recognition. Collectively taken, the teaching of individual Catholic writers indicates that the entrance upon an interracial marriage is a morally good act despite certain undesirable circumstances that might accompany it.

These conclusions presume that the marriages in question have been entered upon in accordance with the dictates of Christian prudence. This prudence is based upon the principles of Christian faith and refers all things to the supernatural end of man, namely, God as He is known and loved on earth and as He is possessed in heaven. Christian prudence is not only concerned with man's destiny here on earth but also with his eternal destiny. In entering upon an interracial marriage when all the requirements of Christian prudence are fulfilled the individuals concerned act without reproach. In this evaluation it was recognized that there are advantages and benefits of sacramental and even natural marriage, the desire of which constitutes a motive of such a high order as to transcend other considerations of a lower order of importance militating against entrance upon an interracial marriage. These benefits involve a relationship to the ultimate end of man and as such they are of a higher order than mere temporal considerations.

The various objections which may be placed against interracial marriages, some of which are more or less grave, do not seem to be of sufficient weight in light of the principle of double effect to forbid interracial marriage when the parties themselves desire the exalted benefits of marriage and in their prudent judgment choose this particular type of marriage partner and as the prelude to great natural and supernatural benefits seems to be sufficient reason to contract such a marriage. Finally, it is to be observed that since the force of moral and social objections to these marriages varies so much with local and personal circumstances, Christian prudence having been observed, the charge of indiscretion cannot be leveled against them as a general rule.[7]

It is difficult to imagine two religious bodies further apart than the Roman Catholic Church and the Unitarian Universalist Association. But if we can be confident that Father Doherty's conclusions on "interracial marriage in the light of Catholic morality" are accurate, the following quotation from an official of the Unitarian Universalist Association shows a similar emphasis on the two individuals contemplating marriage "rather than upon the survival" of the religious institution:

A marriage, either interfaith or interracial, is a matter of primary concern to the two contracting parties. The Church would certainly support the action of those persons who, whatever the difference in religion or color, would wish to marry.[8]

While Roman Catholicism and the Unitarian Universalist Association agree on a common end although through totally different means, nevertheless the commonality of their end is extraordinary. Homer A. Jack of the Unitarian Universalist Association of Churches and Fellowships in North America informed me that the following resolution was approved by consensus at the fifth General Assembly meeting in May 1966:

Marriage between two persons is a sacred human institution. Persons who enter into the marriage bond should be able to do so with complete freedom of choice, since the choice of a marriage partner is a personal, not a public, decision. All laws which prohibit, inhibit, or hamper marriage or cohabitation between persons because of different races, religions, or national origins should be nullified or repealed. Adoption agencies are evidencing a more open attitude regarding the adoption of children of races other than that of the adoptive parents. This new attitude is commendable, especially in view of the pressing need of adoptive homes for children of mixed or minority races.

For Jews, "intermarriage" normally means marriage *outside the faith*—with the black-white issue injected by the insoluble problem of whether Jews are a race or a religion or both and in what proportion. Rabbi Arthur Hertzberg of Temple Emanu-El in Englewood, New Jersey, agreed that Rabbi Gordon's book *Intermarriage* "is generally accepted as an authoritative guide." Since Rabbi Gordon extensively treats the subject of black-white marriages and Judaism, it is well to quote here Rabbi Hertzberg, who puts the same Jewish perspective on black-white marriages in a nutshell, but with a slightly different emphasis:

I would add only one thing, that the essential argument from the Jewish point of view against intermarriage is not really a calculus as to whether it is likely to work out pleasantly for the young people concerned. It is, rather, a feeling that the bastion of Jewish continuity is the family. So long as that remains Jewish there is some guarantee that the tradition will continue with it. Therefore, Jews are so strongly concerned about intermarriage because they wish to insure the survival of their tradition.

I am sure what I am writing here is not far different than what comes through quite clearly in Rabbi Gordon's book. The position of Judaism on interracial marriage is, therefore, not at all a concern with the issue of race. It so happens that there are very few Negro Jews, but it is the non-Jew, rather than the Negro, who is the prime issue before the bar of Judaism. I do not mean to deny that individual Jews are particularly edgy about an interracial marriage for reasons of prejudice or of private concern as to the future of such a family, but that is not the issue that faces Judaism as religion. The leaders of the organized Jewish community are, almost without exception, hospitable to the interracial couple which has solved the religious question by opting together for Judaism.

The Mormons, officially known as The Church of Jesus Christ of Latter-Day Saints, replied to my request to President David O. McKay with the following statement signed by the secretary to the First Presidency:

> I am directed to tell you with reference to interracial marriages that the Church has never looked favorably upon such marriages. There have been few exceptions to the general experience that has extended over the past 135 years, that marriages between Caucasians and non-Caucasians are frequently unhappy and not infrequently lead to split families.

On June 10, 1966, Monroe H. Fleming of Salt Lake City wrote me the following:

> In this state we are faced with a Mormon theology that proclaims the inferiority of the Negro in the sight of God. We find this to be a dangerous doctrine and ministers, teachers and various groups are working hard to expose this doctrine to the world.

The polarization of these two statements from Salt Lake City increased my curiosity and led me to dig into the reasoning behind what seemed an official Mormon statement of opposition to black-white marriages.

John J. Stewart's *Mormonism and the Negro* seeks to make a theological case against black-white marriages:

> Briefly the LDS policy on Negroes is this: Negroes and other people with Negroid blood can become members of the

church and through righteous works receive patriarchal blessings, enter the temple to perform baptisms for the dead, become heirs to celestial kingdom and otherwise partake of many blessings afforded worthy members of the church, but they cannot be ordained to the Priesthood nor are they eligible for marriage in an LDS temple; Negroes and non-Negroes should not intermarry.

I now propose to show three important truths:

That the LDS doctrine of not allowing the Negro to bear the Priesthood is entirely consistent with both of the two great attributes of God himself, the attributes of justice and mercy.

That in this matter of the Negroes not holding the Priesthood we can gain a much clearer insight into those basic gospel principles of FREE AGENCY, FORE-ORDINATION and ETERNAL PROGRESS.

That a belief in the correctness of this doctrine is consistent with other beliefs and practices in daily life which we seldom if ever question.

We believe that we are fore-ordained to the privilege of membership in this church and Priesthood, privileged to be born under the favorable circumstances that we have been, at such an opportune time and place.

Now, if through fore-ordination, as a result of their performance in the spirit life certain individuals were privileged to be born under the most favorable circumstances, then it must necessarily follow that others would be born under less favorable circumstances.[9]

This religious apartheid can be traced back to the founding prophet Joseph Fielding Smith:

Why are so many inhabitants of the earth cursed with a skin of blackness? It comes in consequence of their fathers rejecting the power of the Holy Priesthood and law of God. They will go down to death, and when all the rest of the children (meaning the white and non-negroid races) have received their blessings then that curse will be removed from the seed of Cain.[10]

In his address to the Convention of Teachers of Religion on the College Level, delivered at Brigham Young University on August 27, 1954, and entitled "Race Problems—As They Affect The Church," Elder Mark E. Petersen defended segregation as the principle of God and therefore right:

> Who placed the Negroes originally in darkest Africa? Was it some man, or was it God? And when He placed them there, He segregated them. Who placed the Chinese in China? The Lord did. It was an act of segregation. . . . The Lord segregated the people both as to blood and place of residence. At least in the case of the Lamanites and the Negroes we have the definite word of the Lord himself that He placed a dark skin upon them as a curse—as a punishment and as a sign to all others. He forbade intermarriage with them under the threat of extension of the curse . . . And He certainly segregated the descendants of Cain when He cursed the Negro as to the Priesthood, and drew an absolute line. You may even say He dropped an Iron curtain there. The Negro was cursed as to the Priesthood, and therefore, was cursed as to the blessings of the Priesthood. Certainly God made a segregation there.

The distinguished critic and authority on Mormonism, Dr. Sterling M. McMurrin, a Mormon, traces this religious apartheid back to the 1840's when the early church got into trouble partly because it had two or three free blacks "in full fellowship" when the Mormons migrated to Missouri, where blacks were slaves. This experience produced a sort of Missouri Compromise. Blacks could belong to the church but not to the priesthood. The priesthood is a lay body made up of all male members of the church in good standing who are not blacks. Professor of philosophy at the University of Utah and former United States Commissioner of Education, Dr. McMurrin holds that the Mormons picked up the crude superstition of a divine curse on blacks from Southern white Protestants in the 1840's and that the superstition which interprets the blacks' dark skin results from God's curse upon Cain for killing Abel is not a church doctrine, though many like Elder

Petersen believe it to be a doctrine. The only official practice of the Mormon church is that of refusing blacks admittance to the priesthood. President McKay believes it will take more than a generation to change this practice. Dr. McMurrin states that the whole problem revolves around the singular issue of black-white marriages:

> The problem isn't theological, it's intermarriage. I don't feel that Mormons, depending on where they live discriminate any more than any other Northerner or Westerner.[11]

In his address at Brigham Young University, Elder Petersen provided evidence that intermarriage is the touchstone of tension between blacks and whites via Mormonism:

> He [the Negro] is not just seeking the opportunity of sitting down in a cafe where white people eat. He isn't just trying to ride on the same street car or the same Pullman car with white people. It isn't that he just desires to go to the same theater as the white people. . . . it appears that the Negro seeks absorption with the white race. He will not be satisfied until he achieves it by intermarriage. That is his objective and we must face it.

Elder Petersen closed his address in the following manner which exemplifies the depth of official Mormon opposition to marriage in black and white:

> Now what is our policy in regard to intermarriage? As to the Negro, there is only one possible answer. We must not intermarry with the Negro. Why? If I were to marry a Negro woman and have children by her, my children would all be cursed as to the priesthood. Do I want my children cursed as to the priesthood? If there is one drop of Negro blood in my children, as I have read to you, they received the curse. There isn't any argument, therefore, as to intermarriage with the Negro, is there? There are 50 million Negroes in the United States. If they were to achieve complete absorption with the

white race, where would the priesthood be? Who could hold it, in all America? Think what that would do to the work of the Church?

Now we are generous with the Negro. We are willing that the Negro have the highest kind of education. I would be willing to let every Negro drive a Cadillac if they could afford it. I would be willing that they have all the advantages they can get out of life in the world. But let them enjoy these things among themselves. I think the Lord segregated the Negro and who is man to change that segregation? It reminds me of the scripture on marriage, "What God hath joined together, let not man put asunder." Only here we have the reverse of the thing: What God hath separate, let not man bring together again.

His Grace Archbishop Sion Manoogian informed me through his director of information "that on the question of inter-marriage, the Armenian Church has no official position." Thomas F. Zimmerman, General Superintendent for the General Council of the Assemblies of God responded to my inquiry candidly:

I would have to say that the matter of interracial marriage has never been a topic of discussion in the Assemblies of God. For this reason, no position has been stated and we have no policy that covers this matter.

I am sorry I cannot be of more precise help to you, but since we do not have any action or policy concerning this, I do not have anything to report to you.

Mr. Zimmerman's response, like that of Archbishop Manoogian and those of many other denominational leaders, makes clear the limited number of blacks in their communion, the emphasis upon individual participation in the sacraments or individual salvation, and the very recent awareness of social dynamics whereby religious bodies give consent to the common mores by their silence.

Several religious bodies have not dealt specifically with black-white marriages, but when questioned on their stand, their officials indicate an indirect connection between the church stance on racial justice and black-white marriages. A. Stauffer Curry, director of family education for the Church of the Brethren pointed out that at the 1963 Annual Conference a statement was adopted entitled "The Time Is Now to Heal Our Racial Brokenness":

> This was a call to action on the part of our churches to do something in the area of racial justice. While there is nothing directly on interracial marriage in the statement, it is of course assumed that justice in this area is a part of the overall area of justice in racial relations.

This document has some broad phrases which could possibly be interpreted as supportive of black-white marriages:

> The *time is now* to heal every broken race relationship and every segregated institution in our society—every church, every public accommodation, every place of employment, every neighborhood, and every school. Our goal must be nothing less than an integrated church in an integrated community.
>
> Our witness has not matched our basic belief that every child of God is a brother to every other.
>
> The *call of Christ* is for commitment and courage in such a time as this. This call comes to every one of us, every congregation among us, and every community in which we live. We can dodge neither the revolution nor the call of Christ. Let us respond in works as eloquent as our words, in practices as profound as our prayers, in action as heroic as our gospel.

A similar position has been taken by the American Baptist Convention. R. Dean Goodwin, executive director of the ABC's general program and administration, division of communication, stated that "our denomination has not made any statement directly on the subject of interracial marriage," but mentions a relevant resolution which was passed by the Convention in San Francisco in May, 1965:

We recognize that any form of segregation based on race is contrary to the gospel of Jesus Christ and is incompatible with the Christian doctrine of man and with the nature of the Church of Christ. Whenever and wherever Christians, individually or collectively, practice segregation by action or inaction, we betray Christ and the fellowship which bears His name.

We confess that un-Christian racial attitudes and conformity to the unjust mores of secular society have produced segregated churches which have failed to challenge unjust practices in the world.

Dr. Carl F. Reuss, director of research and social action for the American Lutheran Church, forwarded to me a statement commended by the church on "Effective Ministry in Intercultural Communities." The following excerpt captures the thrust of the document:

Segregation and social stratification, both based on essentially external differences, regrettably occur in Christian churches. Segregation grows out of many different causes such as tradition, custom, and economics, and is frequently interrelated with man's prejudices, fear, envy, and pride. It is not always easy to discern which is the dominant factor. Segregation often finds its support in differences in skin color or physical appearance. Social stratification is reflected in levels of wealth, education, or social standing. Frequently these man-made distinctions of race and class restrict the ministry of love and belie the fundamental unity of the human race in the redemptive plan of God as revealed in Jesus Christ.

Wherever and whenever the churches help to foster race or class distinctions between people, and wherever and whenever they support attitudes of superiority or inferiority between persons, groups, or classes on the basis of race, class, national or ethnic origin, or economic position they violate God's will.

Were His Spirit to rule in men's hearts and lives,

problems of racial segregation and harmful social stratification would diminish. The free and voluntary actions of men who genuinely love neighbor as self because of God's love for them will exceed in justice and equity the compulsory actions forced by decree upon the unwilling.

The above statement was adopted by the Second General Convention of the American Lutheran Church, October 21–27, 1964. This same Convention adopted the following statement which is by far the most specific statement made by any of the denominations on the function of the pastor. In the light of the statement quoted above, this advice may well serve to be enabling rather than disabling:

Particularly difficult is the request to officiate at the marriage of a man and a woman markedly different in such characteristics as religion, race, age, and cultural background. Such a marriage presents complex problems fraught with difficulties. The pastor should insist that the couple examine carefully the consequences of their marriage for themselves, their children, their families, their congregations, and their community. Only when the pastor is firmly convinced that the two are sufficiently strong and mature, both spiritually and emotionally, to overcome the hazards to a sound marriage which their marked differences in background, experience, and outlook impose, should he officiate at the desired marriage.

The Lutheran Church–Missouri Synod has been less direct in instructing its pastors; perhaps this indirectness reflects a more conservative or traditional stance. Its secretary of adult education, Oscar E. Feucht, reports:

Actually our church body as such has made no official pronouncement on interracial marriage, perhaps because it felt that every case deserved to be treated separately and that social implications would have to be taken into consideration by the counselor.

It is quite clear that no national convention of any denomination can speak for all of its constituents, but it can be influential in informing both the laity and the clergy of the plumb line by which their attitudes and actions should be guided. There is a general tendency among many denominations to ignore the specific issues involved in black-white marriages or to ignore the implications of black-white marriages and to deal generally with the whole rub between blacks and whites in our society. Insofar as denominations deal in broad policy statements and do not wrestle with the specific issue of black-white marriages they leave each individual layman or clergyman, on his own, to discover the appropriate response, and this laissez-faire policy is tantamount to placing members of the denomination at the disposal of the dominant mores of the society, a policy which allows the Church to be transformed by the world when its stated purpose is to transform the world through the renewing of its mind.

It is understandable that no in-depth wrestling with black-white marriages should appear in the annual meetings, official publications, and unofficial resolutions of the Christian Science Church since, as David Sleeper, manager of the committees on publication, explains

> that for the Christian Scientist this subject along with a
> number of related matters is for individual determination. In
> general, our church does not make specific rulings on social
> and family matters.

The Evangelical United Brethren Church takes quite a different stance. Cawley H. Stine, director of the department of Christian social action, sets forth its position with candor and reveals the denomination's limited sense of the depth of its involvement in the status quo:

> The position of our Church emphasizes Christian Marriage
> in its truest form. It makes no reference whatsoever to the
> race issue.
> The 1963 Discipline of the Evangelical United Brethren
> Church, paragraph 923, part 173 states "virtue and morality

in society, stability and permanence of free government can
be had only as the Christian home is maintained in its
integrity. . . ."

The Church does not promote neither does it deny the
right of interracial marriage. However, I believe our ministers
would counsel the contracting parties as to the acceptance of
society of such marriage with particular reference to the
possible children involved.

There is a credibility gap in the EUB's position, and this gap
can be demonstrated most clearly by comparing the EUB's position on black-white marriages with that of the Bahá'ís, set forth
than in a pamphlet entitled "Unity from Diversity," which is put
out by the National Spiritual Assembly of the Bahá'ís of the
United States. Dr. David S. Ruhe, Secretary for the Assembly, reminds me that there is "no official position paper as such" by the
Bahá'ís, but that "the Bahá'í Faith believes in marriage. It does
not hold with any concepts of special racial virtues, and holds
that interracial marriages of all kinds are good, providing only
that they are entered into with honor, love and loyalty." In their
pamphlet we have the most specific and thorough and responsible
statement made by any religious body in America, with the possible exceptions of the United Church of Christ and the United
Presbyterian Church in the United States of America:

> The basic Bahá'í principle of the oneness of mankind
> inevitably leads to the free association of peoples of all races
> and nationalities based on equal rights and common
> responsibilities. Among these rights is the right to select a
> mate without regard to religious background, nationality, or
> race.
>   Of all the barriers to the various forms of mixed
> marriages, those against interracial marriage are the most
> difficult to eliminate because of the easily recognizable
> physical characteristics which are inherited by the members
> of various racial groups, especially that of skin color.
> Nonetheless, belief in the unity of mankind demands the
> rejection of restrictions on marriage based upon race. The

Bahá'í position on this issue is clear. "Abdu'l-Bahá, son of Báhá'u'lláh, wrote:

> *"If it be possible, gather together these two races, black and white, into one Assembly and put such love into their hearts that they shall not only unite, but even intermarry. Be sure that the result of this will abolish differences and disputes between black and white. Moreover, by the Will of God, may it be so! This is a great service to humanity."*

Prohibitions against interracial marriage originate in the false belief that some races are inferior to others and that intermarriage therefore causes the deterioration of the stock which is presumed to be better. However, there is no evidence that any race is superior or inferior to any other, and the fear that the offspring of an interracial marriage is likely to be defective is completely unfounded. Geneticists have demonstrated that there are no deleterious biological effects from interracial unions as such. In fact, there is considerable anthropological and historical evidence that some blending of races has produced physical types in various areas of the world that have been superior to the parental stocks. Such mixture is known to have also resulted in a reinvigoration of mental powers and increased diversification of creative talent.

Unfortunately, children from interracial unions are frequently subjected to more discrimination than are children from parents of the same race because they tend to be rejected by both of the racial groups to which their parents belong. Any behavioral disorders which they may have are commonly caused by social and economic pressures and not by inherited predispositions of any identifiable racial character.

While the Bahá'í Faith teaches that racial traits are not important in selecting a marriage partner, it is made clear that the good character of those betrothed and the support from their families is essential to a stable union. "The Bahá'í betrothal is the perfect agreement and entire agreement and entire consent of both parties. They must show forth the utmost attention and become informed of one another's character. The firm covenant between them must become an eternal binding, and their intentions must be everlasting affinity, friendship, unity and life."

Since the solidarity of society ultimately depends upon the stability of the family, it is important for every marriage to bring the families of the betrothed together in a spirit of unity and harmony. For this reason, Bahá'ís are obligated to recognize the wisdom and experience of their parents by marrying only with parental consent. "Bahá'u'lláh has stated [that] the consent of all living parents is required for a Bahá'í marriage. . . . This great law He has laid down to strengthen the social fabric, to knit closer the ties of the home, to place a certain gratitude and respect in the heart of children for those who have given them life and sent their souls out on the eternal journey toward their Creator."

The racial diversity of Bahá'í communities throughout the world is a demonstration of the power of the Faith of Bahá'u'lláh to remove prejudice and create respect for all human rights, including the right to marry without regard to race.

The revolutionary character of this document is unmistakable. Its call for the right of individuals to marry and its call for familial support of individuals who wish to marry is not only a responsible statement of respect for parents by children but of respect for children by parents. The right to marry without respect to color of skin requires a challenge to change the traditional mores.

The dictum of Bahá'u'lláh, "close your eyes to racial differences and welcome all with the light of oneness," is not antithetical to the position adopted by the Fifth General Synod of the United Church of Christ, on July 5, 1963. The UCC in its official statement calls for radical commitment by the church in the struggle of fellowmen:

> To gain acceptance as a person of worth who may marry whomever he loves and whoever loves him. . . .

This position is reinforced by the call for immediate enactment providing

> equal protection under the law, and the repeal of all racially discriminatory laws, such as laws prohibiting marriage across racial lines and racially discriminatory immigration laws.

Prior to merging with the Evangelical and Reformed Churches and becoming the United Church of Christ, the former Congregational Christian Churches developed a publication by its committee on church and race in 1947. In 1960, the UCC Council for Christian Social Action published a discussion paper on "Marriage Across Racial Lines."

Methodists have not taken a position on black-white marriages, and the response suggested by the distinguished Methodist who serves as Professor of Theology at Southern Methodist University's Perkins School of Theology, Dr. Albert C. Outler, is instructive:

> The answer would seem to be, as far as I can discover, that there is *no* official position of The Methodist Church on this specific point—other than the general constitutional rule that ministers are bound to obey the civil laws in the political units where they reside, and this would apply to marriage as a civil contract. Since Methodists have rejected the notion of marriage as a sacrament, the only two aspects under which it *can* be considered as a civil contract—theoretically, at least, as valid when performed by a civil magistrate as by a clergyman—or as a single instance of the generalized theory of interpersonal relations, which has always held that men (and women) are free to do as they will insofar as what they will does not stultify the freedom of others to do what *they* will—within the framework of *public order.*
>
> So much for the theory—or lack of one. You would know, of course, that what really governs such matters, in the absence of a theory or sacramental doctrine, is the mores and prejudices of various communities and the circumstances of the particular people involved.

It may well be that the reasons advanced by Professor Outler were part of the dynamics which led the division of human relations and economic affairs of the general board of Christian social concerns of the Methodist Church to accept the UCC discussion paper as its own study paper, entitling it "A Christian Approach to the Question of Interracial Marriage." This UCC paper, adopted by an agency of the Methodist Church, examines, briefly, the historical development of the issue of black-white marriages, and includes this summary analysis:

> The marital question is usually raised in the form, "Would you want your daughter (or sister) to marry a Negro?" The assumption is that the relation involves a colored man and a white woman. The irony of the situation is that the mingling of races has occurred, for the most part, in the opposite way. For generations white men have taken advantage of colored women who, as slaves or as free women of an oppressed group, had no legal or economic protection. With the insights of modern psychology we can see how this deeply suppressed guilt in our society expresses itself in the reverse fear that the Negro man seeks the white woman. Until our society recognizes and acknowledges this guilt, it has great difficulty in thinking in a rational and Christian way about marriage between persons of different races.
>
> Nothing of this historical background constitutes an argument for or against "intermarriage." But until we honestly acknowledge the facts and guilt of our society, we cannot separate the real problems of marriage from the false problems that often get greater attention. As we see ourselves and our history more clearly, we can face God more honestly and seek His will for ourselves and our society.

While religious groups have taken stronger and more significant stands than social scientists on the question of black-white marriages, they have not departed from the social scientists in holding to the notion of black-white marriages as "intermarriage," which in effect reinforces the notion of these marriages as *outside the par-*

ticular group. This failure is not in keeping with the biblical grounds on which these religious groups stand to challenge custom and eliminate guilt.

For example, the UCC statement or discussion paper holds that marriage "is instituted by God himself (Genesis 2:24)." On this biblical ground, marriage is "a part of God's purpose for the growth of human personality, the nurture of children, and the achievement of the most primary of all communities, the family." It follows then that marriage is basically a call of union of two persons, not two races, and the use of the term "intermarriage" is divisive rather than unitive as demanded by God "in the Christian view":

> Marriage is a voluntary relationship into which people enter not because they must, but because they have so chosen. The Church has sought to give counsel to those entering this relationship and to help them develop Christian homes when the family is established. In the Christian view, marriage involves the union of two persons—not two races; thus it is no more concerned with the color of skin of those marrying than with the color of their eyes or hair.

In adopting the study paper of the UCC, the agency of the Methodist Church also refrained from the use of "intermarriage" when referring to black-white marriages, a step which indicates the depth of their thinking out of the Christian perspective. Even more important, however, is the new ground broken in this UCC study paper with respect to the task of the Church:

> The first task of the Church towards those entering into matrimony is *to offer sound counsel.* It should help the two principal parties to examine their own emotional maturity, their spiritual resources, and their preparation for the responsibilities of establishing a Christian home. When the marriage is across racial lines, the Church should also help them prepare for whatever social tension results from a sub-Christian social climate.

In addition to spelling out specific ways the Church can help, the statement stresses the positive rather than negative approach:

> Although obstacles confronting a couple marrying across racial lines may be greater than in other cases, this in itself is no reason for the Church to discourage that couple from marrying. Obstacles may be a blessing, bringing about a greater cohesiveness and solidarity.

Further, we learn that the second task of the Church is to help those entering upon matrimony to develop a Christian home:

> The Church is called upon by its Lord to minister to all families alike, offering to each the opportunity of worship, fellowship, and service. Those who have established families across racial lines may be particularly in need of the encouragement and support of the Church in stabilizing their family life. Although it may not be able to determine the make-up and behavior of the community, the Church should seek in its own life to show that inclusiveness and fellowship which is the reality and foretaste of the Kingdom.

With all of this instruction, the UCC statement is especially crucial and extraordinary because it, unlike most religious statements on the matter of black-white marriages, does not shrink from the basic task of reforming the society:

> The Church is called upon to oppose those elements in society which are destructive to family life and to promote those elements which contribute to family welfare and stability. It should, therefore, foster a warm and hospitable atmosphere in the community for every family and fight all that is destructive to human dignity such as legal barriers to marriage across racial lines, restrictive housing, unequal job opportunity, and the denial of public facilities and services.

Whether or not there is a theology or theory or sacramental doctrine, the mores and customs really govern people vis-à-vis black-white marriages. Therefore, churches are required by their own biblical and Christian tradition to make possible the living out of their espoused teachings. Herein lies an important distinction between Christians who take seriously the need to reform the society as well as to counsel individuals wisely, and the totally individual instruction of the American Ethical Union as stated by Howard B. Radest, its executive director:

> With respect to your question on the Ethical Culture Movement's attitude toward intermarriage, quite simply the Ethical Movement from the outset has recognized the problem of marriage as a human problem and has tried to deal with people regardless of the labels or adjectives attached to them or the origins from which they come. Of course in our pre-marital meetings with the couple and on occasion with the families involved, the question of religious origin is discussed in order to assess whether or not any potential tensions may be in the situation. If so, then we do try to counsel on how to deal with them. We have, unfortunately, no statistics available. I can only give you an impression that many of the marriages we conduct would be called intermarriages by those looking at it from the outside. I think I should also say that we do not have any policy with respect to insisting on membership in the Ethical Movement as a prior condition of conducting marriage ceremonies or advising people preparing for marriages, and as you know about our Movement there are no creedal requirements.

At its General Convention of 1964 the Protestant Episcopal Church adopted a general statement on "The Church Speaks" which covered "racial inclusiveness." Though the Episcopal Church has a sacramental doctrine respecting marriage, the pressures of our times led Episcopalians to

> solemnly reaffirm the mandate laid upon the Church to proclaim unfailingly in its worship, its sacraments and rites, and in what it does in the world, that racial discrimination, segregation, and the exclusion of any person in the human

family because of race, from the rites and activities of the Church, in any form whatsoever, are contrary to the mind of Christ and the Church which is His body.

The 1964 Convention also felt the need to deal specifically with the matter of black-white marriages. The matter was not resolved, nor were clear and specific instructions worked out for either the laity or the clergy, but a resolution was studied by the influential body, as pointed out in this response from the Secretary of the General Convention:

The matter of inter-racial marriages was brought before the General Convention of 1964, meeting in St. Louis, in the form of a Resolution adopted by the Annual Convention of the Diocese of Central New York and introduced by one of the Lay Deputies from that Diocese. The resolution read as follows:

Whereas, Laws in some States, both north and south, forbidding marriages between persons of different races, have caused grief to some loyal members of this Church and have caused the clergy to act sometimes in ways which have compromised their sense of justice; and

Whereas, It is clearly contrary to the spirit of the teachings of our Lord and of St. Paul that racial, social, or national distinctions be raised as barriers to marriage; and

Whereas, The Church neither encourages nor prohibits inter-racial marriages, but only counsels persons in the proper exercise of their individual freedom; therefore, be it

Resolved, That this 61st General Convention publicly acknowledge that there are no theological or moral barriers to marriages between persons of different races.

The Resolution was referred to the Standing Committee of the House on Christian Social Relations, which reported by asking to be discharged from further consideration of the matter, on the grounds that two prior actions of the General Convention had adequately dealt with the subject. The Committee was so discharged.

The two matters to which the Committee referred were

(1) An amendment to Canon 16, "Of Regulations
Respecting the Laity," by the addition of a new Section
(4), which provided that no communicant or baptized
member of the Church shall be excluded "from the worship
or Sacraments of the Church, nor from parochial
membership, because of race, color, or ethnic origin."
(2) The adoption, concurrently with the House of
Bishops, of a Resolution entitled, "Racial Inclusiveness of
the Church" [set forth above].

We have seen that the Mormons oppose black-white marriages, in principle and in practice, and that many other religious
bodies are concerned to counsel caution if persons to be married
are within their faith, although there are notable exceptions such
as the Bahá'ís and the American Ethical Union. The groups emphasizing the parietal and peremptory prerogatives in support of
"the cake of custom" may be larger in number and more influential than those which are more permissive. One body which appears as close to the neutral zone as any is The General Conference Mennonite Church. According to its executive secretary,
Orlando A. Waltner, the Conference "has not issued an official
statement on the question of interracial marriage":

Without doubt, interreligious marriages are for us less
acceptable than interracial marriages. And although no
official statement on our part encourages interracial
marriages, a number of such marriages have taken place in
our church.
Implication of the section "Our Commitment"
appearing in the Declaration on Race Relations would be
that we permit persons of different races to marry provided
they have similar religious convictions.

A recommendation by the board of reference and counsel to the
49th session of The General Conference of Mennonite Brethren
Churches held in Winnipeg, Manitoba, August 3–7, 1963, led
R. M. Baerg, dean of the Mennonite Brethren Biblical Seminary,
to write:

With respect to the discussion on racial intermarriage, it was stated from the floor that *the Scriptures do not forbid intermarriage* as such; but that both parties contracting such marriage relations should be carefully counselled and instructed as to the social problems they would encounter in a society that is not entirely favorable to racial intermarriages.

The Mennonite position differs little from that expressed by William Culbertson, president of Moody Bible Institute, who might be expected to be of the Mormon inclination:

I do not see anything in the Word of God which proscribes interracial marriage. I do feel, that there are sociological problems that must be faced, which have to do with different cultures, the conditions the children may have to face, and such like. These must be weighed as before God and the mind of the Lord secured by the child of God. So far as Christians are concerned, the mandatory Scripture, in my judgment, is that both parties know the Lord.

It seems to me the kind of marriage you speak about has its special considerations which require much maturity. In any case, maturity should characterize the parties agreeing to enter into marriage at all. In other words, in the language of one of the services, it is not to be "entered into unadvisedly or lightly; but reverently, discreetly, advisedly, soberly and in the fear of God."

It might be anticipated that the most permissive or supportive or open statement would come from the Religious Society of Friends, popularly known as the Quakers. Hertha Reinemann, chairman of the family relations committee of the Philadelphia Yearly Meeting, in cooperation with Ross Roby, M.D., and consultant to the counseling service of the family relations committee, composed a statement believed to be "the consensus position of most Yearly Meetings in the Northeastern and Western parts of the United States," but which is in no way official:

We, Quakers, are often asked for the official stand of the Religious Society of Friends on a number of social problems which have ethical and moral implications. We usually introduce the answer by restating one of the essential tenets of Friends' belief; namely, that each person is free to follow the light that is within him; further, that his conscience, formed by Christian precepts and a very personal sense of the spirit of light and truth, will lead each member into the way that is right.

The various Yearly Meetings of Friends have laid down principles for appropriate Quaker action in books of "Faith and Practice" or "Books of Discipline." However, no specific advice on the rightness or wrongness of interracial marriages will be found therein.

We often turn to a brief historical review of Quaker customs for guidance in answering questions on faith and morals. As a background for the query on interracial marriage, it is well to point out that there was a long period—one or two centuries—when Quakers could not marry persons of different religious affiliation without losing their membership in the Society of Friends. Historically, the Society was made up almost entirely of immigrants or their descendants from the British Isles and, to a very small degree, from other European Countries. It was thus not faced with problems of interracial marriages. On the other hand, there has been an equally long tradition of Friends' concern for interracial understanding, justice and peaceful co-existence, beginning with William Penn's design for peace and justice, between whites and Indians, and continuing with active participation and leadership in the anti-slavery and civil rights movements.

We are aware that there are now numerous members of meetings, particularly in the urban and Northeastern parts of the United States, whose marriage partners are not Friends; and stricture against such interreligious marriages—which at the same time, might also be interracial—has long been abandoned. There are also some marriage partners, belonging to a non-white race, who are members of the Society of Friends.

Many Friends feel that Quaker principles demand complete approval on the part of the Monthly Meetings to whom application for a contemplated interracial marriage is made, and wish to support such couples wholeheartedly. But there are also many Friends who feel that interracial marriages present such insuperable difficulties for the marriage partners and their children that they cannot look with favor on them.

As can be seen, there are no uniform positions on interracial marriages in the Society of Friends. It can be said, however, that there is a most sincere effort to receive requests for interracial marriages and act upon them with a special measure of love and understanding on the part of most Monthly Meetings in order to further our goal of Christian Brotherhood.

We began this chapter with the cue given us by authoritative researchers that religion is not opposed to black-white marriages *de jure,* although a number of religious bodies are opposed to black-white marriages *de facto.* It is the *de facto* opposition of most religious and nonreligious people in America which is our basic concern. The variety of responses from religious institutions to my queries about their stand on black-white marriages makes clear that only the exceptional religious organization is willing to confront the common mores, and in such organizations it is the voice of the hierarchy in particular which is willing to challenge the mores, and not the members at large. The reports from what may be viewed as nonrepresentative sources—but sources that must be accepted as indicative of the thinking of religious bodies in the United States—are important as set forth here because they reveal the real ethos of our society, and how this ethos is continued and supported in conscious and unconscious ways by that religion which gives first allegiance to custom rather than to God in a matter vital to human welfare.

In reviewing the general acquiescence of religious institutions to social custom, it is most exceptional to find ecclesiastical bodies expressing unadulterated hatred of blacks by direct opposition to black-white marriages. While no Southern-based body responded to my query, we would not expect to find a body such as the Southern Baptist being so bold as to rule blacks out in the way the Mormons have. Thus, beneath the surface, the issue of black-white marriages as a singular instance of policy among denominations turns out to have extraordinary depths of evil or demonic institutional collusion, not because love of blacks is circumscribed or because hatred of blacks is vociferous—but because indifference is the dominant response to black-white marriages. There is no doubt that all religious institutions are fully cognizant of marriages in black and white as the real test of full communion and acceptance into the fellowship of the concerned and the caring. Black-white marriages are the touchstone of commitment to a truly human or Christian society, if what the gospel denominations preach and the social concerns departments they support are to be taken seriously. Caring in this sphere, like charity, should begin in the churches and then spread abroad, where it is not abroad to be spread into the churches, if the churches are to be about their business of responding to God rather than to man-made commandments.

So, the important question for religion vis-à-vis blacks in America and social justice is not whether religious bodies oppose black-white marriages *de jure*—the real question is what action churchmen are taking to undo their support of the segregation of blacks from whites which has occurred throughout our history and which makes this society the racist society it is. The unacceptableness of black-white marriages by religious bodies is due to their unacceptableness by the customs of the society which is due to mores which hold blacks to be inferior and whites superior. This unspeakable assumption is unquestioned or unchallenged in large measure because religious bodies believe it and therefore support it by their indifference to and silence on the question of black-white marriages.

There is no doubt at all that if the churches were serious about the matter of the equality of blacks and whites they could launch an educational program through their church schools, women's circles, adult educational groups, and other communication avenues that would reach every constituent from the cradle to the grave and teach consistently and on a regular basis that black-white marriages are good and right and valuable without reservation. Such a program is within the bounds and easy management of religious institutions, which some day must pay for the generations they have told their parishioners it is understandable that they do not wish their sister or daughter to marry a black. The only way the churches can attack the decadent mores they support and show they have overthrown their duplicity in this vicious collaboration is to teach every member of every congregation in every hamlet, village, town, city, and metropolis to say "Yes, I want my sister (daughter) to marry a black," though she may not be so fortunate. American Christians could take a cue in this regard from Professor Otto Piper, who declares in his *The Biblical View of Sex and Marriage* that churches and every other form of government

> have no right to prohibit inter-racial marriages. Such a prohibition is a denial of the unity of the human family established by the fact that notwithstanding racial differences God has called all mankind to salvation. Whether or not one should actually conclude an inter-racial marriage is a question of expedience rather than of principle. It seems, for instance, that in not a few cases marriages between whites and colored people in the United States encounter special difficulties, since the colored community looks upon the white person as an intruder while the colored person is shunned by a section of the white group. However, the difficulties of this problem might conceivably motivate some Christians to enter deliberately into such a marriage in order to relieve some of the existing prejudices.[12]

A substantial beginning toward being radical and relevant in rooting out the evil which plagues Christians and their non-Christian brothers and sisters has been made by a significant number of denominations which, like the United Presbyterian Church in the United States, has set forth *a bold call to suffer:*

> Believing that racial segregation is a problem of such magnitude and urgency that it takes precedence over other social issues in American life today,

Acknowledging that the continuing tensions with regard to race relations expose the faithlessness of the church, Being convinced that the General Assembly has stated the position of our church so clearly and explicitly that further exhortation can only emphasize the gulf between what we profess and what we do,

The 169th General Assembly makes bold to call the members and ministers of the churches to the vocation of suffering for the sake of truth and justice, for "we should not be surprised at the fiery ordeal which comes upon us" (I Peter 4:12) when we seek to obey the call of Christ, and to encourage and support one another in bearing witness to the gospel according to which God makes no distinctions as to race or origin, and expresses our sense of fellowship with those of our own and other communions who have suffered for their witness to the gospel in this matter. (1957)

In 1965 the General Assembly made its first official statement concerning black-white marriages in a resolution which followed upon the previous call to suffering. The 177th General Assembly

Recognizes that the issue of interracial marriage is a reality that cannot be ignored and finds no scriptural or theological grounds condemning or prohibiting the marriage of a man and a woman of different races.

Urges United Presbyterians to work with others for the repeal or nullification of laws that prohibit interracial marriage.

The call to bold suffering and its link with support of black-white marriages can only be meaningful if Presbyterians and other like-minded Christians really suffer. The only real suffering white Christians can engage in to bring about racial justice is suffering through changing the mores of its fellowships and by extension those of the society with respect to creating a climate in which black-white marriages are accepted, supported, and viewed as right and natural. When whites ask what they can do amidst this human revolution in which blacks are doing their "own thing" in separation from whites, the answer is for whites to take the initiative in their own immediate fellowships to create a climate of acceptance of black-white marriages, for on this acceptance lies the acceptance of blacks, which is the objective blacks seek. Whites must take the initiative in accomplishing a climate of acceptance for black-white marriages since they took the initiative in preventing blacks from being totally acceptable without reservation in the most intimate and public and respectable spheres of human diversity in unity.

The cardinal error of white Christians is their insistence on regarding all human beings as individuals in a racist society, which means that the emphasis upon personal worth is sheer rhetoric. With this orientation, white Christians are honestly seeking to avoid the error of apartheid, which persists in ignoring the personal worth of individuals

> because it always treats them as members of a particular ethnic group and in so doing personified the racial group, the tribe, the race. Indeed, it declares in effect that the individual has worth only as he has a value to the racial group to which he happens to belong. Such a theory must be condemned as unethical. It is at this point that *apartheid* demonstrates most clearly that it is immoral, because it seeks to deal with people not as persons, but as members of a particular group.[13]

Our society is not an apartheid society, but it is nearly so in that it is racist, which means black people qua black people are not acceptable. To treat each black as an individual has less meaning at this juncture of history when it is the black group which is despised and rejected. The thrust must be toward the acceptance of the black group and when the black group finds acceptance, it will then be possible for whites to act meaningfully with respect to the individual worth of black persons. That is why whites who are Christians and who seek justice must undo the injustice of the past rejection of the black group through a dynamic educational program throughout the length and breadth of religious institutions which makes real the only reality, that blacks are acceptable marriage partners for white brothers and sisters.

Christians have largely transcended the peremptory or authoritative forces such as the clerical and legal factors which enforce the mores against black-white marriages. Christians agree, largely, with the position that there is nothing intrinsically wrong with black-white marriages. But they still hold to the enforcement of peremptory factors such as parental wishes, moral commitments, and social customs in the belief that these extrinsic factors make black-white marriages wrong. Now this concern with extrinsic factors is really a Roman Catholic position, consistent with its teachings that are always and everywhere geared to the social climate in which the Church abides. Father John La Farge and Monsignor Francis Gilligan are in the mainstream of Roman Catholic feeling when they say that individuals at the present time should not marry if they are black and white because of the opposition of public opinion, which should not be changed but respected:

> Even though the biological and social evils of miscegenation have not been proved and are probably incapable of proof, a marriage between a Negro and a white person in the United States at the present time, would place a considerable handicap on the moral life of the contracting parties. For that reason it would be wrong in an overwhelming number of cases for a member of either race to enter into an interracial marriage.[14]

Protestants have followed Roman Catholics in very few pragmatic areas since the Reformation and in many instances (on the issue of birth control, for example) have led many Roman Catholics to come around to their way of acting if not thinking. Protestants would not be true to themselves and their call to be bold in suffering for racial justice were they to follow the Roman Catholic inclination in the sphere of black-white marriages, for as the late Bishop James A. Pike reminded us,

> to be true to its character, the ethic of the reformed Churches would have to start with the assertion of the positive responsibilities of the individual.[15]

Christians are keenly aware of the fact, or ought to be, that the issue of black-white marriages is not in essence the question of the compatibility of one black and one white person. In essence the issue is the acceptance of blacks by whites so that blacks can accept whites. It is simplistic subterfuge to approach a black-white marriage by asking individuals to change to meet social custom instead of by changing social custom to meet the right to marry as a basic human right and the right to marry a person of one's choice as a necessary corollary which belongs to all by reason of nature. It takes no imagination to list the difficulties of black-white marriages:

1. A black-white marriage conjures up the fears of mongrelization and challenges the assumption of white superiority and black inferiority which seeks to destroy the fact of human equality.

2. A black-white marriage calls into question the preconscious white folk religion that blacks and whites are by nature incompatible.

3. A black-white marriage overrides, in the name of equality in the quick and justice on the make, the political, social, economic, and cultural motives for segregation and discrimination in the intimate spheres.

4. A black-white marriage conjures up the guilt and despair of sex and racism in our history, which leads to the personal abuse being cast upon those who dare to untwist our twisted history.

5. A black-white marriage requires the prudence of those to be so engaged to consider, in addition to the ordinary concerns of any marriage, personality, cultural, educational, and social backgrounds and common cultivation of relatives and friends, as well as economic and residential conditions.

6. A black-white marriage rubs against the assumption by those external to the union that it is subject to social, economic, and moral handicaps from which other marriages

are exempt, which leads to external forces working against rather than in support of the marriage by acquiescing to instead of challenging to change the popular beliefs in the inevitability of (a) isolation from familial and social ties; (b) nonacceptance in communities; (c) overall discriminatory practices; (d) the loss of status to white parents and to a lesser extent to black parents; (e) the relegation of children to the status of being black; (f) the limited and infrequent acceptance by homogenous groups of other couples (g) denial of one's racial-ethnic heritage.

The religious man, no less than the humanist, knows that these difficulties are clear but untenable barriers, and as often as not they are excuses for the perpetuation of the barriers, when what is called for is a change in the environment and the change comes about through eliminating the pressures which act against the white sister's brother or the white brother's sister engaged in a black-white marriage. A black-white marriage has a number of positive factors in its favor:

1. A black-white marriage begins in the fact that the blessings of marriage may be experienced in any kind of marriage.

2. A black-white marriage requires more maturity which means that for mature persons entering therein the marriage is based upon religious and/or humanistic convictions grounded in a free choice among alternatives, so that one's own views and those of others have been thoughtfully considered, a process in which an adult is most likely to be sympathetic and understanding toward the views of others and toward the views which they have felt they must make on their own premises.

3. A black-white marriage usually includes a commonly held and articulated basis of ideas, purposes, and motivations which are more thorough and substantial than in other marriages.

4. A black-white marriage has the resources of marital health and growth in our day through common involvement in the most significant of all possible interests, the acceptance of blacks without reservation.

5. A black-white marriage is inherently alive to the ultimate peril of man, his enslavement to things and to people.

6. A black-white marriage witnesses in itself to the truth that true love may sometimes be a lifelong martyrdom.

7. A black-white marriage calls for a change in individual attitudes and community customs, behavior patterns, values, and social sanctions which are destructive.

Marriage in black and white may seem to be too surrounded by difficulties to be condoned, but there is not a single shred of justification for such worship of custom on the part of Christians. The Christian understanding of marriage begins in the affirmation of the dignity of sex as a natural fact of human beings and holds that two people who are sexually attracted to one another may be moved by God to enter into a lifelong alliance for better or for worse. Marriage is a universal institution, a social arrangement by social groups to insure order, stability, and permanence of group life. Marriage is not a private arrangement of individual men and women, but a form of social life prescribed by human groups. Yet, while marriage is a social custom and legal form, it also serves to protect the divine meaning of sex, sexual mutuality and fellowship—in health and in sickness, in poverty and in wealth, in social acceptance and segregation.

Christians have unconsciously or consciously turned over their understanding of marriage to experts on family and marriage as a means of denying the value of black-white marriages. In modern textbooks on marriage an erroneous idea is frequently encountered that needs to be dispelled:

They [experts on the family and marriage] speak very confidently of sublime, ideal, model, and happy marriages, and from this supreme ideal of marriage they seek to derive its general meaning. But such lofty flights of the imagination mean little to the average person. Equally mistaken is the notion that love alone imparts value to marriage.[16]

For the Christian, the validity of the marriage vow is not contingent upon the partners' mutual suitability to one another, although people seek a marriage partner who seems to give promise of a harmonious relationship. But it cannot be predicted what the partner will become in five, ten, fifteen, or twenty years, so for the Christian it is evidence of divine grace that persons should be ready to promise each other lifelong fidelity. That is, for the Christian, marriage is more than social or ecclesiastical custom. Marriage is holy only because two persons accept it as God's way of lifelong union. Marriage is holy, further, because within it the virtues of mutual responsibility and dedicated service are implemented by faith, and not by race or mores.

Sex plays a decisive part in life in general and in marriage in particular, for the sexual impulse penetrates our entire nature and manifests our will to live. Marriage is based upon the willingness of two persons of the opposite sex to establish an enduring fellowship conditioned by their sexual union, regardless of skin color. The sexual relationship brings with it tensions from within as well as the external pressures from without, but love and fidelity and trust are not limited to black-black or white-white marriages, for

> Christian love is sure that God's work which brought the couple together is more real than are the outward conditions, and thus either spouse is not chiefly concerned with his own burden but with the other spouse's problems, and he will therefore help the other bear the load (Gal. 6:2). Surprisingly enough, the additional sacrifice and patience demanded to render such assistance do not increase one's own encumbrance, but actually diminish it.[17]

The central fact of the voluntary joining of two individuals in marriage does not mitigate the need for an environment which holds the same convictions and ideals and seeks the same goals in life as the black-white couple do. Thus, beginning in their own environment, churches can create a climate in which a black-white couple is greatly helped, and, in turn, such marriages can help the religious environment to be true to itself:

> By means of its customs a community expresses its sense of responsibility for the cultivation of certain values. The custom serves to exclude or repress all attitudes and behavior patterns that conflict with the values recognized by the community. This goal is attained mainly through social sanctions for those who violate the custom. Thereby custom limits drastically both the incentives and opportunities to disregard or destroy these treasured values.[18]

There is no reason churches cannot create environments which are supportive of black-white marriages and place high value on them, so that the behavior patterns of members which conflict with these values produce sanctions of them. According to the Protestant understanding, marriage is founded upon the voluntary union of a man and a woman who are held together by their permanent devotion to one another, which means that every "outside encroachment" contradicts its very nature because individual commitment is first and foremost. While marriage is not a purely private matter, and is socially useful, it is important that communities do not set up provisions irreconcilable with or inimicable to the Christian faith. Where this is the case the Church is called to direct action for fundamental change.

With respect to black-white marriages, the Church is responsible for the creation of an environment which is in keeping with the Christian faith:

> The biblical interpretation of the significance of faith in God as creator raises questions of vital importance for people on both sides of the current crisis in race relations. Here are some of the questions it raises for the advocates of segregation as the Christian solution to this problem: How can you possibly justify the attachment of so much importance to differences in the color of human skin? Do you not thereby deny the notion, stemming from the biblical view

of God as creator, that the only difference of really decisive
religious significance is that which separates, not one group
of men from another, but every man from his creator? Since
you are dependent on your Maker for all you are and have
and hope as the man who inherited parents of another race,
what right have you to treat the color of your skin as a
ground for favored (or, if you insist, separate) treatment at
the hands of men? [19]

The environment needed begins and ends in the faith put into action that

the death of Jesus Christ annuls the divisions that heretofore
have separated men into superior (fellow citizens) and
inferior (strangers and foreigners), privileged and
underprivileged members of the community of God's people.
. . . And if we are children of a common Father through
Christ, then we are brothers to all other Christians,
irrespective of race, color, or nationality. And if we are their
brothers, dare we offer them anything less than full fraternity
in the family of God in Christ? [20]

In the end, the Christian community is tested by its equality of acceptance of blacks as well as of whites, a reality which cannot
begin in our racist society apart from the full acceptance of black-
white married people into "full fraternity":

The Bible sees men as equals, not in native capacity, not in
physical development, not in cultural progress, not in social
poise, not in political know-how, not in spiritual maturity,
but in more fundamental and ultimate respects. Men are
equal in their dependence on God for their place in creation;
they are totally dependent on God for their place in creation.
Men are equal in their dependence on God for their
membership in the covenant. Men are equal in their
dependence on God for their anticipation of a glorious
future; they are totally dependent on God for their
anticipation of a glorious future. [21]

Beyond the need to create an environment, there is the need for the Church to produce counselors sensitive to and aware of all the forces of society opposing marriages in black and white, counselors who work out of the churches the following pattern:

> There is in most of these situations a special reason why the counselor should lean over backward in openness as to the answers the parties may reach. Usually one or both are being subjected to pressures from parents and other relatives and perhaps from the family priest or minister, who talk little of independent decision on the merits and much of "loyalty," "apostasy," "superstition," "giving up your religion," and often with all the emotional stops pulled out: "It will kill your father!" "We won't be able to face our friends." "We've always been . . ." etc. One can sympathize—and should in conference—with these quite natural family reactions, but it is important that there be at least one person in the picture who treats the parties as adults, respecting their integrity and trusting them to make honest inquiry and attempt sincere decisions.
>
> As soon as the matter of family pressures comes out in the discussion (and the counselor should ask questions to bring it forth) the counselor should set them in the proper priority scale. It's not that they should be ignored, but that they should be faced as a secondary question after the main question has been faced and answered.[22]

Religious bodies, caught as they are between the push of the gospel and the pull of a racist society, have an important undertaking ahead of them with respect to black-white marriages. To this point religious bodies, by and large, have been parochial, parietal, protective, and prosecuting in the name of racism, though they have not been generally racist. It is time now—past time—to attune religion to the demands of the biblical faith and to the acceptance of blacks as sons and daughters of the same creator. The place to begin is with denominational wide re-education which leads to a "Yes" across the nation wherever the question is raised or implied: "Would you want your sister (daughter) to marry a black?" There is no more difficult task for the churches, but it is an impossible possibility for religious bodies which purport to believe in the forgiveness of sins, the good news, suffering, the victory of death to the old ways and resurrection to the new way of life. If churches take seriously their responsibility of creating a new climate in America where black-white marriages are acceptable, they may well find that many are cold but few are frozen. Christians have a unique opportunity, for they have a unique commandment, coupled with the belief that the religious unity of couples is vital. There is one way out of the collusion between churches and the society in our history: the price paid for this collusion of forces which opposed the full acceptance of blacks by denying black-white marriages must be paid for by the suffering which comes in the creation of a new society:

> But when all is said and done there is of course much left to
> be desired in any mixed marriage. However helpful the above
> suggestions and guides may be in a given marriage they are
> but makeshifts designed to "shore up" the situation. In the
> long run the best single thing a marriage can possess is a
> common religious grounding, just as the best thing an
> individual person can possess is a sound religious
> orientation.[23]

If we can affirm the unity of blacks and whites through the forthright actions of churches, laying their life on the line to teach the brotherhood of man in every community by holding forth that blacks are beautiful partners for life, we may overcome the judgment of Whittaker Chambers:

> At the heart of the crisis of our times lies the cold belief of
> millions, avowed and unavowed, that the death of religious
> faith is seen in nothing so much as in the fact that, in general,
> it has lost its power to move anyone to die for it.

I am not antisemitic, as this section on blacks and Jews will demonstrate. The candid criticism I have made in my other books of blacks and WASPS should place me in a favorable position to criticize the stance taken by Jews in general, and religious leaders in particular, vis-à-vis the issue of marriage in black and white.

It is perfectly clear today that Jews comprise the best friends and best enemies of blacks. This assertion is amply illustrated in the number of marriages between gentile blacks and assimilated Jews, probably a very significant percentage of all marriages in black and white.

Nevertheless, there is a strong Jewish strain which opposes the marriage of a Jew to a black as vehemently as it opposes marriage between a WASP or a white Roman Catholic to a Jew. Liberal Jews who are concerned to be known as the friends of blacks contend that the bond of affection between these two groups ought not to be transcended into marriage between the individual black gentile and the white Jew. These liberal Jews contend that blacks and Jews have in common an experience of suffering, that both are outcasts in most nations of the world. Jews often set forth their success as a closed socio-religious society as the pattern of success which blacks would do well to imitate. Of course it is not possible to define what a Jew is, whether being a Jew be a matter of religion or culture or some variation of both. To be black by definition in America is to have one drop of African blood in one's veins. In effect, to be a Jew or to be a black comes down to so identifying oneself for a myriad of reasons.

Of course, Jews have going for them the tradition which hangs, tightly or lightly, on a distinct religion. Blacks, for the most part, have no distinct religion, but have adopted or adapted many kinds of religious traditions, including Judaism, Islam, Christianity, and many varieties of these religious traditions. This is an important distinction between the two groups. There is one more, and it is that while blacks have suffered in the United States, Jews have not been oppressed here as a people.

The success of the Jews in America and elsewhere led C. P. Snow, the noted British author and physicist, at a Founder's Day address at the New York School of Hebrew Union College-Jewish Institute of Religion, to declare his preparedness to believe that Jews have a superior gene pool to Anglo-Saxons and other people.* The failure of blacks in America has led Arthur R. Jensen, educational psychologist at the University of California at Berkeley, in the March 1969 issue of *The Harvard Educational Review*, to intimate there are differences between blacks and whites, concluding that it is "not an unreasonable hypothesis that genetic factors are strongly implicated in the average negro-white intelligence difference." **

Jews have not publicly declared their superiority; they have successfully demonstrated it. Blacks have challenged the assumption held by some that they are inherently inferior, yet they have still to demonstrate this reality as a group in the face of unprecedented obstacles. We have here in the success of the Jews in America and elsewhere, and in the failure of blacks, a basis for the tension that exists between them, a tension that is based upon exploitation of suffering. Suffering, or the fear of it, has led the Jews to close ranks even against blacks, who suffer even at their hands, and to suggest the pattern blacks should follow.

Blacks and Jews may have some common identification in such styles as the wearing of beards, but even here the difference is significant. Jews wear beards as members of a group who wish to signify their religious orthodoxy. Blacks wear beards in an attempt to suggest their manliness and virility, beyond the suggestion of ethnic identity.

If the Jew is a friend who has experienced elsewhere the suffering blacks experience here, Jews and blacks may be said to be enemies with respect to their ultimate objectives. The religious and cultural exclusiveness which Jews cherish and by which they have gained unprecedented success is understandable from the Jewish point of view. In their struggle for ethnicity blacks have neither a universal religious uniqueness nor a universal cultural uniqueness to draw upon; even their real claim to being the only group in America which has made a distinct contribution to Western civilization through jazz finds expression and exploitation by other groups and may be said to belong to the public domain. The future of blacks has yet to be worked out along politi-

---

* *The New York Times*, April 1, 1969, p. 37.
** *Ibid.*, March 30, 1969, p. 52.

cal, economic, cultural, and religious lines. That future is taking shape now whereby ethnicity and black exclusiveness toward other individuals and groups is in tension. The question to be answered is the way in which blacks will become ethnically one without being exclusive in the way that Jews and WASPS have been. The concept of a united black people for inclusiveness and openness on the part of individuals appears to be paradoxical, but the reality of this paradox is the essence of the black struggle.

This struggle for unity from and with diversity is the impossible possibility of black people, for blacks are a diverse people of many ideologies who share a common fate. They are caught between the social, political, economic, and cultural exclusiveness of WASPS and the religious and ethnic exclusiveness of Jews.

We have concentrated throughout this book on the struggle between blacks and WASPS vis-à-vis marriage in black and white. Nowhere is the tension between blacks and Jews more strenuous than on the issue of ethnic unity and marriage across the color lines. The fact that a considerable number of black gentiles marry white Jews puts in dramatic and provocative relief the "friendly enemy" differences that exist in the intuitive and rational world views of the two groups, although some individuals choose to suspend or ignore these differences.

The best way to get at this testy matter is to grapple with the Jewish tradition on matters of marriage. The most important work on intermarriage to date is the book by that title written by the late Rabbi Albert I. Gordon. This work demonstrates his enormous grasp of interfaith, interethnic, and interracial marriages. Here in summary form is set forth the wisdom of Judaism.

Rabbi Gordon was an extremely competent social scientist, an extraordinarily able defender of Judaism. These two professions are compatible and clearly serve to enrich Rabbi Gordon's point of view and therefore all who are interested in these two dimensions. Nevertheless, it is a highly spurious business to defend the faith by the use of social science research, just as it would be spurious to advance the cause of social science by the use of religious affirmations. To be sure, religion and social science bring forth knowledge which illuminate one another's theories and

practices, but this relationship is of another order than the com-
bining of the two for the protection and maintenance of religious
borders.

Indeed, Judaism is not concerned about religious "imperialism." Its concern is the weakening of acknowledged religious
groups through infiltration, the refusal of romantic love to respect
religious territory. The purpose of Gordon's book is to state the
case for religious pluralism; that is that Jews, Roman Catholics,
and Protestants (and by implication any other religious body) are
"separate but equal" religious communities. These communities
understand the benefit to each in this arrangement; no religious
body has as its mission the conversion of any other, though there
are imperialistic fringe groups. Thus, *Intermarriage* does not primarily seek to instruct the major religious bodies in America. Its
fundamental message is for individuals who ignore the group
values for the sake of personal values, who allow themselves to
consummate a "mixed marriage." What gives force to Judaism's
stand or forces Judaism to take this stand is clear in the following
sentences:

> For reasons which to date have not been fully explained, the
> number of divorces and separations between intermarried
> couples in the past decade has been two to three times as
> high (some authorities say that it is four times as high) as
> those divorces and separations involving marriages of
> persons of the same religion.[24]
> The [total] divorce rate is obviously high. It is my conviction
> that the rates of divorce, annulment or separation will
> continue to increase with the increase in the number of
> persons whose religious, ethnic or racial backgrounds differ
> from that of their marriage partner.[25]

Judaism is right in what it affirms: the reality and integrity of
religious communities in America and their right to expect continued existence because of their avowed values. Judaism is wrong
in what it denies: the right of individuals to intermarry without re-

gard to "religious, ethnic or racial backgrounds," and to expect support from American religious and other communities. Judaism acknowledges its bias and then brilliantly marshals statistical evidence through such scholars as Rabbi Gordon to support and confirm its conviction: intermarriage increases the rates of "divorce, annulment or separation," therefore, the case against marriage in black and white. Everyone ought to be concerned with the fact that "the total divorce rate is obviously high." But the real problem is less intermarriage in general than it is mixed marriages where one partner has no religious identification. Judaism ignores this fact and its suggestions of avoidance are at best ameliorative because its fundamental concern is with encroachments upon religious territory. Is it enough to attack the symptoms and not the disease, the results and not the causes? Judaism does not appear to be interested in causes which are so difficult to discover and which might just undermine the case for religious pluralism, for as we shall see, religious communities may be contributing to interpersonal conflicts because of their prior commitment to unhealthy group well-being rather than to healthy individual well being where there is a conflict between the two. To put it boldly, arguments against black-white marriages is to religion what blood and purity arguments against intermixtures is to racist theories—both oppose "imperialism," and wish only to keep their inherited lines pure. In a word, opposition to black-white marriages is as pseudo-religious as racist doctrines are psuedoscientific.

We will not see the day when arguments for religious purity will be as unacceptable as the arguments for purity of race presently are. Whether or not "races" remain pure, they do remain intact as identifiable groups and perhaps it will always be so with religions. Marriage in black and white is not a threat to "religious, ethnic or racial" groups, nor is it set forth as a solution to the conflicts between these groups by this writer. Judaism attacks intermarriage for the defense of its own religious bias by suggesting that intermarriage is a threat to religious groups. Some people see intermarriage as a solution to group conflict, but the fact that their position is wrong in that it is untenable is no reason to oppose intermarriage as a right of individuals or to refuse to give in-

dividuals who wish such marriages the needed support. Such de-
liberations will not stop intermarriage, if anything they will
increase them and insure their failure.

Of course Judaism's stance results from its being a precious
and rare commodity for which Jews do not wish to compete on
the human-world market. Jews believe Judaism will exist only as
long as internal restrictions are respected by external tariffs. Judaism is very much for interaction between members of the various
religious groups without intermarriage. Intermarriage only involves the minority within any group. To be sure, the smaller the
group the more impact an intermarriage will have upon it, but it is
useless to attempt to reverse the irreversible by "parochial" arguments. In fact, the case for intermarriage is the case for religious
pluralism—freedom of choice. Without freedom there is no
choice, without choice there is no freedom! These vital options
will not exist or be enhanced by restrictions; they will be increased only through making a group uniquenesses available to
all. There is a large secular market in which to sell the "better
mouse trap"—without danger of imperialism.

The best spokesmen for Judaism are not inflexible reac-
tionaries; usually they are rigid in their thinking, which leads
them to be as provoking as they are provocative, but this quality
is typical of conservative religious leaders. It would be one thing
were their conservative thinking mere reverence and respect for
honored traditions in the defense of which they present Judaism's
best. However, the crux of the black disagreement with Judaism is
Judaism's acceptance and justification of reinforcing the current
mores, customs, and values as if they were right (and therefore
laudable) because they exist as dominant in the mainstream. It
comes to this: Judaism takes the most reactionary convictions in
the society and uses them to support the traditions it wishes to
conserve via the technique of quantity as opposed to quality of
opinion. With regard to intermarriage, Judaism sets up for attack
those opinions which are most ideal and visionary. The dynamics
of change in our time lead Jews to look to the past for guidance
rather than to direct the present by the impending future. Urbani-
zation, cybernation, technology, anonymity, and mobility are all

forces which faithful Jews recognize as determinative in our time. Faithful Jews' deep suspicion of contemporary forces is that these forces free individuals to make decisions apart from systems, especially religious systems. When we are in a time of revolutionary change and our way is not sure, we tend to look to the past if we are afraid of venturing forth into the future with uncertainty. In this kind of conservatism, the Jews are like all men. But the camel's nose is under the tent.

It is less the faith of Judaism and more the faithful Jews who view the family as "the principal means of socialization in our day," and fear college youth, whom they view as disinclined "to accept parental attitudes with respect to social, cultural and religious values." [26] It is among the college students that faithful Jews perceive radical and rapid changes taking place, changes that undermine past loyalties:

> The admonitions of parents, of family and of the church are no longer accepted without debate. Intermarriage with a person of another religion, color, class, or ethnic group is far less unusual in these days than it was but a generation ago.[27]

These weakening social forces, once the determinative controls for youth, are now replaced by the peer group structure, and among the brightest youth there is a demand for an individual, internal direction that means autonomous or heteronomous ethics. These are contributing factors in the rise of mixed marriages:

> The barriers that separate individuals, religions, ethnics and races from each other must, in view of many young people, be broken down. Some believers in "one world" assume that nonidentification with their parental groups will hasten the day when prejudice, hatred and even war will be vanquished. How realistic such a view is remains questionable. It is equally uncertain whether, by the elimination of these religious and other divisions presently existing among men, we shall gain more than we may ultimately lose.[28]

Youth has always been the time for idealism. What makes the youth of today different is not their ideals but the context of their ideals within an age called "the triple revolution." While they may not make their ideal reality, the point is they may come too close in a time when the dynamics are for the first time on the side of youth. Of course, the risk is that the old systems will go, or at least become powerless; win, lose, or draw. The pragmatist who views himself as "realistic," because of his classical stance, is terrified at the prospects, though he knows that what we have bequeathed the youth may not be worth perpetuation—for example, bigoted family life, provincial religion, a racist society, the opportunity for the fool or the mad man to destroy civilizations. The point that many faithful Jews and gentiles miss is that youth are not accenting "nonidentification with their parental groups" as the means of commitment to a better society than they have known, but rather ignoring what seems to be inappropriate, unfitting to their vision. Obviously there is good in past systems and groups, and these will not "fade away." Basic groups will always exist for those who value them, but new forms and patterns may well emerge that will make the tried and untrue obsolete for some. The future-oriented will be experimental, and there is room for this.

Faithful Jews do not wish to risk the good. They have known in past systems and groups that uncertain good may or may not come about in new forms. Their liberal method for expressing traditionalist views fails to hide what is basically a closed world view vis-à-vis the conflict between generations. This conflict is necessary for creativity, though faithful Jews imply the gap needs to be closed to preserve a continuity with the past, not a selective part of it. It is the system that faithful Jews deem valuable in the belief that there can be progress within it, while the younger generation asserts there can be progress beyond the old system, though that progress will bring with it another system that is open for individuals as well as pluralistic and tolerant of various groups. Faithful Jews are not at all sure that an evolving new system of responsible individual freedom will be open to the existence of religious groups for those who wish them, and, if possible, faithful Jews are most pessimistic as to whether "we shall gain more than we may ultimately lose."

Faithful and traditional Jews see youth as change agents. Faithful Jews believe it is imperative to protect their tradition and Judaism from the change mounted by youth. For example, faithful Jews tend to support college fraternities and sororities because they are institutions of conformity, not unlike religion and the family. Self-examination on the part of Greek organizations, spearheaded by predominantly Jewish systems, has led to less exclusiveness and close-mindedness than in the past. Alarmed by any threat to the traditional pattern of in-group unity, faithful Jews perceive the push by Jews or blacks for inclusive fraternities and sororities as dangerous. So dangerous in fact that a desperate warning is broadcast:

> Minority groups that advocate the letting down of barriers in fraternities and sororities must accept the responsibility for an increase in intermarriage that follows naturally therefrom.[29]

The Greek system of secret societies is generally supported by its advocates because of its long association with institutions of higher learning. These secret societies produced many of the administrators of colleges and universities today who remember with nostalgia their small group of likeminded persons. Despite the arguments for the Greek system and the many values it gives to individuals, the system is deadly and dying. Perceptive youth generally perceive fraternities and sororities as antiChristian, antihuman, antidemocratic, antieducational, and antiAmerican. Fraternities and sororities are instruments of the past, and in looking to them as sources of group survival, despite their evils, faithful Jews disclose their disparagement. Especially is this case when the Greek system is grasped to discourage marriages in black and white.

Faithful Jews hold that marriage between blacks and whites in the academic world, the most conducive of all environments outside of the entertainment world, is so low a priority as to be almost negligible. The controls may be weakening, but they are

effective in so delicate a sphere as marriage because they are nurtured in the young at the earliest age. These controls include parents, the family life, prejudice, religious life, religious leaders, education in the home, education in the schools, group isolation
devices, consciousness of kind, and primary group loyalties. Thus,
with specific respect to interracial marriages the group opposition
to them is so strong that faithful Jews' implicit if not explicit negative response to these occasional occurrences must result from a
prior commitment to group survival at the expense of individual
rights and freedom, even in isolated instances where the group
cannot be threatened by individual variations. What faithful Jews
in fact do is to demand that the individual conform to group
norms rather than support the norms of the individual when they
are superior to the group norm, or to deny the individual support
in following the group norm to its logical conclusion, intermarriage. In the name of group survival faithful Jews reinforce and
call forth all the prejudices of the society and conclude, in effect,
that evil in the cause of what they hold to be good is not vice but
virtue.

So, for faithful Jews, the fraternities and sororities are not to
be rooted out. Like the family and the church they are instruments of conformity which know the good for the individual better than he does and therefore are just practical when they use
prejudices and all other social devices for the protection of the
group and the protection of the individual against himself.

The opposition of faithful Jews to intermarriage is not based
solely on their vested interest in group survival, however. They
really believe, and call forth every conceivable evidence from all
religions to support them, that intermarriage is not in the best interest of individuals. It never occurs to them to admit that religion
(along with individual and social forces) is a reservoir of prejudice
and discrimination, which may require religion to change. I think
faithful Jews do religion a gross disservice when they demand that
it dictate the terms on which two persons may come together and
when they unwittingly use racist arguments for religious survival.
The extremity of their position is based on the false assumption
that "Marriage between persons of different faiths apparently
weakens the ultimate religious beliefs of such persons." [30] After

all, the basis of pluralism in America is that the differences in rituals are modes of traditional preferences which do not conflict with
basic beliefs and values. The difficulty lies with the children of
mixed marriages in which one partner has no religious identification. But even if faithful Jews can show that people of two
different faiths who join in marriage experience difficulty, and
consequently are prone to annulment, separation, or divorce because of conflict over the rearing of children, this problem does
not lie with the couple but in religion and society.

Surely faithful Jews are not saying that in this age of the rise
of the individual and his increasing exercise of freedom of choice,
events can be reversed to force him to respect boundaries which
are unintelligible to him, but which cannot be used to make religion more tolerant. As faithful Jews put the case, there is something terribly wrong in religious systems, if not in the heart of religion. What we need and what we can have are religious groups
that survive on the basis of their openness rather than on the basis
of their exclusiveness. It is possible for religion to be strong and
alive without being provincial. It is God that is sacred, not the
systems; surely God is not to be found on the side of a prejudice
that ostensibly seeks to support him. If we are to increase faith,
we cannot do it by condoning devices that threaten marriages.
Faithful Jews want to reduce marriage conflicts by increasing the
differences between religions, but this suggestion leads not to the
best in religion, but only to a commitment to formalism at best
and a disrespect for individual persons at worst. We must either
find a way to increase the value of religion without its exclusive
disvalues or to increase the values of individuals without regard to
religious systems.

If religion interferes with the success of marriages in black
and white, then religion need not be eliminated, it simply must
change. It may be true that many faithful Jews believe that "to
marry someone of another religion is often regarded as a form of
desertion." But the Roman Catholic Church has certainly shown
that popular beliefs may not be the beliefs of true faith, that popular beliefs can in time be changed in line with true faith, and that
the accent must be in this direction. To assume that institutions
are not in need of self-criticism which has a healthy respect for

their failures and attempts to correct them is as nonsensical as assuming that institutions should only be concerned with their weaknesses and not with their strengths. To be sure, there are all kinds of social and religious obstacles to successful intermarriage, and they must be taken into account. There are also all kinds of ways in which religion could *begin* to eliminate these barriers because their elimination need not be detrimental to the survival of religious groups as vitally alive options. One does look to religion to be on the frontier, overcoming detrimental forces which invade against the union of two people.

One of the great difficulties with minority groups is that they want to have their cake and to eat it as well; they want full participation without any elimination. This is understandable, a dilemma whose dynamics are creative. The rich contributions minority groups have to offer have resulted from great suffering. This suffering makes their group life a precious heritage we must not simply protect but nurture as well. However, it does not follow that increasing the barriers for those persons of minority group heritage who wish to go beyond them is the way to insure the preservation of this heritage.

Jews may be the most opposed religious or secular group in principle to intermarriage because they are a socio-cultural as well as religious minority. Jews are few in number and wish to keep these few together through "intrabreeding" rather than through intermarriage. Thus for Jews, conversion before marriage is not much better than intermarriage because "an alien element has been introduced." It would be too much to expect a dynamic openness that truly trusts in God and the future among minority religious groups, which have suffered for so many centuries at the hands of the majority, though this openness to God and the future through reformation via revolution in the present, without fear of survival, can and should be expected of those in the other major religions.

Faithful Jews would largely accept the following quotation by Rabbi Louis Finkelstein as in agreement with their own position:

Jews are hostile to intermarriage with people of another faith. This is not too well understood. Jews are not hostile to intermarriage with people of another race, if they are Jews. The basic doctrine here is that the home is a sanctuary. It cannot be so maintained if either the high priest or the high priestess, so to speak, belongs to another faith. That is something Jews do not like—marriage outside of their fold—because it means the children will not be Jews, or will be only half-Jews. . . . Judaism does not consider it an unreasonable sacrifice for a Jewish man or woman to shun marriage or even the thought of marriage to a non-Jew.[31]

While faithful Jews would largely agree with this statement, they would not generally agree with the one sentence, "Jews are not hostile to intermarriage with people of another race, if they are Jews." This concept is crucial. If only faithful Jews could accept this sentence and recruit blacks, their position would be more bearable because it would then be more understandable. While it is true that no major religion in the world is in principle opposed to marriage between blacks and whites, they all are in practice. In fact most of the major religious leaders in America and most of the practitioners of Protestantism, Roman Catholicism, and Judaism oppose marriage with a black of the same faith.[32] If a black Jew asked a white Jew for the right to marry his daughter and the decision rested with the most faithful Jews, they would point up all the social barriers and strongly advise against it despite the religious unity of the couple involved. Contrary to the above quotation by the distinguished Dr. Louis Finkelstein, Chancellor of the Jewish Theological Seminary in America, Jews are hostile to marriage with black Jews in America, as Rabbi Gordon made clear throughout his book. In this respect, Jews are not different from Protestants and Roman Catholics. In America, when it comes to marriage between blacks and whites who are Jews, brotherhood takes on a different color.

Faithful Jews use extreme caution in setting forth their opposition to marriages between blacks and whites, even in their private conclusions.[33] Faithful Jews provide no encouragement or suggestions for resolving the difficulties of black-white marriages, despite the fact that they are seen to be inevitable. In Gordon's words:

I believe that Negro-white marriages will increase
slowly—but that they *will* increase. Such interracial
marriages are likely to occur more frequently than hitherto
among college-trained Negroes and whites, and in much the
same way as our interviews-in-depth have indicated.[34]

Instead of helping persons engaged in intermarriage with the
knowledge gained from "interviews-in-depth," faithful Jews such
as Gordon concentrate on reiterating the need for blacks to gain
equal opportunity and on emphasizing the belief that those who
dare to engage in this union will face major problems, "involving
personal insecurity and other psychological and emotional problems as well." [35] In fact, Jews and WASPS are united in their
argument against such marriages—they appeal to the victimization of children:

> The uncertainty about where and how one will live, "being
> neither White nor Black" is about as great as any problem a
> human being is likely to face.[36]

This argument shows a woeful misunderstanding or misinterpre-
tation. A black child is a black child, however light or dark he is
(a Walter White, for example), whether he is born of black-white
parents, of a light-black and a dark-black parent, or, of two light-
black parents. The suffering and joy in being black is the same for
all blacks regardless of parentage and includes employment,
housing, and education. It is inconceivable that a religious people
could think that who your parents are matters if you are black,
unless such people believe that being black is so bad that two
black people should not have children, whether they themselves
are either indistinguishable from being white or coal black for
that matter. How do Jews and WASPS think blacks who have not
"passed" but who could have, and their children, have survived
these generations? This is precisely the point that religious Jews
do not understand. Blacks accept being black, believing that a
black "by any other name would smell as sweet."

The tradition of religious Jews, which opposes intermarriage
on social, cultural, religious, psychological, and historical

grounds, even while some of Judaism's constitutents admit such marriages are on the increase, is not especially helpful when one of its spokesmen informs us that blacks have problems, as will their children, unless the purpose of such information is an attempt to persuade Jews not to take on the burdens of blacks at the level of social, sexual commitment; for there is absolutely no difference between what occurs to blacks whether they marry blacks or whether they marry whites, and the same is true of their children. Try as I may to believe differently, there is only ignorance or intolerance in this traditional view:

> The children of the racially intermarried are likely to be faced with the same discriminatory practices as are their parents. Unless a miracle occurs that will eliminate discrimination from our society—and that does not seem probable—we may expect such children to suffer the same indignities as do their parents.[37]

It is most difficult to determine whether religious Jews really know what they are saying and believe it if they do:

> Whether people, however much they may love each other, have the moral right to create such a problem for a child is, of course, debatable. It is my belief that interracially intermarried parents are committing a grave offense against their children that is far more serious and even dangerous to their welfare than they realize. The Negro in the United States suffers greatly. He is most often provided with the poorest housing available, the least desirable job and faces the unwillingness of people to accept him socially. The children of Negro-white marriages are thus easily hurt, even by their well-intentioned parents.[38]

My family and I live in an all-white section of town; my oldest son being the only black boy in his school. He plays well with both the boys and the girls of his neighborhood and enjoys a fairly wholesome life, except that his parents are black. Recently, a family who do not live in our block, sent their children into our neighborhood because of its extra play facilities. My son and his usual friends and neighbors somehow joined in a snowball fight that became directed at this set of children from outside our usual environs. They then chased the children, who naturally ran to their father. Not understanding the children's play, this father unwisely took up his children's cause, and gave the kids from our block hell. And, almost by instinct, he turned to my son's friends and said to them, "Get that dirty black Nigger friend out of here." My son is nine years old. To be sure, I threatened this man to within an inch of his white life, and God only knows why he still moves about today, though when he sees me now he is so polite and courteous you would think he was my slave. The point is, how would it differ any more for my son if my wife were white? Do Gordon and the faithful Jews really believe that it is all right for the black children of known blacks to suffer? In my book, Gordon and the faithful Jews he speaks for are for blacks as long as blacks "stay in their place," which they wish to define.

Tradition-oriented and faithful Jews are often brilliant social scientists and defenders of the faith, but they are dead wrong in both instances vis-à-vis marriage in black and white. It is unbelievable that they should declare it "debatable" whether or not a black-white couple "have the moral right to create such a problem for a child." Such a position is immoral, clearly discloses bias, and demonstrates that, at least from the black point of view, faithful Jews as religious leaders or social scientists must be viewed with suspicion:

> The Negro-white families interviewed by the author were unanimous in their belief that their children were likely to find their teen-age period (when partying and socials were being emphasized) the most trying period of their lives. Refusal of whites to permit such interdating is quite general in the United States. Permission on the part of some white parents to allow interdating is sometimes given only because the Negro-white youth is a rarity in a particular neighborhood or community. The subsequent resentment built up by children of interracial marriages against these attitudes must be regarded as unhealthy and even dangerous.[39]

If faithful Jews are leveling with us, if they are serious, they have just argued not only against marriage in black and white but against integration as well. I, like a number of other blacks, have lived the majority of my life, as child and adult, in white communities, and the same is true for my children. There are to be sure all kinds of difficulties for black children in such neighborhoods which "must be regarded as unhealthy and even dangerous." So, black people should now not only refrain from marriage with whites but from integrated housing as well. It cannot be denied that the same problems which face black children of black-black marriages face those of black-white marriages, and difference that makes no difference is no difference. Blacks who have teenagers in white communities have always had to find ways for their children to meet other blacks, and only occasionally have blacks permitted their children to date only whites or be concerned to do so. Of course there are problems for blacks, but they have endured and whites who marry blacks will also, as will their children. I am suspicious of opposition in principle, even on religious principles, to marriage in black and white, for I fail to see any difference between being black and being black.

One more word in this regard. Faithful Jews write time and again on how important it is for parents to create an internal security for their children, but Gordon implied that something extra here occurs within a black-white family that does not occur within a black-black family:

> If parents, however happy they may be themselves, are
> disturbed or unhappy about the manner in which they have
> been received by other persons, this attitude is more than
> likely to manifest itself in their relation to their own children.
> They, in turn, respond to the world of men in accordance
> with the attitudes and beliefs that have become part of their
> natures.[40]

Since a black man cannot jump out of his skin, he must learn ways to survive with some success. Black people cannot live without being insulted, rejected, disapproved of, in the daily round.

What possibly could be worse for a black-white couple and their children? Faithful Jews seem to have a block when it comes to black children. I wonder what their response would be to sterilizing black-white and black-black couples so that they would not bring black children into the world and with them the intolerable burdens they assume to be inevitable?

As a rule of thumb we certainly must agree with faithful Jews that the more people have in common, the better their chances for success in marriage. Thus,

> if interfaith marriages require great courage, then interracial marriages may be said, under present conditions in our society, to require even greater fortitude.[41]

Let us assume that a black-white couple accepts these premises and still decides to be true to one another. Faithful Jews have little to say to them except that "the information we have acquired about interfaith and interracial marriages ought to be heeded" if " 'success' in marriage is the desired goal." [42] Faithful Jews can add that with regard to black-white marriages "the American people do not, to this date, accept them as proper." [43] Faithful Jews are fundamentally sympathetic; it is too bad that blacks are not "free, white, and twenty-one." Fortunately, things are changing. Until they do change, it is best to keep in mind these popularly held perspectives on black-white marriages:

> Neither Negroes nor whites want it especially. Negroes are, supposedly, more "at home" with Negroes. Whites are generally more "at home" with whites. People of similar backgrounds, experiences, and hopes tend to remain together just as Catholics tend to create Catholic neighborhoods around a church and Jews like to live among their fellow Jews. Protestants, too, do very much the same thing and understandably so.[44]

One would have thought an oppressed minority would be familiar with the social response of "feigning attractiveness" and would have recognized its existence in the etiquette of black-white social relations.

Beyond the detailed, painstakingly documented, but overblown argument against intermarriage, persons who contemplate or are involved in intermarriage might hopefully look to the expert for guidance:

> Mixed marriages, in my view, need not necessarily prove harmful to and destructive of our society. They may, however, dull the impact of that distinctiveness and uniqueness that often give races and religions meaning and actually contribute to the improvement of our society.[45]

But this statement is as far as Gordon and most faithful Jews will go, for they are concerned not to support the minority for many good reasons, which trespass against the social, psychological, cultural, and religious forces of separation:

> Viewed in terms of the short-time situation with which we are generally confronted, intermarriage appears to the major religious bodies, as well as to national ethnic and racial groups, to constitute a betrayal of the ideals and values which each professes. It appears, also, to constitute a betrayal of family and group values. A deep hurt is often created in family and friends whose values are spurned. Pride is affected. Families, friends, religions and races, knowing that their "values" differ from those of others, believe that their unique way of life is somehow endangered when mixed marriage occurs. To minority groups—racial, cultural or religious—the possible extinction of the group as the result of intermarriage looms as a very serious threat.[46]

The above quotation is essentially the central thesis of Gordon's argument against marriage in black and white. It is the case that a black-white marriage appears to others, aside from the couple, as "a betrayal of family and group values." However, appearances do not constitute reality, they reflect a relative perspective, and all perspectives are relative. By the time intelligent, mature, and alive persons are ready for marriage they may well discover that to accept provincial, specious, and prejudicial "family and group values" would be to them a self-betrayal. In fact, it is more often the case than not that such perceptive persons believe themselves to be most loyal to the "family and group values" when they act upon the principles espoused rather than the practices followed. They have a solid point when they say their family or group is really part of a community engaged in betrayal when they teach the acceptance of persons on their merit but accept them on their prejudices. In this respect at least, such communities have uniqueness and meaning which do not "contribute to the improvement of our society." It would be one thing were they to keep their prejudices to themselves—to permit people to choose the group prejudices and individuals while allowing and encouraging others who wish to reject them; but these communities are not satisfied until wrong *as they define it* is declared right. Unfortunately, the concern which discourages black-white marriages is not with the right; it is with the preservation of the system—"my religion, right or wrong."

Of course pride is affected when mature young people accept all the teachings of their communities but come to a different conclusion. Indeed, this is what occurs most often, a linkage with the past teachings rather than their elimination. To honor one's father and mother and relatives is not to unnecessarily hurt their feelings, nor is it to avoid hurting their feelings when these feelings are prohibitive rather than liberating in such critical situations as marriage. In fact, hurt feelings may be an opportunity for growth. Surely parents are honored when children follow them at their best rather than at their worst, though it is true that the real meaning of contemporary parental teaching is to accept the worst and make the best of it. Tradition-oriented Jews are basically paternalistic; children never become as wise as parents and individuals can never become wiser than the group. They believe religion, "like a good parent," demands certain obedience even if persons do not find such obedience in their best interest. I would prefer a group to think of parents as responsible, and by responsible I mean that a parent would nurture the child with a wisdom that would guide the child toward making his or her own decisions in such a way that the parent would willingly, happily learn from them. Children should not be grist for the group mill which parents may use in one manner or spare in another. Children eventually must go their own way, and good parents will stand by whatever they do, unless loyalty to a system or tradition says they must do otherwise. In this context, the words of Jesus are impelling and compelling:

> But from the beginning of creation, "God made them male and female." "For this reason a man shall leave his father and mother and be joined to his wife, and the two shall become one." What therefore God has joined together, let not man put asunder.[47]

There is a hard saying of Jesus which the traditionalists ignore in their preference for group norms over individual norms, when in truth there is no contest between the two but a flexibility which allows the better of the two to reign:

> Then Pharisees and scribes came to Jesus from Jerusalem and said, "Why do your disciples transgress the tradition of the elders? For they do not wash their hands when they eat." He answered them, "And why do you transgress the commandment of God for the sake of your tradition? For God commanded, "Honor your father and your mother," and, "He who speaks evil of his father or mother, let him surely die." But you say, "If one tells his father or his mother, What you would have gained from me is given to God, he need not honor his father." So, for the sake of your tradition, you have made void the word of God. You hypocrites! Well did Isaiah prophesy of you, when he said: "This people honors me with their lips, but their heart is far from me; in vain do they worship me, teaching as doctrines the precepts of men." [48]

It simply is not the case that marriage in black and white appears to blacks in America as a "betrayal of the ideals and values" American blacks profess, unless one makes the Black Muslims spokesmen for all black people in America. The arguments in opposition to marriage in black and white which faithful Jews attribute to Judaism and to the beliefs of other religious groups in America are not the responses given by blacks when they are generally confronted. Of course it would be hoped that the rise in black pride will continue among blacks whereby they will engage in mutual self-help to increase their ability to meet opportunity and to demand that equal opportunity. But blacks do not have ideals and values different from the best of this society. The "distinctiveness and uniqueness" of blacks may be their demand for justice and liberty for all, and thus for themselves. Blacks are different in that what is in their best interest is in the best interest of all. The very equal opportunity they seek can be gained only as it is increased for everyone else. The same is true of justice, liberty, education, and life chances beyond employment. There are subcultural differences in tone, interpretation, and even in passion in the expression of blacks' ideals and values, but these differen emerge from the majority demand that blacks remain within their community for their religious, cultural, and social life. Furthermore, the majority culture has not to date permitted the black male to assume the leadership role expected of other males, and thus while the black family has always been stable, marriages have not been stable among a minority of blacks, where poverty and fertility are the rule.

Blacks not only do not have a different set of values and ideals from the best of the society, however poorly the society allows the best to be expressed, but the one thing blacks supposedly have in common, they do not—skin color. Blacks are as white as snow and black as coal and brown as fall, and of all color variations thereof imaginable. The one thing they do have in common is a "color stigma," the force of white preference for whites, the preconscious white folk religion that relegates blacks inferior by virtue of the whites' irrational color prejudice. This second-class citizenship demands that blacks think of being black first and of being Americans second, which results in black pride in being black. But being black is not a matter of pigmentation, for then blacks would have to discriminate among themselves. Being black is a matter of positive identification with the suffering and inequality which the "color stigma" inflicts, regardless of pigmentation.

Blacks must deny what faithful Jews affirm. There are, to be sure, blacks who do not accept whites when they marry blacks, and reject blacks who marry whites, but this reaction is a temporary one and lasts only until the black-white couple prove their identification with the color stigma. How could it be otherwise? Even though this society forces a consciousness of skin color to the point that whites and blacks alike are on the lookout for who may be black, blacks cannot themselves tell who is or isn't. After all, blacks do not lose a child through marriage with whites—they gain one. All one has to do to be a black is declare oneself to be black by identifying with the suffering, a declaration that may be obvious in marriage in black and white. The exceptions prove this rule. Blacks cannot lose identity through any action, including marriage with whites. Individuals who wish to "pass" for whites and do so in some substantial numbers are no threat to the existence of blacks qua blacks. Instead of marriage in black and white being a betrayal, it is an affirmation of black ideals and values. For blacks are not about keeping the burden of color stigma unto themselves. They are about making democracy work through this color stigma and thereby eliminating it. The more people who wish to join in this ideal and value the merrier. Blacks know they cannot lose true pride or true identity through winning others; they can only win through others' losing their false pride and false identity.

In their attempt to destroy the color stigma, blacks are not about the elimination of color or of ethnic, cultural, and religious differences which "contribute to the improvement of our society." They are only about the elimination of those ideals and values within these differences which disrupt and delay improvement. The reason why blacks qua blacks (individual preferences notwithstanding) cannot oppose black-white marriages qua black-white marriages is that their uniqueness lies in being black; their separate religious, cultural, and social life is a reality with opportunity, but it is a means rather than an end. Black communities will always exist in America, at least for the centuries immediately ahead, and what blacks demand is to be black through any of the various divisions of the society which are meaningful: religion, culture, language, institutions, and structures. They want it to be all right to be black, to be black and marry whom it pleases them. In the past interbreeding between blacks and whites has taken place without equal opportunity, consent, or consignment. Blacks are permanently shaped by this reality, they cannot become more or less black, they can only become black. In the past, cohabitation between blacks and whites was largely clandestine. Thus in a day when social and sexual intercourse has begun to take place in public, and with the pledge of allegiance to blackness, it should not be surprising to discover that blacks accept marriage in black and white as right in principle and practice for those who choose this way. Marriage in black and white may brighten, it will not "dull the impact."

Faithful Jews reserve their biggest attack upon marriage in black and white for the position which holds that black-white marriage is the way to instant human brotherhood, the bringing in of the Kingdom of God. The acceptance of black-white marriages by blacks is based on their awareness that they have always been attractive to whites. Otherwise the question "Would you want your daughter to marry a Negro?" would have no meaning. Blacks know what whites wish to hide: that blacks and whites are one in blood, genes, and culture, and thus they love and hate each other with such passion. Blacks as a group are not interested in marriage in black and white, yet neither do they fear it; they do not have elaborate arguments or practices to discourage it. Blacks see no relationship between accepting the reality of marriage in black and white among individuals and pushing for marriage in black and white as means to human brotherhood. Rather, blacks know that human brotherhood will come only when it is all right to be black, therefore it must be all right to be anything that increases human brotherhood. In contrast, faithful Jews believe there is only one way to the goal of real humanness. Exclusiveness is the voice of the past. Blacks are the people of the future for their destiny is one with all mankind. For blacks there are more ways than one to real humanity, and they wish to be and will be found moving down all of them at once. Blacks are for the best which is not the same for all. In a word, faithful Jews are understood to be sincerely reasonable, but wrong:

> Belief in the distinctiveness of a certain culture or religion
> and the desire on the part of some individual or group of
> individuals to perpetuate that distinctiveness because of its
> demonstrable superiority does not, of itself, make any person
> less a proponent of human brotherhood.[49]

They are wrong because the above statement, in the context of the whole Jewish case, is a defensive opposition to marriage in black and white qua marriage in black and white, a position they equate with perpetuation of distinctiveness, when in truth there are many ways to perpetuate "demonstrable superiority," and the best ways are not to keep people out but to welcome them in. Religion cannot be defended on the same basis that one defends a private club, an exclusive social group. Faithful Jews love polarized intermarriage and in-groupness. The future and truth lie not in extremes, but in the flexible and imaginative many ways. There is no way to human brotherhood—human brotherhood is the way. Whatever ways human brotherhood calls us to support, many will be called and some will be chosen.

For the sake of the one way approach to human brotherhood—"the desire to perpetuate one's own religion or to prevent its assimilation"—it is not necessary to eliminate or attack or discourage a human way that may not be for brotherhood so much as it is for interpersonal humanness—marriage in black and white. Religion when pridefully deployed "becomes a divider rather than a binder." Faithful Jews hold that

> diversity in color, race, or religion, is, then, neither a blessing
> nor a curse in itself. It may become one or the other,
> depending entirely upon how diverse peoples use their
> diversity.[50]

The case for group survival and strength is made in this statement. Blacks know that their "diversity in color, race, or religion" is viewed and used by the majority of whites as "a curse in itself."

This negative white reaction has prompted in blacks the advocacy of "diversity in color, race, or religion" as a blessing "in itself." The emphasis of blacks is upon diversity. They have learned through long years that for the black group and the black individual, diversity is "in itself" the strength and hope of this diverse people. It is not for "color, race, or religion" that blacks hold out their hand in welcome to "diverse peoples," for they have known singularity or diversity in these differences qua differences to be as harmful as they are helpful. It is the diversity of people in unity that blacks proclaim—diversity in, by, through, and beyond color, race, or religion. Unity that emerges from and depends on the diversity of *all* people, not diversity in *a* united people, insures the best for each individual and group.

Chapter Seven

RATIONALIZATIONS DETERRING
TECHNICOLORED UNIONS IN SPIRIT AND FLESH

As we have seen earlier, the 1967 Supreme Court decision, which lampooned the legality of states prohibiting marriage between blacks and whites, was a historic act. It was more than a symbolic decision, though the heavy hand of past customs and sentiments insure that there will be no significant shift in the rate of black-white marriages. This decision put an end to negative laws designed to keep blacks in their place and signaled the continuation of positive law, affirmative action for the well-being of all citizens. It has taken us a long time to act upon what we have always known to be true: liberty without fraternity is not equality. Without a doubt, the powerful presence of color as an influence in the world and the conscious world affirmation of human rights are forces that help us toward the right. We still have a long way to go, but this decision makes it clear that we are no longer restrained by the myth, "we cannot legislate morals." There is one more myth that has been toppled, the myth that there is a rank order of rational change so that relations such as prejudice must be modified first and others later. We have awakened to the only reality, the necessity and wisdom of moving on all fronts at once. In waiting for the majority to catch up with the minority we deny the latter their rightful opportunity. By supporting the majority and the minority in their rights we penalize neither, admitting that all men are equal but some are more equal than others.

The free choice of the minority will never be the freedom chosen by the majority, and this difference of choice particularly applies to black-white unions. There is a minority who have discovered that the "crisis in black and white" is not primarily the result of economic, housing, and educational barriers but of the barriers in our minds that must be struck down through restructuring our thinking action. Those who are free from color prejudice and choose to marry have eliminated another area where there was once a barrier in the mind. Such people are too evocative for us. We wish they were not so free of the barriers we have raised. We like barriers and we like them high. We feel safe beneath them and secure behind them. We are only shaken when in our midst there are those who live without these indispensable fortresses.

Some of these barriers are rationalizations spun out of whole cloth. Our experience is that such barriers, like laws, are necessary to curb the few who would otherwise increase and thereby disrupt the good of the order. Perhaps, in time, these rationalizations deterring technicolored unions will go the way of the laws. On the way toward the future, the majority will insist upon its prejudices. Understanding these rationalizations may help us to see why a minority must take them with a grain of salt. Myths have meaning and relevance; they do engage reality and speak of truth found there through experience. But myths are selective, they disclose a partial truth, they are not representative of "the whole truth, and nothing but the truth." All of us live by our myths, and mistake our limited perspective as the truth. This tendency is understandable, but it is not acceptable, particularly as we seek to force upon those who perceive a different version of reality our version of reality as synonymous with the whole of reality.

Here an old Russian proverb applies to blacks and whites alike, both to the majority who oppose black-white marriages and to those of the minority who engage in them: "We do not hate the wolf because his fur is gray, but because he eats our sheep."

MARRIAGE IN BLACK AND WHITE
IS INAPPROPRIATE

The inflexible racist argues and acts on the belief that blacks are monkeys rather than human beings, a presupposition which leads to the conclusion that the two species are not fit for cohabitation. One cannot cross apes and humans and achieve human results. The flexible racist contends that there is a "white race" which is superior to the inferior "black race" and that any black-white marriage deteriorates the presumed superior stock. Until recent years these views were seemingly reinforced by laws that were interpreted to be forms of protection for the human species against an unwitting interpenetration with and by an inimical species which only appeared to be human. Historically, the first law prohibiting marriage in black and white was enacted in the Colony of Maryland to curb the frequent marriages between white indentured women and black slaves. The children of these marriages which took place before the law were black. A later law allowed a free white woman to marry a black slave provided the permission of the slave master was obtained. This law granted the woman her continued status of freedom but gave the slave master and the clergyman involved the power to inflict deterring penalties. However, since it took six or seven years for an indentured servant to become free, the laws were real deterrents. They also reflected the truth that free people of the same standing in the community, however high or low, find each other and marry irrespective of color, unless prohibited.

The dynamics of our "one world" are such that clergymen who focus upon the color of people's skin rather than on their strength of purpose, integrity of character, and awareness of problems, are the exception. Moreover, the role of the family is in transition from one of an institution to one of companionship:

> In the past the important factors unifying the family have been external, formal, and authoritarian, as the law, the mores, public opinion, tradition, the authority of the family head, rigid discipline, and elaborate ritual. At present, in the new emerging form of the companionship of the family, its unity inheres less and less in community pressures and more

and more in such interpersonal relations as the mutual affection, the sympathetic understanding, and the comradeship of its members.[1]

To say today that a black-white marriage is inappropriate is to say less about the social mores and still-strong taboos and more about the personal prejudices one holds for oneself. One man's prejudice is another man's freedom. In our mobile, urban, technological, electric, and anonymous society it is more difficult than not to call forth enforcements through the ties of neighbors and relatives. In this context, the reality must be faced that the blessings of marriage may be experienced in any kind of marriage. Thus, we must declare that if two persons find marriage in black and white appropriate for them, it is appropriate. Otherwise, instead of persons marrying for the best of reasons, they may be conditioned by our unfitting negations to marry in support of a cause.

INTERCOLORED INTIMACY
MEANS SOCIAL OSTRACISM

This century's once downward trend in marriage between blacks and whites appears to some researchers to be on the upswing now. In the past few white men married black women. Those who did were largely European born, and their foreign values did not place a "color stigma" upon blacks. If few American white men married black women, nevertheless in extramarital relations the white man has been more involved with black women than black men have been involved with white women. A partial explanation for the infrequency of marriage between white men and black women was the penalty to his employment security which the white man assumed to be automatic. The trend toward more white men marrying black women is indicative of the attractive role of color in a society no longer rural or small town oriented. One can make one's way in urban and technological America quite apart from one's familial relationships.

For good or ill, anonymity in a mobile society means that people are employed on the basis of their personal competence and ability. In our pragmatic society the results that one brings forth are what counts, not the personal life.

Most of all, the transition in the family role from that of an "institution" to one of "companionship," means that one has a greater dependence upon the singular primary group rather than on the extended kinship relationship of the past. Internal family strength offsets the other forces which once were so indispensable to family well-being. These developments in our society benefit the technicolored family as much as the white-white or black-black family.

We live at a time when those who are alive only to the small world in which they live do not often find it within their power to marry a black, but there is every expectation that some persons will. Indeed, there is a growing willingness on the part of both whites and blacks to engage with persons of the same socio-economic-political-educational level. There are far fewer black-white marriages than we as a society are ready to welcome.

With respect to whites marrying blacks, everything depends upon the presence and interaction of blacks at all levels of life, their sheer availability. With respect to blacks marrying whites, everything is dependent upon the acceptance of black-white marriages in a given community. At least with respect to New York, San Francisco, Chicago, Detroit, and Los Angeles these two factors are on the rise.

Thus, the only ostracism faced by couples in the middle class range comes from their former home environment, not from their present or any likely future one. Irrespective of our heritages, we choose our friends on the basis of common values and interests. For the most part, we have few, rather than a great many, very good friends. Home entertainment and occasional outings to social clubs open to the public are far more prevalent than belonging to private and exclusive clubs. There are some personal insults which a black-white couple might confront, but they occur so seldom that even such a disturbance is something less than unsettling. No, social ostracism is hardly a reality, though if it were, along with personal insults, the cost is not prohibitive.

If we were concerned to answer the question why the majority of blacks and whites do not intermarry, it would be enough to assert that the WASP ethos of this culture has determined from the beginning that there would be no social equality between blacks and whites and that strong taboos have permeated WASPS and blacks and immigrants alike.[2] There are whites, too, who wish to retain their economic dominance and therefore exploit the fears of the larger society. Despite these realities, our concern is simply to recognize the minority in our culture who triumph over the taboos and who would fare much better were these social taboos rejected by us all as past inheritances we should forsake for our future. Groups will remain relatively stable; the restriction of blacks to ghettos insures this stability. Our rise in individualism and decline in institutional controls means there will be some problems in the culture during this transition period, at least until we discover ways for mature individuals to do what pleases them, and it pleases them to do the fitting thing. Though still numerically small, people are intermarrying at an increasing rate due to a number of factors,[3] discussed in Chapter Six.

CHILDREN OF INTERMARRIAGES ARE NOT FULLY ACCEPTED

It is widely held that neither the black nor the white community accepts children born of technicolored marriages. This is the most often repeated argument and is generally considered to be the most persuasive, particularly when a strong couple is considered capable of making the necessary adjustments. I have witnessed the most liberal minded mothers and fathers come to tears over this one, stating unbelief that one of their children would bring forth a child by a black person with the full knowledge of the great evil that will be thrust upon them. When one infers from this implication that blacks qua blacks ought not to have children the tears dry up.

The only validity to this argument bears not on the children born of an intercolored marriage, but on the children born out of wedlock to a white woman by a black man and sometimes vice versa. Actually, this kind of "interbreeding" is on the decrease with the rise in black pride and black opportunity. The point is that such cases, where the child is not accepted, are due to the fact that marriage has not taken place and that the relationship was not a responsible one.

The fact is that a child born of a black-white couple will be lighter than the black partner. A light child has always had the best of it in the black community because of the feeling that being the light child is nearest to the majority group and therefore has advantages which do not accrue to the darker child. But even this advantage is waning in an age of the "instant Negro." However, the chances are also better for a light child to gain acceptance by his white grandparents. Since the child is considered black in this society, from the child's perspective there is no more difficulty getting along with children than experienced by a black child of black-black parents. By the time the child enters college or is ready for work, the color of his skin has traditionally been a definite advantage to him which he may or may not wish to use. Thus, whether on the family, personal, or social level, the child of a black-white marriage has all the disadvantages of being black mitigated by some of the advantages of being light or white.

The child of black-white parents has one more option, whether an advantage or not: the child can choose, if he or she is light enough, to be white. Among the many who "pass" each year the majority are males. Women may not have the opportunity or the inducements to "pass" as often as do the men, probably because being light in a black world is an advantage and women have been encouraged to conform more to the customs of society and to the expectations of the family.

BLACK FEMALE IS A PURE SEXUAL ORGANISM

It is a common saying, if not a common practice, that "a white man is not a man until he has slept with a nigger." Some white men are bent on the belief, and the action that follows from it, that every black woman irrespective of her cultural achievements and character reputation is fair game. This myth that black women will go to bed with anyone, especially a white man, may grow out of the advantages taken by whites in the period when black men could not protect their women. Whatever the source of this myth, one of its results may be a hatred of white men by some black women who deem involvement with them even in marriage a "slut" relationship.

The opinion that black women are of all creatures the most sexually awakened and powerful may in large measure be due to the inferior status they are granted in comparison with that ascribed to white women in the society, to the fact that they have, until of late, been forced to care for their families through domestic work where they have been in more intimate contact with whites than black males. That white men get excited in the presence of black women leads the latter to feel unduly "eyeballed" in certain circumstances, since they are not so much admired as women, but as objects of prey or pay. Some white women feel that black women are unfair competition because they are held to have a primitive passion which is ever ready and inexhaustible. The black female as the sex militant is largely the outgrowth of unfulfilled needs in white men.

The truth is that black women have no more raw sexuality than do white women. Indeed, the lower proportion of black men to black women has led to frigidity among some black women. Of course it is true that the self-fulfilling prophecy works here as elsewhere. If whites believe black women to have a savage potency which is unmatchable, it should not be surprising that whites find this potency in black women.

It is the cheap way in which white men have engaged black women I find the cruelest dimension of black-white relations in the society. White men have failed to be serious in their relationships with the black woman in comparison to the seriousness of relationships between the black man and the white woman. The clandestine and illicit relations engaged in by white men on the basis of brute power do not indicate much more than superior force. What is important now is to forget the underhanded and irresponsible ways of the past and to insure that the present and future be dominated by public, open, and responsible relationships. When the white man discovers that a relationship with a black woman cannot be on his terms, that the black woman is not an animal to be attacked, the love between black women and white men may grow, and the white male fascination with the black woman as an organism may die. When viewed as a "black beauty" instead of a "black beast" the black woman may prove to be far less alluring, savage, and sexy.

WHAT THE BLACK BUCK WANTS
IS A WHITE WOMAN

More black women have been attacked and seduced against their will by white men than have white women been attacked and seduced by black men. It is also true that more black men have gained white women out of mutual admiration and love than white men have gained black women on a serious, equal basis.

Still, the black male is seen as one bestial in nature, the great "walking phallus," whose only desire is to sleep with a white woman. Fascination with the black man's genitals seems to be a preoccupation among some whites. I recall, in the neighborhood in which I was reared, one of the white fellows talking with another about a white girl by whom they both were gratified. The gist of the conversation was that this girl had an affair with a black man, and this fellow wouldn't touch her again "with a ten foot pole" because "once one of those black bucks tears into a white woman there is no way on earth for a white man to satisfy her."

This vision of black men engenders in white women a belief in the extraordinary gifts of the black man; he is seen as the summit of sexual engagement. Some women take this myth so seriously that they seek out black men and, having found one or more, will have nothing to do with white men. Frantz Fanon, in *Black Skin, White Masks,* suggests that some white women become so taken by this myth that they dream of being savagely raped and ravaged by a black man.

What is certain is that those who spin this myth tend to bring blacks and whites together around the sole concern of sex as often as they do to prevent interrelatedness. The woman who takes this myth for reality will find no difference in the genital length or circumference between blacks and whites nor within their groups. It may be that some blacks are better lovers than some whites, but this possibility has everything to do with their concentration upon technique as opposed to their natural endowments.

Since black men have been kept away from white women

through isolation, laws, punishments such as lynching for "eyeball raping," and myths, it does seem natural to assume that given an opportunity the black male will try to see what it is he has been denied. Of course the legend that black men want white women because they find them so desirable is countered by the belief of white folks that black women are the living end of sex, and logically one would conclude that the two most sexual beings on earth (black males and females) could and would be satisfied with nothing less than each other.

Our fundamental belief is not that black men want white women, it is that white women want black men. The onus placed on the black man—that he is a romantic figure to whom white women are attracted—is the way to project our deepest fears. Given equal opportunity, we fear that the white woman would choose a black man, and therefore, the black man must be viewed as the wolf seeking to steal the innocent sheep. Somehow, the power of the black male is thought to be such that the white woman cannot say "No."

What the black male wants in this society is equal opportunity to be a man, with all of the implicit and explicit rights, privileges, and prestige. He wants to be treated as an individual who has the opportunity to develop his ability and be respected for his merit. Instead he must live in a society that not only fails to give him his due but actually works against his being responsible. As if this were not enough, the society has created the most evil myth imaginable to insure that he is kept down, "in his place." The myth cannot be changed or eradicated, but it is possible to radically change the society so that such myths have no place of power or meaning for the callous.

WHITE WOMANHOOD IS UNTOUCHABLE
Nothing is more revolting or shocking to a white man than to see a black man with a white woman. Unlike a white man with a black woman, who may be her employer or sugar daddy, the black man has to be up to no good. Lurking beneath this view is the belief that the black woman is an easy target for the white man's frustration, particularly in light of the assumption that all white women are to be praised. In a black-white involvement the

white woman is never suspect, only the black man; conversely, never the white man, only the black woman.

White women have been brought up with one or two beliefs about black men. The first is the belief that all black men are rapists in constant heat and desire for a white woman. When the white woman holds this belief, she is overly conscious of sex as something that will ruin her for life. The second belief is the assumption that all black men are to be treated as "dumb male animals," a belief that supposedly eliminates any sexual attractiveness between the two. In this latter belief a supposed freedom of interaction between the two is implied: the black man knows that to touch a white woman may mean instant death, while the white woman knows the black man to be potent among his kind.

Of course it works out that white women are extremely drawn to black men in either instance, though the necessities of the environment may result in suppression or repression of this sexual attractiveness. Above the Mason Dixon line, some white women often act in public as they have behaved in secret below the line. Just as white men have seduced black maids who had no recourse but to submit in their home, so it is that white women have seduced black servants with the same authority and results.

The free association between blacks and whites with an "understanding" has been traditional in the South. In the North, blacks and whites have generally been reared apart and do not meet until they leave the neighborhood for college or employment. In these circumstances there are two kinds of women especially attracted to blacks. There are the white women involved with black people in such issues as civil rights and peace movements and those who become involved with blacks through other areas of mutual interest where they simply back into each other or accidentally find each other. There are white women who have been reared in such a fashion that they never have known a live black man until they meet one outside the "white noose." These situations are worth recalling here because they typify experiences common to white women in the North, and the Southern dominant mode is breaking up in favor of the Northern pattern.

The white woman is first of all a woman and secondly a follower of the dominant white mores. The overwhelming majority of white women, like white men, will not venture beyond the bounds of conformity. Neither the white woman nor the white man are antiblack, except as the culture makes them so. But this same culture will make some white women attracted to the green grass on the other side. All women have within them that dimension of Eve, the possibility of being lured by forbidden fruit. Few of them will be or are reduced to the ways of the snake in the seeking of a black bedfellow at dusk. Most white women are curious, fascinated, and attracted to black men as much as they are revolted, disgusted, and turned off by them.

TECHNICOLORED MARRIAGE IS A SPECIAL CASE IN INTERMARRIAGE

Among minority groups (racial, religious, or ethnic) there is a tendency for the man to out-marry with more frequency than the woman, and the following factors are largely responsible for the higher rate of out-marriage among males:

1. The women in these groups have fewer opportunities for meeting the men in other groups than the minority men have for meeting women outside their own group.

2. Religious and other institutional controls of behavior may exert a stronger influence on minority women than on minority men.

3. Men take the initiative in dating and courtship.

4. Marrying a woman in the majority group, or a woman in the minority group whose appearance and manners closely approximate those of the majority-group women, is a symbol of success, of prestige, of being accepted in the larger community.[4]

These reasons for the male minority member marrying out seem largely plausible. It would appear to be very normal, desirable, and to be expected for people who interact with common values and goals to intermarry. In fact, the more such interaction occurs, the more intermarriage is assumed. This pattern is true of Jews and of Catholics. It is also true of Orientals in America.

What seems unreasonable here is the implication made in No. 4 above that male minority group out-marriages are not so normal and expected because of interaction but because of a special desire on the part of these males. There is also implied here a belief that there is something wrong when such actions occur, that one ought to marry within his minority group because most people do. So, if one does marry outside of his group, there has to be more than naturalness, i.e., the absence of prejudice involved; the desire for "success" or "prestige" is the motive. This interpretation does not appear to be a fair representation of reality especially if one takes into account the low sex ratio per 100 of Oriental men to women, for example. Of course the prestige factor may come into play with some individuals, but people who fall in love and marry are not generally so callous.

The interpretation cited above is even more suspect when it is elaborated by the following statement:

> In the case of the Negro in the United States, it may also mean the realization of a wish, perhaps an unconscious wish, to have children who will be nearer to the ideal physical type of this country.[5]

Among black men there has been a tendency to marry the "light skin" woman not so much because she is "a symbol of success, of prestige," but more because her features are more in line with dominant beauty features of the culture. Certainly black men have not married light skinned women in the hope of "being accepted in the larger community." Surely the black man does not marry a white woman for the purpose of the beautiful children they will bring forth, even if this is a happy result. Most of all, such views are dated in this new era when "black is beautiful," when color is desirable.

It is widely believed that since marriages are not the norm they are not normal. There has to be something unacceptable about people who marry in black and white. Those who take this stand and spread this message usually analyze the culture by accepting its values as the way things should be and are without making judgments upon it. Judgments are reserved for the individuals involved who are believed to be sick people in a healthy society, though I believe they are, more often than not, healthy people in a sick society. These improper judgments inveigh not simply against marriage in black and white, they cast in the wrong light what would otherwise be considered healthy social intercourse between blacks and whites.

There are no more potent rationalizations deterring technicolored unions in spirit or in flesh than the psychological ones. Black men are supposed to marry white women because of their rebellion against the society or their parents, because of their affinity for the exotic or a need for "kicks," because of their hostile desire to get even with white men for their past history of raping black women and holding black men down, for the flattery of being loved by a member of the dominant group, and because of their attraction to forbidden fruit. White women are supposed to marry black men because of their desire for attention, their pity for the underdog, because of a guilt and need to atone for whites' mistreatment of blacks, because of their rebellion against societal and parental authority, their attraction for the exotic, the lure of forbidden fruit, and because of a desire to prove their lack of prejudice.

In contrast, people may marry "their own kind" for the most weird reasons, yet these reasons do not make each marriage suspect. Some black-white marriages may well occur for less than the best of reasons, but to conclude that ulterior motives are primary says more about the individuals making these interpretations and about the society in which we live than about the couple who intermarry.

We may not wish to accept the times in which we live, but the old assumptions that discredit the involvement of blacks and whites no longer can be trusted. In fact, it is no longer typical of black-white marriages that the "majority woman" is of a lower socioeconomic status than the minority man she marries. The marriage of Margaret Elizabeth Rusk and Guy Gibson Smith may not be typical of black-white marriages. What is significant about this marriage is symbolic: the future should be our guide in the present, not the past.

In these critical days, perhaps marriage in black and white

cannot be perceived as a simple moral right to be cherished. In a time of domestic crisis progress can best be made, for if we do not advance on all fronts at once we shall advance slowly and perhaps not at all. If we do not support people who are in the right, we inevitably support those in the wrong. If a minority is not free, the majority is bound. If through inertia, indifference, or inaction we fail to give aid and comfort to those who wish to do the right, the many in the wrong who wish to inflict harm will assume they are doing *the* right. We need not be concerned to establish the principle of healthy black-white unions; that has been done in practice. We need to be concerned to establish the practice of healthy black-white intimacy, that it may be done in principle.

Chapter Eight

REASONED OPPOSITION TO BLACK-WHITE MARRIAGES

T he issue of intimate relations between blacks and whites in the United States is usually described in print as an exotic or daring affair. It would appear impossible for people of different skin colors to enter into a wholesome relationship as a natural course in human destiny. Obsession with subterranean racism and sex distorts our perception and thus the reality of black and white intimacy. Those who engage in such intimacy are understood to be rebelling against their parents or social values and are considered to be psychologically perverted or socially deformed, marginal misfits or pursuers of forbidden fruit. There is no doubt that such people are to be found in our society, and they do make good copy. My experience discloses that intercolored involvements often are internally wholesome, and that the disquieting effects result from external interferences. What is disturbing to me is our American way of accepting and defending these deranged social mores as if they were sacred and therefore inviolable. The thrust of our society has become one of placing the onus on individuals who find themselves intimately related across the artificial barriers of skin color, instead of actively changing the social customs toward a more open society of mutual support. This fundamental sickness and irresponsibility calls us to positive response and change.

It is not up to Americans to decide for or against miscegenation; our history has already determined that miscegenation is not to be the planned pattern. It is up to Americans to determine whether or not persons engaged in intercolored relationships shall find encouragement and reinforcement so as to increase the healthiness of their relationship and therefore of the nation, as well as to make us aware of our sickness, so that we act before we become sick unto death. Because I believe that healthy intimacy between blacks and whites will contribute more to our maturity as a people than will desperate reaction or indifference, and that marriage in black and white is of great symbolic value because it does point to our real concerns and needs, I think it will be helpful at this juncture to take a candid look at the intelligent opposition. My interest in this entire issue is not the result of armchair speculation or of mere academic curiosity. My interest grows out of a concern for the welfare of my two sons, who daily move in a white society and one day soon will be called upon to decide for or against healthy-mindedness in black-white social intercourse.

The thrust of this book does not run counter grain to the dominant concerns of the American black minority. It is not difficult to determine the order and priorities of black America's wants. They are, unmistakably, equal opportunity and results in employment, education, housing, law courts, politics, police enforcement, and public facilities. Among the least concerns of black Americans are the desegregation of churches, integrated social clubs or social life, and black-white marriage or sexual intercourse! However few, blacks and whites *do* intimately relate and marry. Moreover, the number who do will increase, albeit those who do will constitute only a permanent minority among both groups. It is the emergence of intercolored public, rather than unnatural intimate, associations that the majority of blacks and whites cannot escape, though it concerns them so little. As a matter of statistical fact, intercolored unions ought to concern us little. It is a different matter when the issue is posed as a moral, human, or political one. It is in the American tradition to aid the underdog, to nurture and cherish the minority against the tyranny of the majority, because the dissenters are in their right and may be right, if ahead of their time.

It is not insignificant, then, in the light of the democratic dynamics to set forth here the basis of the white majority's and black minority's opposition to black and white marriages. In addition to the American Creed of "liberty and justice for all," there is a pervasive religious and social fundamentalism that determines intercolored intimacy unacceptable.

The intellectual Protestant white moderate liberal admits there is an irrational color prejudice—what I call preconscious white folk religion—but he would call it a "color stigma." The color stigma is to his mind indistinguishable from the stigma attached to Jews and to Catholics in kind or degree. His faith is in integration through social interaction and consequent acculturation, assimilation. The immediate task is to do what can be done now: desegregation in all spheres of society and mutual aid among blacks to increase ability so that opportunity can be taken advantage of immediately. Full opportunity for the black follows desegregation, which increases social interaction and results in assimilation. Since it will take decades of legal enforcement and, perhaps, special efforts in employment for the black male who has not been allowed to take the male lead demanded in the society, as well as special endeavors for black youth, integration as full assimilation will take generations. It is nonsense, pure fantasy, to now seek more than full opportunity in employment and education. Thus, marriage in black and white, which presupposes equality of opportunity, education, and a common style of life, is out of sight and therefore should be out of mind and action. In calling for integration *now* in employment and education, as the means to assimilation in the future, the white moderate liberal sees interaction between blacks and whites as a necessity. The more interaction, the more integration—and the less prejudice. Of course there is little interaction through interpersonal cooperation between blacks and whites outside of employment, because there is increasing discrimination with respect to housing and therefore education. Marriage in black and white cannot be a goal, now, because it would increase prejudice and pull support from surefire full opportunity. Equal status, as opposed to equal opportunity, is a hoped for result of integration, not a process to be pressed.

Black-white marriages are not the end result for the white liberal moderate. His continuum is not integration toward assimilation, and in this end he opposes the white moderate liberal. The white liberal moderate sees disvalue in black people losing their uniqueness. The objective he sets forth is inclusion, or full citizenship—the opportunity to share the wealth and health of the society without giving up differences which can enrich. The white moderate liberal believes the eventual goal is for black people to rise to the level of middle class white people on all fronts, and when black people have achieved this level, the "color stigma" will vanish and intermarriage will result. On the contrary, says the white liberal moderate, our society is a dynamically pluralistic one. Witness the change which has come about through the inclusion of Jews and Catholics. It is through their advancement as religious bodies with competence, skill, and reserve that we have a pluralistic society in the twentieth century. They did not become WASPS. Neither do black people need to become WASPS to gain inclusion. Indeed, black people are looked to as a cohesive group to continue the reformation of this society beyond that accomplished by Jews and Catholics so that not only they but all persons will be included "without regard to race, creed, religion, national origin, or condition of previous servitude." The test of democracy rides with blacks and has implications for the clash of color throughout the world. The color stigma is present; what needs to be eliminated is not color but the stigma. The way is through black people insisting upon being included in the society at the same time they uplift themselves through community efforts of mutual support. In the decades ahead this process will enhance the meaning and value of color through group solidarity while eliminating the stigma, the handicap of color which prevents its inclusion. The American way is that of pluralism, solidarity at the risk of separatism, but neither separatism nor assimilation is the objective. The objective and process is full participation combined with the preservation of identity. Thus, if marriages in black and white occur, they will be a by-product, a spinning off of the main process. They will also be incidental and minimal. Assimilation through marriage is not desirable because black people are for pluralism, and pluralism is the American way which requires group solidarity.

Marriage in black and white as a process worthy of support is opposed or ignored by the white moderate liberal because his hope is in equal opportunity with interaction on the way to assimilation whereby there will be no differences between whites and blacks. Marriage in black and white is not in the white liberal moderate's picture because his hope is in pluralism through black internal uplift and an outward pressure. Both positions are based on the assumption that the blacks are a total group in the society, that black people rise or fall together. These positions hold in common the presupposition that color stigma or prejudice can and will be eliminated in the end. They further assume that the model of the immigrants' entrance into the society is an analogy of significance, that black people are on a continuum with Jews and Catholics.

It is precisely at this point that the white liberal disagrees. The comparison of blacks with other immigrants ignores slavery and the white view of blacks as inferior primitives. Both the fact of slavery and the inferior status ascribed to blacks are manifested in white attitudes toward blacks vis-à-vis assumed subservient roles and marriage. The key test of a society is who is accepted for marriage. Not only WASPS but Jews and Catholics view blacks as the out-group for marriage. Of course it is true that the once prevalent Jewish orthodoxy which led the Jewish father to mourn his son or daughter as dead following marriage with a gentile appears similar to white reaction to marriages between blacks and whites. But the color stigma did not and does not follow marriage between persons of different ethnic, national, or religious groups. They can melt into the society even though they may not have family blessings.

It is also the case that prejudice between whites and blacks which does not manifest itself on the job, in functional relations, is manifested in social relations. The same person who can interact well with blacks on the job will exclude them from the neighborhood, and consequently from the school and family. This exclusion occurs because prejudice responds differently to the differing reference groups and reference group conflict. Thus, prejudice is ego fulfilling in relation to some reference groups and not to others. Interaction is not linear; it does not lead to modification of prejudice on all levels, but, indeed, reinforces prejudice in some areas while decreasing it in others. To view the black as an immigrant obscures the fact that in many metropolitan areas throughout the North and South blacks have been educated, do gain high economic rewards, are professionals, and have a style of living compatible with middle class whites. Yet these blacks who have been in society for generations are not accepted; in many areas they do not gain their full citizenship. Of course, if the argument is that all blacks must reach a high level before inclusion or integration and assimilation will take place, it supports the theory of irrational color prejudice, preconscious white folk religion.

To be sure, the outpouring of blacks into the urban centers from rural areas of the South has increased the ghetto-like existence of blacks, but this fact only exposes to view what was previously ignored. To assume that in time, since we are over the hump of the in-migration from rural communities in the South, interaction will take place, overlooks the fact that whites could isolate themselves from blacks without imprisoning them in ghettos. The fact that blacks regardless of the level they attain are not readily accepted into any neighborhood of their financial ability and choice means that prejudice does not subside with black achievement. Whites believe that blacks inherently have different values that threaten all whites. Blacks therefore must be locked out. Where there are exceptions to the rule, the rule is that only a few Negroes can be allowed in the neighborhood to prevent movement toward the "tip-point" when whites move out en masse. This rule appears to be a permanent one and applies everywhere in the United States. This special rule for blacks is held by Jews and Catholics who, like WASPS, inflict the color stigma on blacks.

It is to the credit of the white liberal that he does not hold out the hope of inevitable assimilation or of group solidarity as monistic patterns for the blacks. He does not think these patterns insignificant, only insufficient. He sees full well that the opportunity for blacks to gain full citizenship is better now than at any time in history. The previous attainments of Jews and Catholics aid this. A dynamic and expanding economy makes it possible for the absorption of blacks into the labor market, even if special help for the black male and black youths is demanded. There is pressure, too, from the role of the United States as a leader in the world, as well as pressure from within through the presence of Asians and Africans here as diplomats and students who must be treated with equality. There is also pressure caused by the rise of blacks in Africa to positions of leadership in their nations, though this new leadership represents but a paper revolution since African blacks are still dependent upon economic ties to former powers. Yet, all of this pressure for progress can be stymied by a Vietnam war. The white liberal knows that there is no guarantee to keep other wars and distractions from preventing the movement toward the inclusion of blacks in this society. Thus, the white liberal adds to the objective of inclusion or integration an attack upon prejudice. It is the white liberal's conviction that as long as there are enforced ghettos, there will be little interaction of the kind that changes reference groups on all levels. Thus the attack upon prejudice requires a changing of interracial patterns. Without these changes, equal opportunity in the short run will not bring equal status in the long run.

The key thrust must be for open housing, says the white liberal. But here is the rub: blacks do not push for open housing because they have assumed that whites do not want them, and they do not want the discomfort that comes from being with whites. Black communities have become deeply rooted as a result of prejudice, and as a result, blacks have vested interests in the black community which would be eliminated if they moved out. Moreover, only a few blacks could move out. They must face token integration, which many blacks deem not worth the effort. The few blacks who are able and willing to move out help themselves to a certain degree, but they do not remove prejudice so much as they become the exceptions that prove the rule. The selective few blacks who integrate neighborhoods do not help erase the stigma of color as it applies to the whole black group, nor from themselves. In fact, token integration tends to give false comfort to whites or the feeling there are major changes taking place. There are, as it were, two different directions in which the black community is moving at once. The tiny middle class moves up, and the vast majority moves down. In the light of this movement, the question of marriage in black and white is irrelevant. It is not an immediate solution, nor is it a long range one. Black-white marriages do not affect color stigma as it relates to black people as a whole either for good or for ill. Neither equal opportunity nor equal status will come until changing interracial patterns are brought about on all levels. In the meantime, we must settle for better life chances available to individual blacks amidst prejudice, among which may be marriages in black and white.

The white radical parts company with white liberals of all shades and challenges reactionary whites head-on. He accepts as reality irrational color prejudice, preconscious white folk religion. Neither time nor efforts by blacks to uplift themselves while putting pressure on the larger community to give them opportunity will bring equal opportunity or equal status for all blacks. Color stigma is dominant among the white majority, which refuses to accept persons on the basis of merit. The majority insist upon ascription of status by skin color on a group basis. The entire white society accepts this basis; it is not different whether the white members of this society be Jews or Catholics or WASPS. Indeed, blacks operate on the same basis. The very tone and structure of our social system prevents individual achievement overriding color as in Bahia, Brazil. The white radical concludes that equal opportunity without equal status is neither possible nor desirable. The strategy of equal opportunity is seen by the white radical to be both complex and circuitous. It is a suspension of encounter with reality, a secular postponement of future rewards which, like heaven, will not come to pass. Some blacks will benefit more than others from pluralism, but all blacks will be subject to color stigma. The only fitting response that will eliminate the suffering of blacks, the white radical claims, is assimilation through marriage now. Of course the white radical is stuck with the reality that there is no place to begin this interbreeding. The minute number of whites or blacks who would agree with the white radical do not constitute a large enough group to make any change in the social system. Logically, the white radical is difficult to counter; but men do not live by logic alone. Logic in and of itself is unimportant—it is meaningful only within a system of social relations. It is true that black people believe in and work for freedom of choice among all people within our social system to a greater extent than whites, but they join with whites in ruling the logic of white radicals out of bounds. It is not surprising that blacks reject the white radical's proposal of marriage for different reasons than do whites. They certainly do not accept the faith that "Negroes are inferior by nature to superior whites," the irrational color prejudice that is the preconscious religion of white folks.

BLACKS ARE EQUAL BY NATURE TO WHITES

Black Nationalism rejects marriage in black and white because they accept the condition of "separate but equal," the operating policy of the white majority in all things social. The significance of Black Nationalists is that their response is not a defensive one. They have no secret hope of joining with the whites in a distant future any more than in the immediate present. They are for separatism with equality if they can get it, but separatism without equality is to be preferred to assimilation. Intimate association with whites is demeaning. Marriage with them is degrading. Such interactions sap the strength of blacks, cuts into their common bond of color. The badge of color is not viewed as a sign of servitude, it is a reality to be nurtured and cherished. Black men and women are of many hues and colors, more beautiful than whites, "the blacker the berry the sweeter the juice." Black Nationalist pride is based on the reality that color cannot be eliminated. Therefore, color is not simply to be tolerated, it is to be glorified. This view effectively counters those white liberals and radicals who perceive color "blindness" to be a possible and worthy goal. It is not true, of course, that marriage in black and white is an admission of white superiority and black inferiority by blacks and whites, or vice versa. It may break the psychological bond, but the biological bond has been invaded by white genes beyond recall. If sophisticated blacks cannot accept the logic of Black Nationalists, they are forced to concede to their spirit. There is no way out of being black; being black is the way in and up. If Black Nationalists are reactionary, the values they sustain in the blacks who follow them are canceled by the rejection of them by those blacks who marry whites. Unlike whites, blacks do not lose a son or daughter through black-white marriage in a racist society, they gain one. Except for the few who opt out altogether, there is no way but home for blacks and for those with whom they intermarry, psychologically if not socially. It is not possible, except for the callous and indifferent, to escape being black and sharing this experience with the white partner. Marriage in black and white is not a way out of suffering, though it may be a way through it for blacks or whites.

Civil rights leaders and workers condone at most the right of the individual to marry whom he pleases. A black-white marriage is not conceived by them as a good or a value, but a choice not to be encouraged or discouraged. Civil rights people wish to ignore such marriages because they see them as tactical errors, poor strategy on the way to integration. They tend to one or the other of the white liberal positions and oppose the white radical. Their refusal to give positive support to such marriages does not mean they oppose them either in principle or in practice. It is believed that marriage in black and white is a "red flag" inciting the white majority to withhold concessions in the sphere of "freedom now." At bottom they believe there is enough flexibility and slack in the American system for the inclusion of blacks, but it is touch and go. They oppose or do not support marriage in black and white for the same reason they do not demand radical changes in the system. Marriages in black and white may be right but they are definitely too radical. Success in the short run is preferable to success in the long run, and more certain.

Upper class blacks do not so much as entertain marriage in black and white, though they oppose it the least. This is the group which has the life style, the education, the employment, and the values of the white upper middle class. The major distinction between them and whites is their color. Marriage in black and white might well be readily entered into by members of this group if all the barriers in the society were down. As it is, a black-white marriage, for the most part, is seen as just another burden to bear. No matter how high the upper class blacks climb, they are subject to the same caste system, the same victimization as other blacks, in kind if not degree. They perceive that only a radical shift in American values will eliminate blacks as victims. The social system requires blacks to think of themselves as blacks first and as

Americans second, however much they desire not to do so. Thus, pride of a different kind from that of the Black Nationalist forces upper class blacks to accept the American way: limited integration and equal opportunity for themselves without equal status. This is a special burden upper class blacks, partially integrated or assimilated as they are, must bear. They often prefer to live on the "gilded edge" of the ghetto though they could well afford to live in white communities and then move out wholesale into white communities. There is no point' for them to push in this area of marriage without the reward of total acceptance in all areas. Thus, upper class blacks have spun their own social system with minor feelings of inferiority or deprivation only at the point of equal education for their children. This deprivation is overcome by some through private schools. Yet, they are the "race leaders" thrown into contact with whites on all levels, occasionally social ones, more than any other group within the black subcommunities. When the best in the white and black communities meet, they know there is no reason not to find acceptance even in a black-white marriage. Whites oppose marriage even at this level, though there are exceptions, because of the color stigma of their friends, relatives, and neighbors. Upper class blacks dare not "sell out."

The black middle class differs from the Black Nationalists in principle but not in practice. Middle class blacks are content with their lot within their own churches and clubs and neighborhoods. They are hard working, law abiding, style conscious, consumption oriented, and desirous of an expanding good life. Their basic objective is neither integration nor assimilation nor inclusion but to live well and better. They wish to rise neither into the black upper class nor horizontally out into white communities. They want little more than a fair break for their children, not in housing but in education. Separate education is believed by many of this group to be equal education. If it is not, the very foundation of their life is threatened. Yet it is well known that separate education is not equal education, that residential separation increases at least educational inequality—though we have yet to see whether ghetto schools controlled by ghetto residents who have been poorly educated can bring about as good or better education for black children in the ghetto. Interaction with whites is demanded when it comes to jobs and rights; it is spurned vis-à-vis social life. Marriage in black and white frequently occurs among the members of this group, but it is a strain on their uptight life and exposes the black middle class's weaknesses with respect to black cohesiveness. Social isolation leads to ignoring the frequency of marriages in black and white.

Lower class blacks are either of the organized blue collar variety who have middle class aspirations and orientation, or of the unorganized "fun morality" variety. These two groups entertain conflicting guiding values. Marriage in black and white is perceived with suspicion at first, though it is entered into with some regularity. These marriages rub against black ethnicity and the rising pride in blackness emerging in the bottom level of the ghetto.

In addressing students on campuses across the country, as well as in all-night sessions with friends in various cities across the nation, I invariably find present black men who are the strongest advocates of Black Power and who at the same time, in the presence of their white wives, berate white people as racists. Often the white wives are more vociferous in their disapproving of whites than their black husbands. The paradox of Black Power advocates married to white women, as in the case of students courting white women, is fascinating to say the least.

On the face of it, Black Power intends to emphasize black ethnicity. Black ethnicity appears to mean black pride, black beauty, black protection, black cohesiveness, and black celebration of blackness as the highest good.

The strong advocate of black ethnicity (which is an inextricable corollary of Black Power when viewed from the popular perspective), to be consistent, should practice what he advocates—or so it would seem to the uncritical observer. That is, to take on the role of Black Power and black ethnicity requires the courting and marrying of black women exclusively. After all, it can be argued, black ethnicity is about the black male coming into power and commanding respect and therefore reversing the role previously held when he could not protect his black woman and when he could not attain roles comparable to those made available to the white male. The black woman who is ugly by black standards would seem not to exist, and even if she did, black ethnicity would require the black man to forsake all others for her comfort and welfare.

There appears to be a discrepancy between the strong and persistent and sincere expression of black ethnicity and the marriage of its proponents to white women. This discrepancy does not hold, of course, for the black man who does not advocate black ethnicity as *the* way. It does not hold for the black man who was raised in a small Midwestern town, a small far Western city, a Southern urban area, or an Eastern suburb, in a family where integration was taught and caught. A distinction is made here between the black man who advocates black ethnicity and the straight middle class oriented black man.

There are those who would be quick to say that a black man who advocates black ethnicity, yet marries white, and continually issues tirades against white people in public to the applause of his white wife, who outdoes him in blasting "honkies," is sick. Others would hold that he has failed to think through the meaning of the ideology he espouses and tabs him as inconsistent, the most damaging description the cool rationalist can unleash. Still others would hold that he is irresponsible. Some contend that such persons illustrate the self-hatred so evident among blacks, or at least that such a person, like most blacks, is in a state of perpetual ambivalence between the love-hate of being black on the one hand and the hate-love of wishing to be white on the other.

It may well be that some of these Black Power advocates can be classed as aliens to black ethnicity, betrayers of black ideals and ideology, self-hating blacks, and split personalities to be avoided and certainly not to be trusted. Yet, the truth may be much more difficult than what appears to those whose immediate tendency is to castigate or ignore such personalities. It is possible that seemingly unstable persons are indeed riding neither horn of that dilemma we may call black-white hatred exclusively, but courageously grasping both horns of the dilemma and riding through the middle. Such persons may be affirming both their blackness and their whiteness at a point in history where neither alone is beyond the need of searching criticism and deep caring. Such persons may not at all be living in the present as if it were the idyllic future, but may well be taking on the full wrath of the present in order to carve out in the now a new humanity for the future.

We cannot write off such persons who speak black ethnicity and act black-white togetherness as sincerely wrong. It is incumbent upon us to see that they exist in a paradox and, in fact, that they reveal the fundamental paradox of the American culture that cannot be avoided unless this society is left to whites, which would be the highest treason to blackness. The American culture has grasped us all and shaped us into being antiblack and prowhite—no one can escape from this reality in innocence. On their way to working out of this detrimental American dilemma, it may be necessary for them to pass through pro-blackness and antiwhiteness on the way to a new society that affirms blackness and whiteness as of equal worth. Down this road, the most militant advocates of the new America may be living out in their lives the push of pro-blackness and the pull of pro-oneness in their proantiwhiteness. Obviously, there are some whites who are more pro-black than some blacks, just as there are some blacks who are more pro-white than some whites. After all, some are born black, some achieve blackness, and others have blackness thrust upon them.

Most of all, antiblackness or antiwhiteness, which leads to hatred of blacks or to hatred of whites and therefore to the denial in principle, beyond expedience, of the right to black-white marriages, is antiAmerican democracy and Christianity, both of which have deeply informed this nation in peculiar ways. Obviously, Americans do not really believe in the principles of democracy or of Christianity, which is precisely our fundamental problem. The principles of democracy, we believe, should be believed in and therefore in moments of stress or public exposure we affirm these principles so as not to expose our real disbelief in them. Thus, on the principles of democracy and Christianity we are fundamentally ambivalent—we do not believe in them, but we believe we must pretend to believe in them. The drive of this generation of youth toward the resolving of this ambivalence or hypocrisy with respect to the principles of this nation is what we find rubbing us the wrong way; we do not understand a generation which takes these principles seriously and to heart when we have for so long operated on the system that principles are for patriotic public show, not for private action. Clearly, our practice of democracy and Christianity suffers from the same ambivalence. Therefore we are doubly ambivalent, for we practice what we believe and what we believe is that which is in our self-interest. The practice of democracy and Christianity has been on the side of antiblackness and pro-whiteness and therefore antimarriage in black and white, but at the same time practicing equality of blacks and whites as long as the functional aspects of living are segregated from the social intimacies. Yet, this nondemocratic and unChristian practice runs counter to the basic principles of each, and the very fact that we do not believe the principles of each frustrates us when the principles are believed and practiced. It is the emergence of the truth of the principles without ambiguity as priorities over conflicting practices whereby the living out of the principles leads to new practices that proves the paradox of ethnic oriented black men courting and/or marrying white women who have opted for the principles and the practice by opting for blackness as the way to turn themselves around within the society they are seeking to turn around. In this attempt, blacks and whites together are not betrayers of their true selves; they are not betrayers of black people, of white people, of America.

One further point is significant in this matter. Ethnicity is really against the mainstream of American life. Put another way, ethnicity is at best transitional. To be sure, immigrant groups like the Irish expressed their ethnicity and pushed it to the point whereby we celebrate March 17 with them and thus propelled themselves into the mainstream. Nevertheless, it is difficult to disentangle Irish ethnicity from its Roman Catholicism. The American way of life holds that one can and should identify oneself only with his religion (Protestantism, Judaism, Roman Catholicism, Eastern Orthodoxy) but not with his national origin or ethnic heritage (one cannot identify as an Italian or German or Spaniard) except as one's ethnic heritages represent minor contributions which do not get in the way of being an American. That is, ethnicity is really transformed by the American melting or transmuting pot into a peripheral concern, the sure test that one has met the test of being an American. For example, it is all right to be an Irishman once a year, as long as one is an American the rest of the year. Since Protestantism, Judaism, Roman Catholicism, and Eastern Orthodoxy all hold in common the values of God and country, the identification of oneself with one of these religions is acceptable and valuable because religion-in-general is compatible with and supportive of the American way of life.

The exception in this area appears to be the not so clear case of the Jews. Jews are not clear whether they are a religion or a culture (or both and in what degree). Actually, the only cultural distinction of Jews is their universality. Jewish culture is actually the composite of all cultures in the world, intertwined with the constance or uniqueness of Judaism. The ethnic push of blacks is in the direction of Jews, and must therefore be caught in the same kind of unclarity or irresolvability. But blacks in America do not have going for them a long and separate history within other societies from which to build up a historically unique religion as do the Jews, so that the cultural distinctions of blacks are not supported or hidden or reinforced by religion. Blacks seek ethnicity without a separate religion. Every other immigrant group has been able to find their way and status beyond ethnicity in religion, except for the Jews, who are caught in an identity crisis of their own choosing. The identity crisis of blacks is the result of an extrinsic force rather than an intrinsic one. We should not be surprised to find, therefore, blacks acting black and speaking black along with blacks speaking black and acting white, as well as blacks speaking and acting both white and black. The very ambivalence of the American culture produces this near madness. Anyone who isn't insane in our society ought to have his head examined, and such an examination might lead to the realization that it is less the mind and more the heart and spirit of America that has to be changed.

Since blacks and whites as groups at all levels do not widely sanction marriage in black and white, it would seem unwise and unproductive to promote such wedding ceremonies. But marriage in black and white is really about something more profound than a couple engaging in marital vows, it is about the union of a people. It is my view that the black community will and should grow as a dynamic force in our society. That in the process it should increase internal pride, value, power, capital, ability, and skill to both play the game according to the present rules of the society and to radically change them in the process for the common good. Separation is to be opposed as a way of life, though not as a means toward black solidarity for the good of blacks and therefore for the good of the American society as a whole. Full citizenship in the societal community is not in conflict with black identity, if it is with black separatism. Moreover, blacks cannot pull out and make it easy for their racist friends to fully take over and make this society white without question. It is the quality of the black communities as they continue to expand that is of moment. They must be enriched from within, become vitally alive in cooperation with all segments of the community for the mutual good of all.

However, to affirm the inevitability and good of black communities is not to affirm that blacks should be monolithic. There should not and cannot be a monolithic community of blacks in which all blacks must live and move and find their being. The dynamics of this society are such that some blacks and some whites will meet, fall in love or out of love, relate intimately, marry, and divorce. This reality does not mitigate in any way black solidarity and mutuality. There are differences within the black community as there are within the white community. Black individuals do not rise and fall with the black group. Some will be more fortunate than others within and without the black community qua black community. Experiences, needs, opportunities, patterns, expressions, and fulfillment vary from individual to individual, as much across the color line as within it.

It is imperative to realistically face marriage in black and white, though it be a peripheral concern of both blacks and whites. Such interrelations will not cease and desist if ignored. The dynamics of our society are such that individuals, though not groups, find increasing interaction the rule. It is sheer madness to assume there will not be those who find each other attractive and marry, not to spite, but in spite of, the customs and beliefs held by blacks and whites alike. A society which fails to give support, encouragement, and opportunity for such couples to grow with the same life chances as "intraracial" couples is as demonic as one that legally supports separation. The test of this society in comparison with South Africa is not at the level of the majority but at the level of the minority. Ten per cent of this population should certainly do better in our white racist dominated society than the heavy majority of blacks in the white racist dominated society of South Africa. The quality of our life of pluralism is in response to the inevitable free choice which falls outside of being Jew, black, Catholic, or Protestant. It is not enough to tolerate a dissenting minority; that minority must be given every opportunity to vitally live.

There is no question in my mind that full citizenship for blacks in this society is decades away. Equal status is light years away. It could be considerably shortened were whites to do what it is in their power to do, the right and good for blacks and therefore for this society and men everywhere. Whites are too dependent upon blacks to force them to give up as little equality of opportunity as possible. Why, in a great society like this one, blacks as a group must be lifted up as culture heroes who carry on their backs the making of a democracy is beyond comprehension. It is commonplace to hear that the test of democracy resides with the initiative of blacks. By and large this is condescension, a super demand made of blacks to compensate for the lack of sterling character among whites. Without blacks' pressing for equality for all, there will be little for others and even less for them. If only blacks were united in their efforts for a radical change in the structures and system of the society—a guaranteed income for all, for example—instead of the middle class work ethic. But this is wishful thinking.

Amidst inequalities between blacks and whites, it is sheer fantasy to demand equal opportunity for all blacks before there is support for some blacks who choose to marry whites. It is not for strategy purposes that the majority whites fail to support whites who choose to marry blacks. What is reflected here is their lack of magnanimity.

Personally, I find marriage in black and white a symbolic but vital solution to the racist issue. Intermarriage in black and white is not an unpopular name to be espoused, an impossible loyalty to uphold, a forsaken belief to revive, or a lost cause to be defended. Black and white intimate social intercourse is an occasional reality which may or may not lead to an occasional marriage. Such a marriage may not be our choice or what we would consider the wisest selection in this the best of societies, but for those who take this way and encounter the abuse, it is for us to perceive what we are and what we must become. In response to the few blacks and whites who do marry we are called neither to cheer nor to despair, but to magnanimity.

Chapter Nine

THE CASE FOR MARRIAGE IN BLACK AND WHITE

alvin C. Hernton concludes his book on *Sex and Racism in America* in the following manner:

> Granted—assimilation may be undesirable for most whites
> and for most Negroes. But in a supposedly democratic
> society, I do not see how Negroes (or whites) can ever realize
> their ambition of becoming free men if, on the basis of race,
> they are still restricted by law, custom, and tradition, in one
> of the most private areas of their lives—the right to marry
> whoever will marry them. I do not see how the society itself
> can really be free, or democratic.
>
> Most of all, I do not see how men, women, and children
> can grow and live healthy, productive lives in a world
> where—even if all other forms of racism and Jim Crow have
> disappeared—the racism of sex still prevails to plague, to
> distort, and to deprave the human conscience of blacks and
> whites alike.[1]

A month before his eightieth birthday, Arnold Toynbee was
asked by J. Robert Moskin, the *Look* foreign editor, "Do you see
any solution for the racial conflict in America?" Toynbee gave
this response:

I've traveled quite a lot in Latin American countries where there's a great mixture of races. There's no serious racial violence; there has been an intermixture in the sense of intermarriage. I've traveled also in Islamic countries, where, again, there's a great deal of intermarriage between the races.

It's curious; some people, of Spanish and Portuguese origin, or Moslem peoples, have no inhibition against intermarriage with people of different physical races, whereas English-speaking, Dutch-speaking, German-speaking people and high-caste Hindus, and Jews, for some reason, we all have this extreme unwillingness to marry people of a different race. I think the only radical cure for racism is fusion, and the only radical way of fusing is to intermarry.

After all, a man in Virginia will not object to having sexual relations with a Negro woman as long as he doesn't marry her; if she's his prostitute or his mistress, that's all right. She's still in an inferior position. But it shows there isn't really a physical antipathy.[2]

We have taken the route through racism and its sexual force in our tortured history. I now wish to briefly state the case for marriage in black and white as the resolution and solution by way of cleansing our American psyche. The case for black-white marriages is not the case Toynbee makes for "fusion" of the races. Fusion is but another term for the old liberal notion of absorbing blacks through processes of assimilation, amalgamation, or miscegenation. It is sheer grasping at a straw to state that the resolution of our black-white conflict will come about through the absorption of blacks. This theory has not worked in the past because there has been no way for whites to put the ideal of bleeding blacks out into action. It will not work in this day of black consciousness and Black Power because blacks rightly and boldly resist what is, in fact, a denial of their rich heritage. Absorption of blacks is not only impossible to attain genetically, it is not only wrongheaded because it is a denial of the virtues and right to be black, it is not only inconsistent with our history—it is no solution or resolution, because it does not have the element of forgiveness and reconciliation within it. Absorption is an attempt to escape from the suffering which whites must go through for their past inflictions upon blacks, inflictions which are condoned in the present through the unacceptableness of blacks.

As we inch toward a truly open and human society, there may well be an increase in the number of marriages between blacks and whites. But the case for marriage in black and white is not the case for the optimum, let alone the maximum or minimum, number of actual marriages in black and white. To be quite candid, I am not the least bit interested in statistics of black-white marriages, whether they increase rapidly or slowly or hold their own in absolute numbers. In fact I do not anticipate a time in our American history when a majority of blacks will marry whites or a dominant number of whites will marry blacks, and I do not either seek or desire such a level of mutual penetration.

It is not the actual number of black-white marriages which constitutes the resolution of racism in America. It is the symbolic significance of black-white marriages that is crucial for the solution. That is, marriage in black and white is the resolution and solution insofar as America has a new heart and a new psyche whereby marriage in black and white is as normal and welcome as marriage in black and black and marriage in white and white. We cannot, and we need not, create conditions whereby blacks and whites marry en masse. We can and we must create conditions whereby every American home anticipates with high expectation the possibility of welcoming into the family a black or white sister, brother, daughter, or son, though this may be a reality for only a precious few. It is sheer rhetoric to proclaim the American dream and espouse the American Creed without at the same time affirming the goodness and desiring the possibility of brotherhood and sisterhood in black and white within the immediate or very near family.

There is no doubt in my mind as to the substantial burden taking this initiative places upon the dominant white element of our society. It is staggering to contemplate. The magnitude of the suffering through humility, forgiveness, and reconciliation is beyond my real comprehension. Yet, the call for a society in which blacks and whites are truly free to marry and truly free not to marry is not only in keeping with our democratic and Christian heritages, it is not artificial or death dealing in its ego denying. Given the American experience, given the black experience, there is no other resolution or solution to racism than the creation of a climate in which marriage in black and white is respected and is seen as a free option supported by public sanction.

This call to marriage in black and white is essential because it is the only concrete way in which blacks can be fully and unreservedly accepted by whites and the only way in which whites can be fully accepted by blacks. The objective is not numerical marriages in black and white. The objective is the full acceptance of blacks and whites each by the other, the test of which is the willingness of the American spirit to accept a black or white within the intimate household. The only alternative to this full and free acceptance is the continuation of racism and its corollary of heightened conflict.

Can this spirit of full acceptance of blacks be implemented? Indeed it can, if we but have the will. In an earlier chapter I set forth the task of the churches in this regard. Churches might well take the lead in transforming their constituents through their institutional life of study, worship, and action. But the acceptance of blacks as potential members of the family can and should be taught and caught throughout our public and private educational systems, from kindergarten through college, just as we have previously taught and children caught the unacceptableness of blacks.

The third immediate action whites can take is the adoption, on a much greater scale, of black babies by white families. There are a good many black babies in need of a home. In part, the fastidiousness of adoption agencies in being extraordinarily cautious about allowing white parents to adopt black babies, like the circumvention practiced by banks in cooperation with real estate agencies in not permitting blacks freely to purchase homes, results from their response to what they believe whites in general desire. Pressure may need to be brought here, just as pressure will certainly need to be brought upon the churches and public school system to teach the full acceptance of black Americans. It simply is a fact that the blacks in our society account for fifty per cent of the poor, that the black population is younger than the white population, that their fertility rate is higher than whites, that the black male has been denied masculine opportunities to provide for the family, and that the youth, who are the majority of blacks in this society, deserve the best that life can afford. A great deal of the basis for the affectionate relationship between some Southern whites and blacks, as well as for the consequent "bad faith," was the role of black women in the nursing and rearing of white children. The good effects of these interpersonal relationships were canceled by the condition of blacks "knowing their place," lack of free and voluntary association, and especially by the hatred sustained for the black group as a whole. Conditions have changed, and while whites still determine the tone and pattern of black-white interactions, whites have the opportunity through the interconnections of poverty and fertility to bring health and life where there is sickness and death. Were white adults to adopt and rear as their own all the black babies without a home, the question "Would you want your daughter to marry a Negro?" would have a positive context. Is there not an interconnection between the reluctance of some social agencies to place black babies in white homes and the unwillingness of white parents to accept them?

There is an interconnection between the subservient role of blacks in the rural Southern past and their imprisonment within the urban ghettos of America with a high fertility rate. Both the constructive and destructive forces of what occurs in these ghettos affects us all. White America, at its best, knows itself to be as responsible as blacks for the ghetto poverty and for its fertility with a vengeance. We may not be responsible for the past, but we are responsible for the present and future. But the past and present conditions must be used to shape the future. White America's response so far to the unequal opportunity of blacks is to claim helplessness and to urge the blacks on toward internal solidarity with mutual self help that will bring pressure upon the white power structure to give concessions. In a word, whites have resigned themselves to applauding the black man, whom they are content to accept, condescendingly, as a culture hero for bringing democracy to a new high. The sterling character of blacks in the face of tremendous obstacles is no substitute for the need of whites themselves to be of sterling character. The cry of whites is that they can only respond to the black initiative for equal opportunity and eventual equal status. However, the initiative belongs to whites as well. Perhaps a little child will lead them. A black child of their very own!

Intimate social and sexual intercourse between individual blacks and whites is *the* solution to their conflict *only insofar as the interaction involves all levels of life.* Functional interaction on the job does not change the patterns of all the reference groups one engages in, and, indeed, functional interaction on one level may increase prejudice on other levels where it is the presupposition of that reference group. We are proposing that, beyond the intimate social intercourse between individual blacks and whites, the way of resolution is for a black-white people to unite as if in holy matrimony and to commence through reeducation in the churches and schools and new associations within the intimate life of the immediate family.

The immediate challenge before America is radical reform in the social structures, which will insure equal opportunity in education, employment, housing, politics, law courts, and public life in general. The present accent must be on lifting up the great majority of blacks who have lost rather than gained through the black movement of integration and civil rights. At the same time, we cannot ignore those blacks—admittedly a minority—who have chosen and received partial integration into the society. Moreover, the great majority of blacks are youth, and of these youth there are too many children without the opportunity of a home. If the initiative of the black movement through power and skill is to increase opportunity for black people as a group, especially for the men and the youth, the initiative of whites may be to bring equal opportunity and nearly equal status for some black children. The emphasis of whites can be on individuals.

Strong, sensitive, and intelligent white adults who are committed may in their wholesomeness provide a healthy home life for black children (the situation today is such that some single adults are permitted to adopt). There is no valid social or psychological evidence to the contrary! In this kind of environment whites are able to provide the necessary economic support that nurtures the best in a child. Where there are other children who are white, the opportunity to create a healthy psychological and sociological environment for both them and the black child is incomparable. Everything depends upon the security created by wise and confident parents in the home; children will take their cue and security from them. The love between the white mother and black child and the protection and guidance of the white father will certainly envelop the child in a bond of affection equal to that experienced by the other children, who are white. Certainly the black child will respond to love; color will make no difference to the child. The difference that color may make to the parents and to the white children will be positive. The child will be brought up as a real son or daughter, though the wise parents and siblings will know it to be a black one, a reality they will not wish to change but to accept.

Once the internal dynamics of the home are becoming vitally dynamic toward cohesiveness, the next step will be taking on the environment. When the black child is a baby, the generally harmful psychological and sociological effects will be experienced by the parents and perhaps by the other children if they are beyond toddler age. Cruel neighbors may wish to inflict some stigma on the child, but the child's innocence will call forth in strong parents a creative offensive which will impel in would be detractors a sense of fair play. Children can but reflect their parents in the preschool years, so that while the white parents of the black child are not engaged in a missionary enterprise, wisdom will lead them to engage their neighbors in the dynamics of respect for personality in their own way.

By the time the black child enters kindergarten the value and joy in being black will have been instilled. Undoubtedly, there will be whites unable to accept a black child as an equal of whites in the neighborhood. The same unacceptance would be true for the black child of black parents, though having a white father and mother would be, more often than not, an advantage. The wisdom of the parents will be put to the test at the time of dating, a matter more of logistics and intrepidity than of anxiety or trembling fear.

Social and intimate intercourse between blacks and whites

within the family is a real option and one that can be disapproved of only at the risk of being inhuman. Its impact and value is interpersonal for individuals. It means, beginning at the family level, that blacks and whites are friends, brothers and sisters, parents and child, neighbors and associates. Intolerance does not grow in this family soil, nor can tolerance be contained in it. Our best hope continues to be the next generation. But this hope can exist only if, as we engage in social change, we create environments where individuals find no root for prejudice. The place to begin is in the family, particularly with the family of whites who are including within their life a black child. Blacks have a long history of rearing white children, a factor which is mainly responsible for their larger tolerance. The next generation will be more tolerant and happier if they are brought up in an environment which induces tolerance. They will also live well with others! This assertion is not a wish or mere hoping but a real possibility. Tolerant adults grow from tolerant children.

Every generation regrets its mistakes and hopes they will be corrected by the next one. Few generations will have the opportunity to live fully and well with people irrespective of their differences open to the next generation if white parents will respond to the call of black babies.

Such a response would not be made in a vacuum. This generation of college students has not been reared in the favorable environment we suggest for the next generation. But they have come to maturity in a time when the civil rights movement has left its mark. Where once black and white students engaged together on the civil rights front, they now work together in the ghettos and in the universities of this country. These encounters have the singular attribute of being clear and right causes calling forth venturous response. Presently, there is a conscious minority which is serious about changing black-white relationships through changing patterns and structures, if not the democratic system. The courage set forth by the creative minority of students against past injustices makes clear their resolve, however inadequate their objective and irresponsible their tactics may be. Undoubtedly, for many, present vigorous action will in time give way to settling-in and finding their place in the decision making processes of the culture. All the prejudices of their past will not vanish! Often their immediate environment and reference groups may call forth compromise, if not silence. But some will have been engaged with blacks as persons, others as friends, a few as lovers. For most of them, then, like the liberal whites of the past, the crux of their identification with the real issues of the culture lies in their ability to opt out at some point. The difficulty with white liberals in the civil rights movement was their available choice to give up and go home after the heat of the day. The black does not have this option, and, to be sure, some whites would not take it. If the conflict between black and white groups is to change into cooperation, the civil rights and university movements have shown us a way. Though the path will not be taken by all groups, it can be by many more individuals. That is, the only way to identify with black people all the way is to identify with them all the way, to take their yoke upon you. The way is that of social, sexual intercourse between blacks and whites. A pattern for white adults is suggested by way of church and public school education and adoption. Young college adults, also a minority in number, can and do sometimes engage in a different pattern of individual, interpersonal worth.

It is to be expected that youth of similar life styles, education opportunity, and ambitions find the snobbishness of social fraternities and discrimination against their friends to be an unconscionable system. Fraternities and sororities alike are dated systems of exclusion externally enforced by alumni who wish to maintain selection on the basis of personality, too often a euphemism for color discrimination. Exclusive college fraternities and sororities lead to exclusive postcollege neighborhoods. Blacks and whites who fight together for principle will produce some who will live together in practice. It is not a long, if difficult, way from the demand that a black be a social brother or sister to the welcome of one as a friend, infrequently a lover, even less often a marriage partner. The obstacles are the same, external influence from adults who wish to impose systematic injustice. Too often black and white college youth who relate intimately as friends, where they are not diagnosed as prey of some psychological disarrangement, are written off as rebels against their parents or society. It may be the case that some are rebels trying to prove something or to be defiant, but then so are the youth who engage in university reform sit-ins, protests, and marches. It is perfectly possible to engage in university reform activity—or to adopt a black child for that matter—and receive condemnation for doing what is believed by the individuals involved to be the right action.

Whatever the motives, black and white youth are increasingly finding each other attractive on the college campuses throughout the country. The only thing they do not have in common, generally speaking, is identical color. In the context of a supposedly free academic community, color is not a barrier for the strong. There is no great breakthrough here for the society as a whole. There is evidence that some individuals in the context of black-white social intimacy find the way that moves from friendship through courtship to marriage. By and large, such couples are intelligent, sophisticated, thoughtful, and mature. The case for black-white social and sexual intercourse is increased by these beautiful people who desire and deserve a chance for life where the question of whether to marry a black or not to marry a black is only as momentous as the question to marry or not marry—and not more so!

We know that prejudice is acceptable where it gives ego strength to the individual who is dependent upon those reference groups demanding prejudice. But in a demonstrative society, where blacks and whites protest together against injustices, there may evolve reference groups where ego strength is provided for those who have overcome color stigma, whereby black preference for blacks or white preference for whites is as acceptable as black preference for white and white preference for black. Individuals find such reference groups within academe. Such enclaves outside academe center around university communities in the Boston, San Francisco, New York, and Chicago areas. Black and white married couples and black and white friendships outside of these fellowships of concern are largely on their own. If, in these areas blacks and whites are really free to marry and really free not to marry, earn a living, find housing and rear their children, continue their friendships, most other American communities are less salient. Although there are not enough communities of support, the fear of facing society alone is not much more difficult for couples involved in black-white marriage, or groups of friends in black and white, than for others given our mobile, urban, and anonymous society. It is less the neighborhood in high-rise middle class apartments that serves as the reference group than the functional groups with whom people hold interests in common.

It is true and a very good thing that some blacks and whites find equal receptivity by both sets of parents during their friendship or courtship and after marriage. Such occasional two-sided support may not be dominant, but it is not unheard of among parents who are loving, particularly in view of the fact that there are some whites who are able to raise a black baby as their own. What is rare at the present time is the acceptance of marriage in black and white throughout the extended family on either side, let alone on both sides. Time and interaction among intercolored people may well produce family bonds whereby relatives on both sides will affirm their relationship out of the creative engagement through a black-white marriage and its offspring. Such an affirmation is too much to expect at a point in our history when we are just released from the symbol of illegality formerly attached to black-white marriages. Public and wholesome social intimacy among technicolored people is only beginning to ascend as a more appropriate response to reality than warring or clandestine encounters. Nevertheless, the entire response of a society to color will eventually change as whites learn fully to accept blacks in and out of the marriage bond.

The case for black-white social intercourse and sexual intimacy is not the case for wholesale black-white marriages—though this fear must be faced, as we have faced it! The case is for a union of one people at every level. Now and then, here and there, we discover individuals who accept their color differences and live together in play, friendship, love, courtship, marriage, and/or through adoption. There never will be the opportunity for every black to marry a white or for every white to marry a black, nor would such a situation be desirable because we need unity in diversity for richness of life, not conformity. While marriage in black and white is no threat to our black and white group identification, those few individuals who do engage in it unleash a challenge that can be ignored or submerged but not denied or eliminated. The challenge for whites is to publicly and intimately accept a black as a friend, a lover, a husband, a wife, a relative, a neighbor, and, failing that, to know a black as a son or daughter.

The case for black-white unions is fundamentally the case for America, an America rid of its evil past of racism, which strides forward with black and white fully accepting one another. Full acceptance is what marriage means—union in mutual fidelity and trust, in adversity and good times, until death parts us.

Our need is nothing less than rebirth as a nation. Rebirth of this nation requires dominant whites to perceive our common history through the black experience—to think black, to feel black, to become black. The real question is, can whites become black, not can blacks become white. The latter is the old question which leaves speculation about genetic manipulation or even black self-hatred on dead center. To be black is really a conditioned experience; it is less a matter of genetics. Given the historic argument that one drop of black blood makes one black, it can be safely argued that it is impossible to know who is black, that what matters is for us all to accept our common blackness as the precious value it is.

Is it an inadequate response, indeed an evasive one, to reply to the question "Would you want your daughter to marry a Negro? that "the Negro would hope to be your brother, not your brother-in-law"? Perhaps it is the first and last response, before and after one has cleared away all implied threats, fears, stereotypes, and rejections. This much is certain: the commitment of some is so infectious that it calls for the commitment of us all when they respond genuinely to the question "Would you want your daughter to marry a Negro?": "Which Negro do you have in mind?"

It is time to throw caution to the wind and to support without reservation black and white social intimacy. In principle it is good, right, moral, democratic, valuable, laudable, Christian, human, and honorable. A responsible society, through education and action in adoption, will see to it that in practice blacks and whites who freely choose life together receive the same positive nurture and chances for success as do the members of every other heterosexual relationship between blacks and blacks or whites and whites. Responsible persons in a responsible society who teach their children from birth to accept all by providing an adopted black child within the family will not wait until their sons and daughters are at the marriageable age to answer the question "Would you want your daughter . . . ?" Responsible adults will have long since made clear their answer, for their daughter will be a "Negro." And if by good fortune, their son as well!

Marriage in Black and White is a call to extend the marital vows beyond individual blacks and/or whites to the group or corporate life of blacks and whites. Wedlock, a contractual or legal union of a man and a woman for life, does not exhaust the meaning of marriage. Marriage is a sacred relationship that can take the form of a covenant between black people and white people for the mutual growth in knowledge and wisdom of this one people. The case for marriage in black and white is the case for an intentional relationship between a black and white people in which faithfulness is expressed in mutual love and respect, their destinies woven of one design, and their perils and joys shall not be known apart from the completion of the unfinished pattern of their redemption.

Chapter One: Cleansing the American Psyche

1. Gunnar Myrdal, *An American Dilemma*, rev. ed. (New York: Harper & Row, 1962), pp. 591–592.
2. Quoted in Erich Fromm's *The Revolution of Hope* (New York: Bantam Books, 1968), p. 169.
3. Franz Boas, "The Problem of the American Negro," *Yale Review*, Vol. X, January, 1921, pp. 393–395.
4. *Ibid.*, p. 395.
5. *Ibid.*
6. Myrdal, p. 54.
7. *Ibid.*, p. 57.
8. *Ibid.*
9. *Ibid.*, p. 69.
10. *Ibid.*, p. 58.
11. *Ibid.*, pp. 57, 58.
12. Thomas P. Bailey, *Race Orthodoxy in the South and Other Aspects of the Race Question* (New York: The Neale Publishing Company, 1914), p. 42.
13. Myrdal, pp. 56–57.
14. W. E. B. Du Bois, "Race Relations in the United States," *Annals of the American Academy of Political and Social Science,* Vol. 30, 1928, p. 9.
15. Robert R. Moton, *What the Negro Thinks* (New York: Doubleday, 1929), p. 241.
16. *Ibid.*
17. W. E. B. Du Bois, editorial, *The Crisis* (January, 1920), p. 106.
18. Moton, p. 239.
19. Kelley Miller, *Race Adjustment: Essays on the Negro in*

America (New York: The Neale Publishing Company, 1908), p. 48.

20. Kelley Miller, *Out of the House of Bondage* (New York: The Neale Publishing Company, 1914), p. 45.

21. Edwin R. Embree, *Brown America: The Story of a New Race* (New York: The Viking Press, 1931), p. 47.

22. Nat Hentoff, in *The Village Voice,* January 7, 1965, p. 5.

23. Abram Kardiner and Lionel Ovesey, *The Mark of Oppression* (New York: Meridian Books, 1951), p. 384.

24. Arnold Toynbee, *A Study of History,* Abrid., by D. C. Somervill (New York: Oxford University Press, 1947), p. 129.

25. Charles E. Silberman, *Crisis in Black and White* (New York: Random House, 1964), p. 109.

Chapter Two: Improvident Ambiguity and Impudence in Our Sexual Past

1. George E. Simpson and J. Milton Yinger, *Racial and Cultural Minorities,* rev. ed. (New York: Harper & Row, 1967), p. 573.

2. Quoted in William P. Zabel, "Interracial Marriage and the Law," *The Atlantic Monthly,* Vol. 216, October, 1965, p. 75.

3. Maurice R. Davie, *Negroes in American Society* (New York: McGraw-Hill, 1949), p. 391.

4. Quoted in Edward B. Reuter, *The Mulatto in the United States* (Boston: The Gorham Press, 1918), p. 128.

5. Davie, *op. cit.,* p. 388.

6. Edward B. Reuter, *Race Mixture* (New York: McGraw-Hill, 1931), p. 37.

7. *Ibid.,* pp. 88, 89.

8. Reuter, *The Mulatto in the United States,* p. 93.

9. Frantz Fanon, *Black Skin, White Masks,* trans. by Charles L. Markmann (New York: Grove Press, 1967), p. 99.

10. Reuter, *The Mulatto in the United States,* pp. 90–91.

11. Reuter, *Race Mixture,* pp. 151–153.

12. Quoted in Reuter, *The Mulatto in the United States,* p. 127.

13. Reuter, *Race Mixture,* p. 57.

14. Quoted in Reuter, *The Mulatto in the United States,* pp. 148–149.

15. Quoted in Louis Wirth and Herbert Goldhamer, "The Hybrid and the Problems of Miscegenation," in Otto Klineberg's *Characteristics of the American Negro* (New York: Harper & Row, 1944), p. 266.

16. Edward B. Reuter, *The American Race Problem* (New York: Thomas Y. Crowell, 1938), p. 137.

17. Reuter, *The Mulatto in the United States,* p. 148.

18. *Ibid.*

19. *Ibid.,* p. 128.

20. *Ibid.,* pp. 109–110.

21. *Ibid.,* pp. 128–129.

22. Quoted in *ibid.,* p. 129.

23. Quoted in *ibid.,* pp. 132–133.

24. Quoted in *ibid.,* p. 134.

25. Quoted in *ibid.,* p. 151.

26. Reuter, *The American Race Problem,* p. 139.

27. *Ibid.,* p. 136.

28. Reuter, *Race Mixture,* p. 41.

29. Reuter, *The Mulatto in the United States,* p. 93.

30. Reuter, *The American Race Problem,* p. 139.

31. Reuter, *Race Mixture,* p. 154.

32. Gunnar Myrdal, *An American Dilemma,* rev. ed. (New York: Harper & Row, 1962), p. 125.

33. *Ibid.*

34. *Ibid.*

35. Reuter, *Race Mixture,* p. 151.

36. Quoted in Louis Wirth and Herbert Goldhamer, *op. cit.,* p. 263.

37. Reuter, *Race Mixture,* p. 167.

38. Quoted in Louis Wirth and Herbert Goldhamer, *op. cit.,* p. 263.

39. Reuter, *Race Mixture,* p. 152.

40. *Ibid.,* p. 167.

41. *Ibid.,* p. 142.

42. Quoted in Louis Wirth and Herbert Goldhamer, *op. cit.*, pp. 264–265.

43. Booker T. Washington, *The Story of the Negro: The Rise of the Race from Slavery* (New York: Doubleday, Page and Company, 1909), p. 227.

44. *Ibid.*, pp. 234–235.

45. Quoted in Reuter, *The Mulatto in the United States*, pp. 140–143.

46. Quoted in *ibid.*, p. 131.

47. *Ibid.*, p. 138.

48. *Ibid.*

49. *Ibid.*, p. 136.

50. *Ibid.*, p. 132.

51. Quoted in *ibid.*, p. 136.

52. Quoted in *ibid.*, p. 137.

53. John Dollard, *Caste and Class in a Southern Town* (New Haven: Yale University Press, 1937), pp. 141, 143.

54. Louis Wirth and Herbert Goldhamer, *op. cit.*, p. 273.

55. Quoted in *ibid.*

56. Quoted in Davie, *op. cit.*, p. 392.

57. Quoted in Reuter, *The Mulatto in the United States*, pp. 164–165.

58. E. Franklin Frazier, *The Negro in the United States* (New York: Macmillan Company, 1949), pp. 313, 314.

Chapter Three: Peril and Paradoxes in the Double Standard

1. Quoted in Maurice R. Davie, *Negroes in American Society* (New York: McGraw-Hill, 1949), p. 390.

2. Quoted in *ibid.*, p. 392.

3. Hortense Powdermaker, *After Freedom: A Cultural Study in the Deep South* (New York: The Viking Press, 1939), p. 192.

4. Ray S. Baker, *Following the Color Line; and Account of Negro Citizenship in American Democracy* (New York: Doubleday, Page and Company, 1908), p. 172.

5. Edward B. Reuter, *The Mulatto in the United States* (Boston: The Gorham Press, 1918), pp. 140–141.

6. Quoted in *ibid.*

7. Quoted in Albert E. Jenks, "The Legal Status of Negro-White Amalgamation in the United States," *American Journal of Sociology*, Vol. 21, March 1916; pp. 672–673.

8. Excerpts from Statutes and Constitutions where quoted in *ibid.*, pp. 666–678.

9. Quoted in Reuter, *Race Mixture*, p. 78.

10. Jenks, *op. cit.*, pp. 670–671.

11. Quoted in Allen C. Brownfeld, "Intermarriage and the Court," *Commonweal*, Vol. 81, February 5, 1965, p. 609.

12.–15. Quoted in *ibid.*

16. Quoted in *ibid.*, p. 610.

17. William P. Zabel, "Interracial Marriage and the Law," *The Atlantic Monthly*, Vol. 216, October, 1965, p. 77.

18. Quoted in Brownfeld, *op. cit.*, p. 609.

19.–20. Quoted in *ibid.*

21. William P. Zabel, "Interracial Marriage and the Law," *The Atlantic Monthly*, Vol. 216, October, 1965, p. 279.

22. Quoted in the *Supreme Court Reporter*, Vol. 87, June, 1967, p. 1819.

23. *Ibid.*, p. 1823.

24. *Ibid.*, pp. 823–824.

25. *Ibid.*, p. 1824.

26. *Ibid.*, p. 1823.

Chapter Four: Passing: Mystery, Magic, Mischief, and the Invisible Color Line

1. Y. A. Robertson, " 'Color Lines' Among the Colored People," *Literary Digest*, Vol. 72, March 18, 1922, pp. 42–44.

2. *Ibid.*, p. 44.

3. *Ibid.*, p. 42.

4. For an extended discussion of these concepts, see my *The Politics of God* (Boston: The Beacon Press, 1967), pp. 103 ff.

5. Quoted in "Shall We Be Mulattoes?" *The Literary Digest*, Vol. 84, March 7, 1925, p. 23.

6.–11. *Ibid.*

12. Caleb Johnson, "Crossing the Color Line," *Outlook and Independent,* Vol. 158, August 26, 1931, p. 526.

13. Quoted in *ibid.*

14.–16. *Ibid.*

17. *Ibid.,* p. 527.

18. *Ibid.,* pp. 527–528.

19. *Ibid.,* p. 528.

20. *Ibid.,* p. 542.

21. Quoted in *ibid.*

22. *Ibid.,* p. 543.

23. Harold Asbury, "Who Is a Negro?" *Collier's,* August 3, 1946, p. 12.

24. *Ibid.,* p. 72.

25. Hornell Hart, *Selective Migration as a Factor in Child Welfare in the United States with Special Reference to Iowa* (Iowa City: University of Iowa Studies in Child Welfare, 1929).

26. *Ibid.,* p. 29.

27. John H. Burma, "The Measurement of Negro 'Passing,' " *The American Journal of Sociology,* Vol. 52, July, 1946, pp. 18–19.

28. *Ibid.*

29. Hart, *op. cit.,* p. 30.

30. Burma, *op. cit.,* p. 19.

31. *Ibid.,* p. 20.

32. *Ibid.*

33. Caroline Day, *A Study of Some Negro-White Families in the United States* (Cambridge: "Harvard African Studies," Vol. 10, 1932).

34. Burma, *op. cit.,* pp. 20–21.

35. T. T. McKinney, *All White America* (Boston: Meaetor Publishing Company, 1937), Chapter I.

36. Asbury, *op. cit.*

37. E. W. Eckard, "How Many Negroes 'Pass'?" *The American Journal of Sociology,* pp. 498–500.

38. *Ibid.,* p. 500.

39. Maurice R. Davie, *Negroes in American Society* (New York: McGraw-Hill, 1949), pp. 394–395.

40. Ralph Linton, "The Vanishing American Negro," *The American Mercury,* Vol. 64, February, 1947, p. 133.

41. Quoted in *ibid.*

42. *Ibid.*, p. 135.

43.–44. *Ibid.*

45. *Ibid.*, pp. 136–137.

46. *Ibid.*, p. 137.

47. William M. Kephart, "Is the American Negro Becoming Lighter? An Analysis of the Sociological and Biological Trends," *American Sociological Review,* Vol. 13, August, 1948, p. 442.

48. John T. Blue, Jr., "A Note on 'Is the American Negro Becoming Lighter?' by William M. Kephart," *American Sociological Review,* Vol. 13, December, 1948, p. 767.

49. *Ibid.*

50. Linton, *op. cit.*, p. 138.

51. *Ibid.*, p. 136.

52. Edward M. East, *Heredity in Human Affairs* (New York: 1927), p. 194.

53. G. O. Ferguson, "The Psychology of the Negro," *Archives of Psychology,* Vol. 36, 1916, p. 130.

54. Day, *op. cit.*

55. Edward B. Reuter, *Race Mixture* (New York: McGraw-Hill, 1931), pp. 70–71.

56. Quoted in Ray S. Baker, *Following the Color Line; An Account of Negro Citizenship in the American Democracy* (New York: Doubleday, Page & Co., 1908), p. 161.

57. Louis Wirth and Herbert Goldhamer, "The Hybrid and the Problems of Miscegenation," in Otto Klineberg's *Characteristics of the American Negro* (New York: Harper & Row, 1944), p. 317.

58. Quoted in *ibid.*, p. 306.

59. Quoted in *ibid.*, p. 319.

60. Quoted in *ibid.*, p. 310.

61. Quoted in *ibid.*, p. 304.

62. Robert R. Moton, *What the Negro Thinks* (New York: Doubleday, 1929), p. 230.

63. Quoted in Asbury, *op. cit.*, p. 12.

64. Quoted in *ibid.*

65. Walter White, "Why I Remain a Negro," *Saturday Review of Literature,* October 11, 1947, p. 13.

66. *Ibid.,* p. 14.

67. *Ibid.,* p. 50.

68. *Ibid.,* p. 14.

69. *Ibid.*

70. *Ibid.,* p. 52.

*Chapter Five: Perspectives of Contemporary
Social Scientists on Black-White Marriages*

1. Robert Watson Winston, "Should the Color Line Go?"
The Current History Magazine, Vol. 18, September, 1923, p. 945.

2. *Ibid.*

3. *Ibid.,* p. 948.

4. *Ibid.,* p. 950.

5. *Ibid.,* p. 948.

6. *Ibid.,* p. 946.

7. *Ibid.,* p. 949.

8. *Ibid.*

9. Melville J. Herskovits, *The Myth of the Negro Past*
(Boston: Beacon Press, 1958), pp. 1–2.

10. Charles S. Johnson, *Shadow of the Plantation* (Chicago:
The University of Chicago Press, 1934), p. 3.

11. E. Franklin Frazier, *The Negro Family in the United
States* (Chicago: The University of Chicago Press, 1939), p. 21.

12. Quoted in Herskovits, *op. cit.,* p. 21.

13. Quoted in *ibid.,* p. 22.

14. Winston, *op. cit.,* p. 946.

15. *Ibid.,* p. 948.

16. C. B. Davenport, "Race Crossing in Jamaica," *The
Scientific Monthly,* Vol. 27, July–December, 1928, p. 225.

17. *Ibid.,* p. 238.

18. *Ibid.*

19. E. B. Reuter, "Civilization in the Mixture of Races,"
The Scientific Monthly, Vol. 31, July–December, 1930, p. 442.

20. *Ibid.,* p. 447.

21. *Ibid.*

22. *Ibid.,* p. 448.

23. *Ibid.*

24. *Ibid.,* p. 449.

25. Davenport, *op. cit.,* p. 238.

26. Reuter, "Civilization in the Mixture of Races," p. 449.

27. Ulysses G. Weatherly, "A World-Wide Color Line," *The Popular Science Monthly,* November, 1911, p. 484.

28. *Ibid.,* p. 485.

29. *Ibid.*

30. Ulysses G. Weatherly, "Race and Marriage," *The American Journal of Sociology,* Vol. 15, January, 1910, p. 453.

31. *Ibid.,* p. 439.

32. *Ibid.,* pp. 442–443.

33. *Ibid.,* pp. 447–448.

34. Quoted in *ibid.,* p. 448.

35. *Ibid.,* pp. 448–449.

36. *Ibid.,* p. 450.

37. Quoted in *ibid.,* pp. 449–450.

38. Melville J. Herskovits, "Race Crossing and Human Heredity," *The Scientific Monthly,* Vol. 39, July–December, 1934, p. 543.

39. *Ibid.*

40. *Ibid.,* p. 544.

41. Franz Boas, "Race and Progress," *Science,* Vol. 74, July 3, 1931, p. 6.

42. *Ibid.,* pp. 7–8.

43. Boas, "The Problem of the American Negro," p. 394.

44. *Ibid.,* p. 395.

45. *Ibid.*

46. Franz Boas, "Fallacies of Racial Inferiority," *Current History,* February, 1927, p. 677.

47. Ralph Linton, *op. cit.,* pp. 137–138.

48. Milton Leon Barron, "Research on Intermarriage: A Survey of Accomplishments and Prospects," *The American Journal of Sociology,* Vol. 57, November, 1951, p. 249.

49.–50. *Ibid.*

51. Quoted in *ibid.,* p. 250.

52. *Ibid.,* p. 250.

53. Kingsley Davis, "Intermarriage in Caste Societies," *American Anthropologist,* July, 1941, pp. 376–377.

54. *Ibid.,* p. 377.

55. *Ibid.,* pp. 377–379.

56. *Ibid.,* p. 387.

57. *Ibid.,* p. 388.

58. *Ibid.,* pp. 338–390.

59. *Ibid.,* p. 394.

60. *Ibid.,* p. 395.

61. E. B. Reuter, *The American Race Problem* (New York: Thomas Y. Crowell, 1938), pp. 379–380.

62. John Dollard, *Caste and Class in a Southern Town* (New Haven: Yale University Press, 1937), pp. 136–138.

63. *Ibid.*

64. Joseph Golden, "Social Control of Negro-White Intermarriage," *Social Forces,* Vol. 36, 1958, p. 267.

65. *Ibid.,* p. 269.

66.–67. *Ibid.*

68. Henry A. Bowman, *Marriage for Moderns* (New York: McGraw-Hill, 1950), p. 80.

69. Harold T. Christensen, *Marriage Analysis* (New York: The Ronald Press Co., 1950), p. 264.

70. Evelyn M. Duvall and Ruben Hill, *When You Marry* (Boston: D. C. Heath & Co., 1945), p. 177.

71. Golden, *op. cit.,* p. 269.

72. Simpson and Yinger, p. 545.

73. Joseph Golden, "The Negro-White Intermarried in Philadelphia," *American Sociological Review,* Vol. 18, November, 1953, p. 572.

74. Sister Annella Lynn, in response to *ibid.*

75. Constantine Panunzio, "Intermarriage in Los Angeles, 1924–33," *American Journal of Sociology,* Vol. 47, March, 1942, p. 690.

76. John H. Burma, "Interethnic Marriage in Los Angeles, 1940–59," *Social Forces,* Vol. 42, October, 1963, p. 156.

77. *Ibid.,* p. 158.

78. *Ibid.,* pp. 158–159.

79. *Ibid.,* p. 159.

80. *Ibid.*

81. Milton L. Barron, *People Who Intermarry: Intermarriage in a New England Industrial Community* (Syracuse: Syracuse University Press, 1946), p. 262.

82. Barron, "Research on Intermarriage," p. 250.

83. Simpson and Yinger, p. 566.

84. Barron, "Research on Intermarriage," p. 250.

85. Simpson and Yinger, p. 567.

86. Barron, *People Who Intermarry,* p. 275.

87. Barron, "Research on Intermarriage," p. 250.

88. Barron, *People Who Intermarry,* pp. 291–292.

89. *Ibid.,* p. 296.

90. *Ibid.,* p. 306.

91. Burma, *op. cit.,* p. 159.

92. *Ibid.,* p. 161.

93. Barron, "Research on Intermarriage," pp. 250–251.

94. S. E. Goldstein, *The Meaning of Marriage and the Foundations of the Family: A Jewish Interpretation* (New York: Bloch Publishing Co., 1942), p. 161.

95. Barron, "Research on Intermarriage," p. 251.

96. *Ibid.*

97. Ruby Jo Reeves Kennedy, "Single or Triple Melting Pot? Intermarriage Trends in New Haven," *American Journal of Sociology,* Vol. XLIX, January, 1944, pp. 331–339.

98. Barron, "Research on Intermarriage," pp. 251–252.

99. Milton M. Gordon, *Assimilation in American Life* (New York: Oxford University Press, 1964), p. 166.

100. Louis Wirth and Herbert Goldhamer, "The Hybrid and the Problems of Miscegenation," in Otto Klineberg's *Characteristics of the American Negro* (New York: Harper & Row, 1944), p. 279.

101. *Ibid.,* p. 278.

102. *Ibid.,* p. 281.

103. Golden, "Characteristics of the Negro-White Intermarried in Philadelphia," p. 179.

104. *Ibid.*

105. Horace Mann Bond, "Two Racial Islands in Alabama," *The American Journal of Sociology,* Vol. 36, January, 1931, pp. 553–554.

106. Golden, "Characteristics of the Negro-White Intermarried in Philadelphia," p. 179.

107. Robert E. Park, "Mentality of Racial Hybrids," *The American Journal of Sociology,* Vol. 36, January, 1931, pp. 550–551.

108. Wirth and Goldhamer, *op. cit.,* pp. 283–284.

109. Quoted in *ibid.,* p. 296.

110. Golden, "Patterns of Negro-White Intermarriage," *American Sociological Review,* Vol. 19, April, 1954, p. 146.

111. Golden, "Characteristics of the Negro-White Intermarried in Philadelphia," p. 182.

112. Wirth and Goldhamer, *op. cit.,* p. 289.

113. Golden, "Characteristics of the Negro-White Intermarried in Philadelphia," p. 182.

114. Wirth and Goldhamer, *op. cit.,* p. 206.

115. *Ibid.,* p. 292.

116. Golden, "Characteristics of the Negro-White Intermarried in Philadelphia," p. 180.

117. Burma, "Interethnic Marriage in Los Angeles, 1940–59," p. 160.

118. *Ibid.*

119. *Ibid.,* p. 165.

120. Barron, "Research on Intermarriage," p. 252.

121. Quoted in *ibid.*

122. Albert I. Gordon, *Intermarriage* (Boston: Beacon Press, 1964), p. 364.

123. Quoted in Barron, "Research on Intermarriage," p. 252.

124. Gordon, *op. cit.,* p. 354.

125. *Ibid.,* pp. 368–369.

126. *Ibid.,* p. 369.

127. Barron, "Research on Intermarriage," p. 252.

128. Gordon, *op. cit.,* p. 370.

129. Golden, "Patterns of Negro-White Intermarriage," p. 147.

Chapter Six: Parietal, Peremptory, and
Permissive Religious Forces

1. Milton L. Barron, *People Who Intermarry* (Syracuse: Syracuse University Press, 1946), p. 47.

2. Albert I. Gordon, *Intermarriage* (Boston: Beacon Press, 1964), pp. 267–268.

3. *Ibid.*, p. 269.

4. *Ibid.*, p. 197.

5. *Ibid.*, p. 164.

6. *Ibid.*, p. 140.

7. Quoted in *Commonweal,* Vol. 52, September 22, 1950, pp. 582–583.

8. Quoted in Gordon, *Intermarriage*, p. 133.

9. Quoted in *Nigerian Outlook,* Tuesday, March 5, 1963, p. 3.

10. *Ibid.*

11. Quoted in *Chicago Sun-Times,* Monday, April 5, 1965, p. 22.

12. Otto A. Piper, *The Biblical View of Sex and Marriage* (New York: Charles Scribner's Sons, 1960), pp. 179–180.

13. The Right Reverend Ambrose Reeves, quoted in Joseph T. Leonard's *Theology and Race* (Milwaukee: The Bruce Publishing Co., 1963), pp. 50–51.

14. Francis Gilligan, *Morality of the Color Line* (Washington, D.C.: The Catholic University Press of America, 1929), p. 92.

15. James A. Pike, *If You Marry Outside Your Faith* (New York: Harper & Row, 1954), p. 87.

16. Piper, *op. cit.*, p. 117.

17. *Ibid.*, p. 157.

18. *Ibid.*, p. 176.

19. Everett Tilson, *Segregation and the Bible* (Nashville: Abingdon Press, 1958), p. 102.

20. *Ibid.*, p. 67.

21. *Ibid.*, p. 122.

22. Pike, *op. cit.*, pp. 176–177.

23. *Ibid.*, p. 167.

24. Gordon, *op. cit.*, p. 4.

25. *Ibid.*
26. *Ibid.*, p. 40.
27. *Ibid.*, p. 41.
28. *Ibid.*, p. 57.
29. *Ibid.*, p. 53.
30. *Ibid.*, p. 91.
31. *Ibid.*, p. 187.
32. *Ibid.*, pp. 267–269.
33. *Ibid.*, pp. 364 ff.
34. *Ibid.*, p. 270.
35. *Ibid.*, p. 263.
36. *Ibid.*
37. *Ibid.*, p. 334.
38. *Ibid.*
39. *Ibid.*
40. *Ibid.*
41. *Ibid.*, p. 349.
42. *Ibid.*
43. *Ibid.*, p. 271.
44. *Ibid.*, p. 270.
45. *Ibid.*, p. 362.
46. *Ibid.*, p. 359.
47. *Mark* 10: 5–9, Revised Standard Version of the Bible.
48. *Matthew* 15: 1–9, Revised Standard Version of the Bible.
49. Gordon, *op. cit.*, p. 359.
50. *Ibid.*, p. 352.

*Chapter Seven: Rationalizations Deterring
Technicolored Unions in Spirit and Flesh*

1. E. W. Burgess and H. J. Locke, Jr., *The Family: From Institution to Companionship* (New York: American Book Company, 1945), p. 7.
2. See my *The Politics of God* (Boston: The Beacon Press, 1967).
3. George E. Simpson and J. Milton Yinger, *Racial and*

Cultural Minorities, rev. ed. (New York: Harper & Row, 1967), pp. 566–567.

    4. *Ibid.,* p. 555.
    5. *Ibid.*

Chapter Nine: The Case for Marriage in Black and White

    1. Calvin C. Hernton, *Sex and Racism in America* (New York: Grove Press, 1966), pp. 179–180.
    2. Arnold Toynbee on "Peace Power Race," *Look,* March 18, 1969, p. 26.

INDEX